CHESTER

A History of The

Edward Giles reported on Chesterfield matches in the early 1950s while he was with the *Derby Evening Telegraph*, which he joined straight from Loughborough Grammar School in 1944, after three years' National Service in the RAF, 1946-49. He moved to the *Bristol Evening Post* as Deputy Sports Editor and Chief Sports Sub-Editor in 1956. In 1970 he joined *The Daily Telegraph*, first in Manchester, then London. He became Northern Sports Editor from 1985 to 1993, when he retired. This is his eleventh book. He is a life member of the National Union of Journalists.

Publisher's Note

Since Desert Island Books was created in 1992 it has never previously been my unhappy task to publish a book that its author would never see. This is indeed Eddie Giles' eleventh book, the last eight of which were published by Desert Island Books. After his seventh, I presumed Eddie had put away his pen for good and taken to his rocking chair and slippers. He would have turned 85 in January 2013 and was in failing health. Then, suddenly, in November 2012 I received an email from him. Unknown to me, he had been hard at work on a final book, motivated in part by a need to keep busy and distract his mind from constant pain. Typical of Eddie, he had said nothing to me about the book for fear that he might never finish it. But finish it he did. His body might have been failing but his mind remained as sharp and alert as ever. There is no hint in the pages that follow of a writer with waning powers. The eloquence, style, rich detail, and knack for unexpected anecdotes are as evident in this book as in all his others. As is Eddie's refusal to embarrass or offend. If a player excels, you will read about it. If he blunders, Eddie would air-brush it from memory. This is a mark of the gentler journalistic age in which Eddie learned and mastered his trade as sports reporter and editor. He had little time for the modern game and its many excesses.

Having received his manuscript, we faced a race against time to edit and prepare the book so that Eddie might hold it in his hands. Sadly that race was lost. Eddie died peacefully on 27 December 2012. He cannot enjoy the book, but you can.

RIP Edward Giles, 1928-2012.

Clive Leatherdale
Desert Island Books

CHESTERFIELD

A History of The Spireites

Series editor: Clive Leatherdale

Edward Giles

DESERT ISLAND BOOKS

First published in 2013
by
DESERT ISLAND BOOKS LIMITED
Unit 1, 36 Clifftown Parade, Southend-on-Sea, Essex SS1 1DL
United Kingdom
www.desertislandbooks.com

© 2013 Edward Giles

The right of Edward Giles to be identified as author of this work has
been asserted under The Copyright Designs and Patents Act 1988

British Library Cataloguing-in-Publication Data
A catalogue record for this book is available from the British Library

ISBN 978-1-905328-76-5

Printed in Great Britain by 4edge Ltd, Hockley, Essex.

Contents

Author's note

To augment the information I have gathered on Chesterfield football club since reporting on their matches for the *Derby Evening Telegraph* in the early 1950s, I have relied mainly on the internet and *Sky Sports* (formerly Rothman's) *Football Annuals*. I am also indebted for the clarification of certain points by Neil Hallam, Jack Rollin, Keith Farnsworth and Stuart Basson, the club's historian.

DEDICATION
To Dr Murray Colburn
With gratitude

1

Date of formation
'something of a touchy subject'

Apart from a couple of short breaks, 1881-84 and 1917-19, Chesterfield has had a football club since 1867. Or was it 1866? As Stuart Basson, the club's historian, has told me, it is 'something of a touchy subject'. Some sources stick to 1866, even though only a few friendly matches were then played, and there is no hard evidence that a club was officially formed at that time. Indeed, as Stuart also says, 'The only two people I know of who have put in the hours over a microfilm reader in the local library are not convinced that 1866 is the correct year.' Yet the issue has been clouded still further by the address of the £13 million B2net Stadium to which the current club (the fourth) moved for the 2010-11 season: 1866 Sheffield Road. Coincidence or portent? If that were according to the postal system, it would place the ground around Dronfield instead of on Whittington Moor.

To quote Stuart Basson again: 'The first reference I have seen to an 1866 formation came in the 1905 *Book of Football*, in an article written by George Oram, a club director, which contained various factual errors. This article formed the basis of others subsequently written about the club, right up to those that appeared in match programmes in the 1990s. My suspicion is that Oram may have over-egged the pudding in order to make Chesterfield older than their near neighbours, the Wednesday.' That Sheffield club came into existence in 1867, but had at least two others ahead of them – Notts County (1862) and Nottingham Forest (1865) – and possibly a third, Stoke City. The Potters have long been credited with an 1863 start, but recent research by their historian, Wade Martin, has found nothing earlier than 1868.

Convinced though so many remain of the correctness of 1866 in Chesterfield's case, the fact remains that the town's first properly constituted football club was formed on 19 October 1867, like the Wednesday by cricketers, at a meeting at the County Hotel, Saltergate. Players were advertised for in two of the local newspapers, and a match was first arranged the following February on a field across which Tennyson Avenue now runs. The visitors, the Garrick club of Sheffield, were comfortable winners, but were beaten at the third attempt in 1869.

Chesterfield FC became independent of the cricketers in 1871, when a new set of rules was drawn up by the president, John Cutts, a solicitor and town clerk, in association with the club's other driving force, C W Rollinson, the secretary and treasurer. After several other venues had been used, a match, against Rotherham, was first played on 4 November that year at the Recreation Ground, which would be the home of Chesterfield football across nearly 140 years, but was then little more than an enclosed field with a small covered section for spectators halfway along the Compton Street side. Before more substantial stands were erected, there was a clear view of the famous crooked spire of the fourteenth century parish church of St Mary's and All Saints that made the Spireites the club's automatic nickname.

The 228ft spire is both twisted and leaning from its true centre by 45 degrees and 9ft 6in respectively. Folklore blames a blacksmith who improperly shod the devil, causing him to leap over the spire in agony, knocking it out of shape. Another tale told is that two imps were sent by Satan to do his dirty work. In reality, it is believed the bend began when the original wooden roof tiles were replaced by heavier slate and lead. The twist, following the direction of the sun, developed from heat expansion and a weight for which the structure was not designed.

The early years of Chesterfield's original football club were deceptively encouraging. In one match Rotherham were even said to have been beaten 1-22, though proof of that has unsurprisingly remained elusive. For the most unusual match played in the club's early years we must surely look to the one against a team called the Original Zulus, a Sheffield club that raised money for families of soldiers killed in the Zulu wars. They wore black jerseys and shorts, blackened their hands and faces with burnt corks, and wore strings of beads. Before the game they went round the town aboard a wagon, stirring up so much interest that a large crowd was attracted to Saltergate. The result was an entertaining draw.

George Whomersley, a Post Office clerk, was Chesterfield's first main marksman. Other prominent members of the team included Tommy Bishop, a tobacconist who was arguably the best local player of those days, John Marriott, later the town's mayor, and Jack Hunter, a Sheffield-born half-back capped by England while with Sheffield Heeley. According to one account, Bishop 'may well have been the first man to receive money for playing for Chesterfield' at a time when the game was widely amateur and largely confined to 'friendly' fixtures. Friendly in quotes because not a few were anything but! There could be quite a rough-house, with as many as fourteen players a side. One match was abandoned almost as soon as it had started when a Chesterfield player, Henry Moss, broke a leg.

Not until 1877 did the Sheffield FA, the first county football association in England, agree to bring their own laws of play into line with those
of the Football Association. It was in a Sheffield FA Cup-tie that, in 1879,
Chesterfield first played competitively, four years after they had joined the
Derbyshire FA. They did well to draw with Wednesbury before going out,
but their next attempt to win this trophy ended in the humiliation of a
0-7 thrashing by Staveley, who had taken over from them as north
Derbyshire's most powerful club. Worse was soon to follow. Players were
tempted away to the more successful Spital club, and those left signed for
another local side, Chesterfield Livingston, when Chesterfield FC had to
disband at the end of the 1880-81 season. Nowhere else could be found
to play after eviction from the Recreation Ground arising from declining
support that plunged the club into a financial crisis. The debt was small,
but nobody was willing to undertake it.

Three years went by before the second Chesterfield FC was formed,
based at the Rec and equipped with some of the original players and others from the Spital and Livingston clubs. One of them, Tommy Severns,
a tailor, was soon among the goals, but there were none for any
Chesterfield player in two thumping defeats suffered before the first silverware, the Alfred Barnes Charity Cup donated by the local MP and colliery owner, was won during 1890 in a match interrupted by a bull's invasion of the pitch. A team depleted when full-back Sammy Martin, a vet,
left at half-time to attend to an injured horse, conceded ten goals to
Staveley. And Old Whittington Revolution rammed home a dozen, the
highest score against any of the Chesterfield clubs (the record reverse in
the Football League was inflicted by Gillingham, who scored ten without
reply in the Third Division in 1987, a week after beating Southend 8-1).

Open to criticism though the Chesterfield teams of those far-off
times could be for defensive fragility, there was certainly no cause to
accuse them of lacking colour. At one stage, the players wore shirts with
the large replica of a Union Jack emblazoned on the front that had
belonged to the defunct Spital Olympic club and been found in the loft
of the Spital Hotel by the landlord. Other club colours in the early days
were cardinal and sky blue, myrtle green and red stripes (reintroduced as
an away strip in the 2002-03 season), and away kits of black and yellow
hoops.

The second Chesterfield club regained top-dog status in their part of
the county in 1889 with the weakening of Staveley through the loss of
key players to Sheffield United. By then popularly known as Chesterfield
Town, though that title was not officially adopted until the re-forming
into a limited company in 1899, they not only won the Barnes Cup again

in 1891, for the second of three times, but also completed a notable treble by also carrying off the Derbyshire Minor Cup and becoming Sheffield League champions at the first attempt. A year later, they entered the FA Cup for the first time, but lost to Gainsborough Trinity in a replay. Their next venture in that competition ended in tragedy. Walter Bannister, the club's first semi-professional, died from injuries incurred during a defeat by Derby Junction. There was another fatality when Staveley's Will Cropper, a Derbyshire cricketer who had played for Chesterfield, was accidentally struck in the stomach by a Grimsby defender's knee, rupturing his bowel.

In the 1894-95 season, Chesterfield reached the FA Cup's first round proper for the first time, then beaten by four goals at Middlesbrough. Until that point the position of the club's secretary had been an honorary one, the line ending with the best of them, Edwin Timeus, a Devonian who moved to Chesterfield to work as an estate manager for the Duke of Devonshire. Timeus guided the Spireites through their first seasons of competitive football during his five years in the post before having to relinquish it as the demands on his time proved too great.

His successor was Gilbert Gillies, the 26-year-old son of an Argyllshire shepherd who had first obtained work as a compositor with the *Derbyshire Times* after being sent to live in Chesterfield with an uncle, a publican. As with Timeus, it was quite a career move to become secretary-manager of a football club, but, as has been observed elsewhere, 'the very fact that they could do so probably cast light on the nature of the role at that time.' The day-to-day running of the club was the secretary-manager's main responsibility. Members of the board usually went to watch a player before signing him, and also selected the team. The trainer decided on tactics – especially at away games, which neither Timeus nor Gillies always attended.

In 1896 Chesterfield were admitted to the Midland Counties League, finishing fourth in their first season and third in the second. This led to their election to the Football League in 1899, the year in which the test match system of promotion and relegation was abolished. Chesterfield and Middlesbrough were brought into the Second Division to the exclusion of Blackpool and Darwen, though that was a bit hard on the Seasiders because Loughborough Town had ended the previous season two points below them, next to last. It took only more season for that little matter to be put right, however. Blackpool were then voted back and Loughborough dropped out after succeeding Darwen as wooden-spoonists. Darwen's concession of 141 goals in 34 matches in 1898-99 remains the worst defensive record in Football League history.

To Herbert Munday, a forward who had joined Chesterfield as a teenager from Eckington six years before, fell the distinction of scoring the club's first League goal, though it was a lone reply to the Wednesday's five in the first match to be played at Owlerton (as Hillsborough was then known) on 2 September 1899. This was the Chesterfield team: Hancock; Pilgrim, Fletcher; Ballantyne, Bell, Downie; Morley, Thacker, Gooing, Munday, Geary. A first League win was gained at the fifth attempt, by 3-1 at Saltergate on the first Saturday of October, against Woolwich Arsenal, a club destined for a far brighter future. Munday went on to become the first Chesterfield player to be selected for the Football League XI, and he achieved another claim to some sort of fame when he snatched the winner in a midweek Sheffield Cup replay against the Wednesday. It gave rise to the frequently asked question at sports quizzes: When did Wednesday fall to Munday on a Thursday?

Chesterfield completed their first League season in a respectable seventh place (out of eighteen, and one above Arsenal), but a cash shortage compelled them to discard a reserve team in the following one. With injuries and player unrest also taking their toll, this resulted in a decline to fourteenth place, only three points better off than Stockport County, who survived with the bottom club, Burton United, only when New Brighton resigned and Walsall were not re-elected. Failure to bring about some improvement prompted Gillies to resign in the December of that 1900-01 season, and an early exit from the FA Cup at the hands of non-League Kettering, in a home replay, also indicated trouble ahead. It promptly came when Chesterfield themselves had to seek re-election, successfully, after sinking to sixteenth in 1901-02. Immediately above them, on the same number of points, were Newton Heath, a club since rather more successful as Manchester United.

Gilbert Gillies continued to live and work, as a journalist, in Chesterfield, and also took up refereeing, before he became Leeds City's first manager in March 1905, chosen from about 100 applicants. He saw Leeds United's predecessors to respectable positions in their first two Second Division seasons, but did not have his contract renewed when it expired during the third one, in February 1908. Three months later, he was appointed manager of the newly formed Park Avenue club in Bradford, and their election to Division Two for 1908-09 gave him the distinction of having managed three clubs in their first Football League season. Again, however, February, three years on, brought a parting. Feeling that he had lost the support of the board after keeping the club in mid-table, he resigned and left football for good. His return to Derbyshire took him into the licensing trade at Matlock.

Following the short reign of Edmund Hind, another newspaperman, as Gillies' replacement, the Chesterfield team that had to seek re-election in 1902 was rebuilt by Jack Hoskin. This son of a local butcher was working as a clerk at a colliery when he was offered the job, but he was also a senior official of the Chesterfield and East Derbyshire FA, an organisation that had been headed by Hind since its inception in 1893, but would be disbanded in 1913 when a 'cold war' with the Derbyshire FA escalated into a full-blown conflict.

Chesterfield's revival to sixth place in 1902-03 included their record League victory, gained by 10-0 against Glossop North End on 17 January with this team: Clutterbuck; Thorpe, Leiper; Haig, Banner, Thacker; Tomlinson, Newton, Milward, Munday, Steel. All the forwards scored, Milward three times, Newton once, and the three others twice each. Joe Leiper strengthend the defence with experience gained as a First Division runner-up and FA Cup finalist with Derby County, and as a Division Two champion with Grimsby Town, but he rejoined his home club, Partick Thistle, before Chesterfield improved again to finish fifth in 1905. That team contained eight locally born players, one of whom, goalkeeper Sam Hardy, Hoskin's main discovery, so impressed despite being beaten six times by Liverpool's coming champions at Anfield that the Merseysiders snapped him up for all of £340 – one of the game's biggest bargains for one of its most talented performers. More about him later.

The reaching of the Cup's second round for the first time in 1905-06 (then beaten at home by Everton, that season's winners of the trophy) was offset by a drop to eighteenth in the League and another application for re-election. No club was voted out that time, but a year on Chesterfield had to go cap in hand to the annual meeting once more and escaped joining the bottom club, Burton United, on the way out when Port Vale, who ended two points above them, resigned. Fulham and Oldham Athletic filled the vacancies. Next season, a first clash with neighbours Derby County, who got through in a first-round Cup replay after being held at home, was followed by a further League reprieve. Again Chesterfield were saved by a resignation, of Stoke City, as the only club below them, Lincoln City, had to make way when Tottenham Hotspur and Bradford Park Avenue came in.

But a fourth successive plea for re-election in 1909 proved one too many. Only one club failed in the vote, and although Blackpool came last, it was Chesterfield, one point better off, who were replaced by the returning Lincoln. Hoskin, who had seen the club through their best seasons of the Edwardian era despite cash-flow problems arising from average home gates of only about 3,000, was surprisingly dispensed with, presumably as an economy measure, by directors who did not value him as highly as the players who had a whip-round to buy him a roll-top desk as a parting gift. A director, Tom Furness, took over, but with such dire results that he was speedily replaced by George Swift, who had begun his working life as an engine fitter at Crewe, but was the club's first secretary-manager with a footballing pedigree. After spells with teams in the Wellington and Crewe areas, Swift had been a full-back in nearly 200 League games, shared between Wolves, Loughborough Town, Leicester Fosse and Notts County.

Swift was recommended to Chesterfield by Gillies, having been with him as trainer at Leeds City. Swift was not blamed for the loss of Football League status in 1909, and faith in him was justified when the Midland League title was won the following year. Bert Munday, who had totalled 106 goals in 314 Second Division games, was a key player in that success, though outscored by Ebenezer Owers' 40 goals in 41 games.

There was to be no prompt Football League comeback, however. Grimsby Town lost their place instead to Huddersfield Town, even though the Terriers had finished fifth on switching to the Midland League to cut the cost of travelling they had incurred in the North-Eastern League. Hilton Crowther, a Huddersfield director, made such a good case in a circular he sent to all the Football League clubs that he secured 26 votes to Grimsby's seventeen. Birmingham, who had been at the foot of Division Two, topped the poll with 30. Chesterfield managed a mere six.

And that bitter disappointment was not all. After only one game of the 1910-11 season, Swift shook Saltergate by resigning, saying that he no longer believed the club could afford his salary. He was later with Southampton in the Southern League.

Munday retired in 1911 with about 230 goals (107 in the Football League) and 600 games to his name in seventeen years with Chesterfield, but the club soon came up with another free-scorer in Tommy Revill, a 19-year-old from Bolsover who bagged nineteen goals in seventeen appearances before his £200 transfer to Stoke. After him came Billy Egerton, who scored five times in the 8-2 defeat of North Shields in an FA Cup qualifying round, a victory remarkable for the fact that Chesterfield were five goals ahead before the advertised kick-off time. The referee began the game early, anticipating problems with the light. Egerton brought in the club's then record fee of £500 when transferred to Lincoln City in January 1914. The previous highest fees had been received for Ellis Gee, who went to Everton for £100 in 1898, and Joe Ball, who cost Bury £400 in 1903.

Full-back Will Cuthbert was another notable acquisition, winning three England amateur caps. He was with Chesterfield around the time they first became Cup giant-killers with a 2-0 win at Bolton before losing at home to Chelsea in the second round of the 1910-11 season. Bolton had twice been finalists, and were set for an immediate return to the First Division as runners-up to West Bromwich Albion. The next big Cup occasion for Chesterfield packed 15,000 into the normally under-popu-lated Recreation Ground for a first-round tie with Nottingham Forest in 1913. The Spireites were convincingly beaten, but went on to take second place to Rotherham in the Midland League.

All, however, was not well at Saltergate. A year later, Chesterfield crashed out of the Cup at West Ham, finding only one response to the eight goals they conceded. Syd Puddefoot, a future England forward, did the hat-trick in seven minutes for the Hammers, then members of the Southern League, and finished with five. Deep as was that dent to Chesterfield's pride, it had been surpassed only a few years earlier by their Cup exit at the hands of Ripley Town and Athletic in the fourth qualify-ing round, a defeat by lowly neighbours that rankled even more than that seven-goal swamping by Staveley.

But, as before, still worse was to follow. In 1914 came the outbreak of the First World War (or Great War as it was then called), and Chesterfield Town FC (1899) Ltd quickly became a casualty. Faced with mounting debts and the loss of key players to the armed forces, the club went into voluntary liquidation in 1915. Out of the ashes promptly sprang a new Chesterfield Town, founded by C W Everest, a local restaurateur who made himself chairman. Success came swiftly as champions of the Midland Combination with a team strengthened by locally based guests from Football League clubs, but demise was not long in coming either. In 1917 the wishfully high-flying Everest was laid low, his club disbanded after an illegal payments scandal. Some 40 players and officials, including the chairman, were suspended by the FA.

The vacuum left was filled by Chesterfield Borough Council, which formed a sports committee with the intention of launching a first-class club to play in a new stadium at the Queen's Park Annexe. Meanwhile, the Recreation Ground was used only for matches in local cup competitions, but it remained the headquarters with the formation of Chesterfield Municipal FC on 24 April, 1919. This made the town's fourth club indi-rectly answerable to the supporters, the town's electors, and it became the one we know today on being reorganised after winning the Midland League title in 1920. Its first manager was Tom Callaghan, a former Glossop, Manchester City and Partick Thistle player who was selected from almost 70 applicants. He was appointed at £260 a year and given a fortnight to assemble a team for two matches at the end of the 1918-19 season. Those he brought in included four internationals, Andy Wilson (Wednesday and Scotland), and three from Northern Ireland, Liam Donnelly (Distillery), Billy Halligan (Derby and Wolves) and Paddy O'Connell (Wednesday and Hull City) – plus Jack Carr (Middlesbrough), who was capped by England a few months later.

Council ties were cut, the word 'Municipal' dropped, to meet the approval of FA and Football League officials who were alarmed at the prospect of democratically controlled football clubs. Not, however, before having already got the wrong side of officialdom in being booted out of the FA Cup for fielding an ineligible player – an offence for which Callaghan was dismissed. In response to a protest South Normanton Colliery lodged on receiving a tip-off after being beaten, an FA inquiry found that centre-forward Frank McPherson, scorer of two of Chesterfield's five goals on his debut, had already played in the competition that season for his previous club, Barrow Shipbuilders. McPherson, who was suspended for a month, maintained he had told Callaghan he was Cup-tied, whereupon the manager made his greatest mistakes by telling Peter Irvine, Chesterfield's captain, to support his claim that no such admission had been made, and by offering McPherson £5 to keep quiet about it.

Met with a double refusal, Callaghan disappeared from the soccer scene. To fill the vacancy he left, Chesterfield put Councillor Tom Priestley, a publican, in temporary charge. So it was that a man who ran a public house, turned to as a stop-gap in an emergency, could be described as the most successful manager the club have ever had. He handed over at the end of December in 1919 with the team at the top of the Midland League, having won ten of the eleven games played under his direction, and drawn the other.

The championship was clinched that season under the management of Jim Caffrey, who had been the mastermind behind that shock 1-0 Cup defeat of Chesterfield by Ripley Town and Athletic in 1912. Caffrey was born in Birmingham, but moved to Derbyshire with his family (originally named McCaffrey) while in his teens, and after working in the mines he went into business as a seed and flour merchant at Ripley Besides becoming secretary-manager of that town's football club, he was secretary of the Derbyshire Senior League, and the organisational ability he showed in those roles prompted Chesterfield to appoint him from the first day of January in 1920 at an annual salary of £300 – a third of which was paid by the Town Council because the club was then still known as

Chesterfield Municipal FC. His original official title was Sports Manager, his duties also including running the town's swimming baths and boating lake.

With Council ties soon afterwards cut, however, and the prospect of a return to the Football League in the new Third Division North for the 1921-22 season, after an absence of a dozen years, there was a growing undercurrent of feeling that a higher-profile manager would be needed, even though the directors made all the important decisions. Consequently, during the 1920 close season attempts were made to force Caffrey's resignation from the Council side of his job. He got round this by making it a summertime one only, but his detractors persisted, and he was finally driven out in April 1922 when the club decided that their manager must be a full-timer. Caffrey's disappointment was offset by the greater security offered as the Council's Sports Manager and Hackney Carriage Inspector.

For the man to follow Caffrey as their manager in the Third Division North (in the formation of which a director of the Saltergate club, Harry Cropper, had some influence), Chesterfield first looked to no lesser a figure in the game than Herbert Chapman, but he not unnaturally preferred the offer he received from Huddersfield Town, members of the First Division. Thoughts of what he might have done in Derbyshire conjured up some tantalising possibilities as he guided Huddersfield to three consecutive championships over the next few years – and then had Arsenal on course for a third in a row when he met his sudden and untimely death from pneumonia in 1934 at the age of 55.

2
Willis Edwards, Jimmy Cookson and Teddy Davison

The start Chesterfield made to their League comeback as founder members of the Northern Section of the Third Division in 1921-22 was hardly spectacular, with a final thirteenth place, 21 points behind the first champions, Stockport County. Even so, the Spireites still acquired a unique, if highly irregular, special place in the record books. The only instance of a player being legally paid more than the maximum wage involved Henry Leddy, a centre-half signed by Chesterfield in March that season at the then maximum of £9. The Football League reduced the maximum to £8 at their annual meeting in June, so Chesterfield cut his pay by £1 for the following season . Leddy took his case to the High Court, won it, and had to be paid the £9.

It was also in March of the 1921-22 season that Chesterfield sold their first £1,000 player, winger Jacky Fisher, to Burnley, and in the following month they brought in a new manager, Harold (Harry) Hadley, who had piloted Merthyr Town, his last club as a player, into the top half of the new Third Division of predominately former Southern League teams (Grimsby the lone exception) the year before.

Both Fisher and Hadley were soon on the move again, however. Hadley, a former West Bromwich, Aston Villa, Nottingham Forest and Southampton wing-half who had played once for England and helped Albion to the Second Division title in 1901-02, left Chesterfield after only a few months, resigning most unexpectedly in August 1922; Fisher returned to Saltergate in April the following year. Hadley was out of management for five years before also having a short stay with Aberdare Athletic, then of the Welsh League on being replaced by Torquay United in the Third Division's Southern Section. After that he put in two more stints with Merthyr, who also dropped out of the Football League shortly before he left them for the last time in 1931. He was finally manager of Bangor City, retiring in 1936.

Chesterfield's successor to Hadley was another Harold known as Harry who had played for WBA. This was Harold Arnold Parkes, also a nippy winger with Coventry City between his two spells with Albion, for whom he played in an FA Cup semi-final (lost to Everton) in 1907 when only seventeen. Parkes, who hailed from Halesowen, was player-assistant manager with the Throstles during the 1914-18 war, while also on munitions work. He then had to give up playing because of cartilage trouble, but kept goal in an emergency while secretary-manager of Newport County shortly before they joined in the Southern League exodus when the Football League expanded to a third section in 1920. He joined Chesterfield after a month of Alderman Harry Cropper's caretaker management, and under his guidance they finished as high as third, twice fourth, and never lower than seventh (also twice) before his departure.

Judged by that record, Parkes was hard done by when sacked at a board meeting held on 25 March 1927. The formation of an 'A' team for promising juniors and local amateurs had increased the strain on the club's already parlous financial situation, but he had come up with several saleable players to ward off the wolves in addition to keeping the team comfortably inside the top half of the table. His worth was readily realised by Lincoln City, with whom, never lower than sixth, he completed ten successive top-seven finishes in the Third North, culminating in promotion in 1932 after twice being runners-up. True, he ran out of ideas after that, unable to avert relegation in 1934 and also powerless to revive Mansfield Town and Notts County before he retired from football in July 1939, but he deserves to be ranked among the leading managers of the lower divisions during that period between two world wars.

While Parkes was their manager, Chesterfield had a goalkeeper, Arnold Birch, who got himself into the record books for scoring five goals, all from the penalty spot, in one season, 1923-24. Birch's story is quite an eventful one. The outbreak of war in 1914 interrupted his footballing career just when he had started trials with the Wednesday, his home club, and on enlisting in the Royal Navy he was drafted into one of the naval divisions raised to make up the shortfall in infantry numbers. When the Germans swept into Belgium, he was among about 1,500 who got away from the trenches near Antwerp and marched into Holland to avoid becoming prisoners of war. The Dutch, who were neutral, interned them, so Birch and his comrades spent the rest of the war at a camp at Groningen. With attempts at escape not officially sanctioned in deference to the Dutch, football matches in the camp were soon arranged, and Birch was also allowed out to play for a local side whose name was translated as Be Quick. He helped them to their divisional championship in 1916.

Chesterfield moved in quickly to sign Birch when he was released by Wednesday in 1923 after being given few first-team opportunities by the Owls since his return. He was a regular member of the League side in his first two seasons at Saltergate, and for most of the next two, getting close to 150 appearances before going to Denaby United. He continued playing for works teams in Sheffield well into his 40s.

The players Harry Parkes inherited on taking over at Chesterfield most notably included George Beel and Willis Edwards. Beel, a centre-forward previously with Lincoln, his home club, and Merthyr Town after having an unsuccessful trial with Manchester United, was Chesterfield's top scorer with 23 goals in the 1922-23 Third North season, but it was with Burnley that he really hit the headlines after his transfer to Turf Moor that took Jacky Fisher in the opposite direction. In his nine years there Beel set the club's existing record with 187 goals in 337 games, including eleven hat-tricks. He was their main marksman in six of those seasons, netting 35 goals, another Burnley best, in the First Division of 1927-28.

Chesterfield's signing of Edwards. a Derbyshire miner, was cheekily enterprising. Having attracted attention as a wing-half with his home club, Newton Rangers, near Alfreton, he was actually on his way to a trial with Blackburn Rovers when Chesterfield nipped in to snap him up for the £10 signing-on fee and a weekly wage of 30 shillings (£1.50). He made his debut at sixteen in 1919, and earned such rave reviews as Chesterfield strongly challenged for promotion to the Second Division in 1922-23 (their final position of fourth earned Parkes a pay rise to £7 a week) that the bigger clubs were soon sniffing around.

Prominent among them were Sheffield United, but they were put off when 'Nudger' Needham, their Derbyshire-born former England wing-half, reported back from a scouting mission that Edwards was too small. True, he was not very tall at the time, but, ironically, he grew to be taller than Needham and went on to be widely regarded as the best wing-half in the country, winning sixteen England caps – exactly as many as Needham had done – and rising to the captaincy of both club and country. He was the first Leeds player to be capped by England.

A move for Edwards from Chesterfield became inevitable when the Spireites again ran into financial trouble despite their success on the field. Debts mounted to £2,000 in the 1923-24 season, and in March 1925, after 70 appearances, off their prime asset went to Leeds for £1,500. That raised the Chesterfield record from the £1,000 they had been paid for inside-forward Joe Cooper (by Notts County) and left-winger Billy Marshall (by Grimsby) besides Jacky Fisher, but in October of the same year it was increased to £2,000 when Cyril Oxley, an outside-right, was transferred to Liverpool. Cooper rejoined Marshall with Grimsby after only one season at Meadow Lane, and it was against Chesterfield, in a goalless game at Blundell Park, that he first played for the Mariners. He

and Marshall helped Grimsby to the Third North title in 1925-26, and
Marshall was also a prominent member of the side when another promotion was gained, as Second Division runners-up to Middlesbrough, in
1928-29.

Between them, Cooper and Marshall totalled more than 500 League
games and over 100 goals for Grimsby before both left after the club's
relegation season of 1931-32. Cooper, who then marked his move to
Lincoln with a debut hat-trick, would have played more than 167 times
for Grimsby but for missing much of two seasons through injury.
Marshall went to Reading, but soon returned to Lincolnshire with Boston
United.

Bargains as both were, Leeds landed a still bigger one in Edwards,
who added almost a dozen matches in the Football League XI to his
England caps, and, never booked or sent off, was just six short of 450
League and Cup appearances for the Yorkshire club in a playing career
that stretched a dozen days beyond his 38th birthday in 1941. After that,
he assisted trainer Bob Roxburgh by coaching the Reserves, and in 1947
took over as manager when Billy Hampson resigned. Although having
only one season at the helm, relegation from Division Two having been
too close for comfort, he was retained on the backroom staff as a scout,
and for a few months in 1958 he was caretaker manager between the
departure of Raich Carter and short-lived reign of Bill Lambton, who
quit when his training methods were criticised by the directors. Edwards
altogether served Leeds United for 35 years, finally working at a Beeston
jam factory after leaving Elland Road in 1960. He was 85 when he died
at Leeds in 1988.

Chesterfield's loss of Willis Edwards to Leeds was offset when the
only transfer fee paid by the club in the summer of 1925, all of £60,
secured the powerful and prolific Jimmy Cookson from Manchester City,
though his impact was not immediately apparent. Cookson had failed to
make City's first team after joining his brother Sam at Maine Road, and
he was at full-back in Chesterfield's reserve side when an injury crisis pro-
pelled him to the head of the senior attack with an astonishing outcome.
He took to that position, in which he had played for South Salford Lads
Club before switching to full-back with Clayton FC, with such gusto that
his 44 goals in 34 games in 1925-26 set a Chesterfield record for one
League season that remains unrivalled. Cookson also scored twice in a
5-0 away victory over Wath Athletic in the first round of the FA Cup on
28 November 1925 that remains Chesterfield's biggest in the competition
proper (though they had defeated Dronfield Woodhouse 11-1 in a pre-
liminary round five years earlier).

The 1925-26 season was the first after the change in the offside law, whereby a player had to have two opponents between himself and the opposing goal instead of three, and individual club records were also broken by Ted Harper, for Blackburn Rovers in Division One, and Ken McDonald for Bradford Park Avenue in the Third North – both with 43. Cookson twice scored four times in a match, against Accrington Stanley and Ashington – a feat he repeated at Wigan Borough's expense on his way to 41 goals in 40 games the following season.

Boosted by that heavy scoring, Chesterfield went 38 games without a home defeat, yet slipped from fourth to seventh in the final Third North tables. At about the same time, Jimmy Cookson's brother Sam, described as 'the best uncapped full-back of his day', missed promotion straight after relegation as Portsmouth kept Manchester City out of the Second Division's second place by a third decimal point on goal-average. City got back as champions the next year, but by then Sam was with Bradford, newly risen from the Northern Section, so Jimmy was the brother who subsequently rose to the top division – but for only one match.

Jimmy's 85 goals for Chesterfield in 74 games and two seasons made him as impossible to hold onto as Edwards had been. His transfer to West Bromwich, then a Second Division club, in June 1927 brought in a new record fee of £2,500, and Albion raked in the dividend of 38 League goals in as many games in 1927-28, 21 in 31 in 1928-29 (when he also scored seven in the Cup), and 33 in 34 in 1929-30. The 100th goal of Cookson's League career came against South Shields in December 1927, in only his 89th match – the quickest individual century of them all. Seven more times he scored four in a game, on one of those occasions setting an Albion record by getting all their goals, including a penalty, in a 6-3 defeat of a not inconsiderable Blackpool team.

In view of all that, fate dealt Cookson a cruel blow when he had to give way to another ace marksman, W G Richardson (the G for Ginger to distinguish him from the other Bill Richardson in the side) after playing in the first sixteen matches of the 1930-31 season. That deprived him of being in at the death when Albion made history by going on to win promotion from the Second Division, as runners-up to Everton, and carry off the FA Cup in the same season by beating Birmingham at Wembley.

With 'Ginger' firmly in possession, Cookson made his sole First Division appearance in a Boxing Day defeat by one goal at Birmingham before going off to Plymouth, then Swindon. He ended his fifteen years in League football with 255 goals in 290 League games – a truly remarkable record. Even then he was not finished. He found time from being a publican to continue playing in the Swindon district until 1952, and lived on to 1970.

In the year West Bromwich pulled off their unprecedented double, Chesterfield also rose in the League, topping the Third Division North by one point from the Lincoln team managed by Harry Parkes. These were the final leading positions:

Season 1930-31	P	W	D	L	F	A	Pts
1. Chesterfield	42	26	6	10	102	57	58
2. Lincoln	42	25	7	10	102	59	57
3. Wrexham	42	21	12	9	94	62	54
4. Tranmere	42	24	6	12	111	74	54

After the misfiring appointment of Alec Campbell to fill the vacancy left at Saltergate by Parkes, the man in the Chesterfield manager's chair was then Teddy Davison, a former Wednesday and England goalkeeper whose association with the Derbyshire club would span some 30 years in two spells. Campbell, the centre-half and captain of Southampton's Third South champions of 1921-22, after having had the unique experience of playing for England's amateurs against the Netherlands while still a schoolboy, was not new to Derbyshire, for he had played for Glossop North End between his years with the Saints.

But his appearances for Glossop had only just got into double figures, and his stay at Saltergate was also short. What would be his only managerial post lasted from April to November in 1927, during which time Chesterfield lost more matches than they won. Back he went south, where he had been a director of a firm of fruit importers, and it was there that he died of pneumonia in 1943, aged 53, while a wartime officer in the Royal Artillery.

Teddy Davison, whose one cap against Wales in 1922 made him the smallest to keep goal for England at 5ft 8in (an inch shorter than Birmingham's Harry Hibbs and Bolton's Eddie Hopkinson), has a special place in Sheffield soccer besides Chesterfield's, having played for Wednesday for eighteen years and managed United for twenty. My old friend and former colleague Keith Farnsworth, an authority on Sheffield sport, has described Davison as 'such a placid and gentle person it was difficult to imagine him in the hurly-burly of professional football.' Seldom as he was heard to offer criticism or complaint, however, it was also recalled by Farnsworth that in one of his games for Wednesday Davison 'was so incensed by a goal scored by Sheffield United's Joe Kitchen that he chased after he referee to protest'. The goalkeeper's view that the ball had been handled into the net was widely supported, and he was sent a card addressed to 'George Washington, Owlerton'.

Neither was Davison short of courage or determination, even at a starting salary with Chesterfield of £6 that was less than his predecessor had been paid. His appointment at the beginning of January in 1928, after starting his managerial career outside the Football League by helping to put Mansfield Town on course for election to the Third Division in just over a season at Field Mill, was soon followed by the replacement of Harry Cropper as chairman by Harold Shentall, who eventually also became a powerful figure in the game nationally as an FA vice-president. Under their direction, Chesterfield found a fresh impetus after a decline in the League and the humiliation of a 1-7 home FA Cup defeat by Huddersfield Town in which even the one reply was an own-goal. From sixteenth in 1928, there was an improvement to eleventh in 1929, fourth in 1930, and first in 1931.

The loss of full-back Charlie Bicknell to Bradford City and Harold Wightman, a former Derby defender, to Notts County (as player-coach) before the promotion push was more than countered by the signing of Albert Bell, a Sheffield-born full-back from Cardiff, half-back David Robb from Wigan Borough, and forwards Harry Andrews (Wolves), Tom Bell (Halifax Town), Bill Baldwin (Scunthorpe United) and Fred Wallbanks (Bury).

Wightman, who during the 1914-18 war had turned out for Nottingham Forest (he later became their first manager), was in the veteran stage when he left Saltergate, but Bicknell, a product of the Tupton village team near Clay Cross, did not play his last League game until 1947, for West Ham at the age of 41. Bicknell joined the Hammers after being a Bradford City regular for 5½ seasons, and he captained them to victory over Blackburn in the War Cup final at Wembley in 1940. His peacetime appearances for his three League clubs totalled 468 (79 for Chesterfield), and to that impressive number he exceeded 200 in the 1939-45 war, more than any other West Ham player.

From 21 December 1929 to 27 December 1930, Chesterfield set a record (since beaten by Arsenal) with a scoring sequence of 46 League matches in which seventeen consecutive home wins were gained. There was also a strong finish to the 1930-31 season with 26 goals in the last six games, all won. Even so, Chesterfield topped the table only once before climbing back there with just one game to go by beating Lincoln 3-2 (after leading 2-0) in front of a crowd of 20,092, Saltergate's biggest up to that time. Chesterfield were also at home for their final match, and they clinched their first rise to the Second Division in storming style with an 8-1 defeat of Gateshead, Davison's home club, that increased their highest number of goals in one season from the 100 of 1925-26 to 102. Lincoln slipped three points behind in losing again, 3-5 at Accrington, so victory in the remaining match they had in hand was made meaningless. Behind the scenes, Davison clarified John Black's role as financial secretary by establishing a clear distinction between how the administrative and playing sides of the club were run. On the field, he further strengthened the team by bringing in the experienced George Thornewell, a winger who had been a recent Cup winner with Blackburn after helping Derby back to the First Division, and Dick Duckworth, a wing-half who was a coach at Saltergate after ending a playing career in which he captained York City to the FA Cup quarter-finals. Duckworth's father was also a wing-half, a member of the famous Manchester United middle line completed by Charlie Roberts and Alex Bell, and an FA Cup final winner with them against Bristol City in 1909. And thereby hangs the tale of the medal that went missing for more than twenty years. Duckworth Senior lost his after attending a Royal Agricultural Show at Oldham, and he was a 71-year-old licensee at Edenfield, in Lancashire, when it was found a couple of miles away in rubble behind an inn at Royton where he had lived for a time.

Although it meant the loss of a future England centre-forward, Teddy Davison pulled off another astute deal in balancing Chesterfield's books with the £1,500 sale to Tottenham of George Hunt not long after signing him for £10. The transfer of Jimmy Bullock, another centre-forward, to Manchester United was most adequately answered by the incoming Albert Pynegar, a Third North promotion winner with Port Vale the season before he also was with Chesterfield. Pynegar's hat-trick in the big win over Gateshead took him to 26 goals in 29 games. Inside-right Tom Bell, another product of the North-East, who, like goalkeeper Bill Dolman, did not miss a match, came next with twenty in 42. Jack Lee, a crowd-pleasing Geordie who had cost only £250 from Arsenal, and yet another from his part of the country, Sid Binks, who moved up from centre-half to partner him at inside-left midway through the season, also got into double figures.

Again, however, success cost Chesterfield an influential member of their staff. This time it was the manager who left. When John Nicholson, Sheffield United's secretary-manager for 33 years, was knocked down and killed by a lorry outside Sheffield's Midland Station while on his way to catch a train for a match at Villa Park in April 1932, it was to Davison that the Blades promptly looked for a successor. Davison had added to his managerial credentials not only by preserving Chesterfield's newly won

Second Division status with a team augmented by the acquisition of centre-half Frank Froggatt, a former Wednesday team-mate who had captained the Owls to promotion (but did not live to see his son Redfern do likewise), and a couple of ex-England men, George Ashmore, a goalkeeper from West Bromwich, and Billy Austin, a winger from Manchester City. With the development of local talent having already been encouraged by the formation of the 'A' team, he had also established a scouting network in his native North-East under the supervision of Harry Dormand, whose ready eye for talent would launch many footballers from that area along a League career with Chesterfield.

Indeed, one of the last players recommended by Dormand to be introduced into the first team by Davison before he left for Bramall Lane was Billy Kidd, a full-back from County Durham who became the oldest to play for Chesterfield when he made the last of his 486 appearances (170 of them during the Second World War), aged 40 years and 232 days, at Southampton on 20 September 1947. And even then it was injury that cost him his place. Not so much Billy the Kidd as Billy the Veteran.

Kidd, originally a miner, first attracted the scouts of League clubs as a centre-forward with the Durham side Pegswood, but he moved to full-back in an emergency – and there he stayed. Dormand was immediately impressed when he saw Kidd in defence, but the signing was far from straightforward. Given a trial by Chesterfield early in 1932, Kidd held out for an improved offer, and he might well never have gone to Saltergate but for being called back two months later (presumably with a rise) when an injury to Joe Weily, a reserve, caused a sudden shortage of full-backs. Kidd's astute positional play, firm but fair tackling, and consistent reliability made him an automatic first choice from then until after that match down on the South coast more than fifteen years later. He was strictly a one-club man, though he guested for a few in Yorkshire during the war, and after retiring from playing he was Chesterfield's third-team trainer until he resigned in 1952 to concentrate on his off-licence business on Newbold Moor. He died in 1979.

As recalled in more detail in the next chapter, Chesterfield slipped back into the Third North in 1932-33, straight after losing Davison to Sheffield United. The Blades were themselves relegated the following season, dropping out of the First Division for the first time, but two years later (when Chesterfield were again promoted) Davison guided them to the FA Cup final, in which they lost to Arsenal by an only goal, and they climbed out of Division Two three years after that. United snatched second spot behind Blackburn by a single point from their Wednesday neighbours on the final day of the last pre-war season of

1938-39 after two third-place finishes – foiled on the second of those occasions only on goal-average as Manchester United went up with Aston Villa's champions.

With war interrupting Sheffield United's recovery, there was a slide from the top six of the first season after the war to the foot of the table in 1949, and a prompt return to the top flight was thwarted as Wednesday turned the tables, finishing runners-up to Tottenham with a goal-average better than United's by 0.008 of a goal. Davison's men were Cup quarter-finalists in 1952, but a mid-table finish in the Second Division – especially frustrating because yo-yo Wednesday went back up as champions – at last brought Davison's reign of two decades to an end. He was dismissed in August 1952, but as one door closed another one opened – back at Chesterfield of all places. Bobby Marshall, formerly a player with Sunderland and Manchester City, and the fourth manager at Saltergate during Davison's absence, had also just left, so John Edward Davison was ideally placed and welcomed back with open arms.

Ironically, Sheffield United were that season's champions under the supervision of Reg Freeman, who had managed Rotherham, one of the clubs for which he had also played at full-back, for almost as long as Davison had been at Bramall Lane. Chesterfield, meanwhile, pitched up halfway down the Third North, to which they had recently returned after eight consecutive seasons (discounting the war years) in Division Two. Davison, whose comeback was especially popular with supporters, did well under severe financial constraints to see the Spireites to four successive sixth places before stepping down in May 1958, and although he was then within a few months of his 71st birthday, he carried on for a while longer as chief scout. He died early in 1971 at Wortley, near Sheffield, having spent all his working life in football.

Unsuccessful though Davison was in his efforts to get Chesterfield back to the Second Division, he at least handed over when they were still a Third Division club – not in the new Fourth Division of 1958-59 that was formed by clubs from the bottom halves of the final North and South sections. He also left a gem of a legacy as a result of his continuance of a youth development policy that produced one of the finest achievements in the club's history. In 1956, Chesterfield's youngsters battled through to the final of the FA Youth Cup. They then lost to Manchester United over the two legs, but by only the odd goal, and the 1-1 home draw was watched by a crowd of almost 16,000 in a season when first-team gates at Saltergate sank as low as around a third of that figure. In goal was a player, carefully groomed under Davison's influence, who went on to attain the game's heights. A chap called Gordon Banks.

3

An epic FA Cup win against Sheffield Wednesday

In the last season of Teddy Davison's initial spell as their manager, 1931-32, Chesterfield entered the fourth round of the FA Cup for the first time with a 5-2 home victory over Nottingham Forest, gaining belated revenge against former holders of the trophy who had knocked them out by 4-1 in the opening round at the same ground nineteen years before. The Spireites went no further, falling two goals short of Liverpool's four as Saltergate's record attendance was boosted to 28,393, but in the next season they pulled off their first really big giant-killing act under the new management of William Henry Tompkins Harvey by beating Sheffield Wednesday on their way to a first appearance in round five.

A third-round pairing with distinguished neighbours was a dream draw indeed, even though it took them to Hillsborough, only about a dozen miles down the road, and pitted them against a club set for a third successive third-place finish in the First Division, straight after two consecutive seasons as champions. What was more, Chesterfield were in the throes of a struggle for Second Division survival they were destined to lose. They had won only three of their first twenty League games of the season before the slight upturn of a sequence of three victories that had been broken by defeat at Bradford City the Saturday before the Cup-tie. In stark contrast, Wednesday, then second in their table, had lost only once in fourteen matches since early October. So it was more in hope than expectation that about 10,000 Chesterfield fans set off for Sheffield, and their worst fears seemed certain to be realised when centre-forward Jack Ball put the home side two up in the first fifteen minutes.

That, though, was when Wednesday made their big mistake. Overconfident, they eased up, and Chesterfield, unfamiliarly clad in white shirts because of a colour clash (Wednesday wore red), hit back to force a replay with goals from their attack leader, Colin Cook, and Jack Lee, a bargain of a winger at £250 from Arsenal. Lee's was the best of the game. He rounded off a top-speed run through the defence with a shot that Jack Brown, one of the six survivors from Wednesday's title teams, could only push high into the air. Lee bravely flung himself at the ball as it dropped and headed it home.

Both sides lost the excellent chance of an outright winner.

Wednesday's was the double miss of a hat-trick by Ball. First he hit an upright with a penalty-kick after Billy Kidd had been harshly judged, in Chesterfield eyes, to have barged him out of possession. Then, unthinking in his eagerness, he did find the net with a tap-in from the rebound, only to have a goal ruled out because he had played the ball twice with nobody else intervening.

Chesterfield's opportunity to snatch victory at Hillsborough came right at the end. Cook, who had scored 70 goals for Crook Town in one North-East season after being rejected by Bradford City, miscued at point-blank range, allowing the goalkeeper an easy save when he otherwise must surely have been beaten.

Unusually, there was a change of referee, with no reason given, for the second meeting at Saltergate the following Wednesday, when a crowd of nearly 20,000 increased the tie's total gate to almost 50,000. There were also three changes in the Sheffield team, right-back George Beeson (influenza) and Jack Ball (injured) reporting unfit, and Harry Burgess losing his place at inside-left. Beeson, a former miner, had been with Clay Cross, his home club, and Chesterfield before joining Wednesday. This was how they lined up, with those brought in for the replay shown in brackets:

Chesterfield: Ashmore; Wass, Kidd; McIntyre, Sliman, Poynton; Austin, Abel, Cook, Bacon, Lee.

Wednesday: Brown; Beeson (Walker), Catlin; Strange, Leach, Malloch; Hooper, Starling, Ball (Millership), Burgess (Stephenson), Rimmer.

Allan Sliman, a strong, attacking Scottish centre-half, had become Chesterfield's costliest player with his £1,800 move from Bristol City. Shortly before the Second World War, he and the locally-born Horace Wass, captain of the club's first promotion winners, were together again in the Southern League with Chelmsford City, where Sliman was manager, at a time when a shock Cup win was gained against Southampton. Wass, whose brother Ted was also with Chesterfield, briefly, before finding more scope with York City, was converted into a dependable half-back or full-back after joining the club as an amateur outside-right in 1920, and he made 413 League appearances (a club record until overtaken first by Ron Powell, and then Dave Blakey, in the 1960s) before leaving for Southport at the end of the 1936-37 season. Also an accomplished batsman, he represented Scotland at cricket – including matches with the South African and Australian tourists – after playing once for Derbyshire in the County Championship. Following wartime service as a physical training instructor in the Middle East, he emigrated to Australia, where he died in 1969 in his 66th year.

Johnny McIntyre and Arthur Bacon, like George Stephenson and Gavin Malloch in the Wednesday side, had formerly played for Derby County. Bacon, nicknamed Rasher, was with Chesterfield both before and after joining the Rams. It was back in Derby that he was killed in an air raid in 1942 while serving as a special constable.

Hard work by the groundstaff averted the postponement of the replay against Wednesday which a heavy snowfall had made look extremely likely two days earlier. There was then such an improvement in the weather that skipper McIntyre was able to set the visitors facing strong sunshine when he won the toss at the kick-off, and dazzling was certainly the word for it as the game began with an amazing reversal of what had happened at Hillsborough. This time an even swifter two-goal lead was gained by Chesterfield. Cook took only three minutes to make amends for missing that late open goal on the Saturday, smashing the ball back into the net when Brown made a poor clearance. Five minutes later, Sammy Abel left the goalkeeper helpless with a first-time shot from Billy Austin's centre. Abel had been snapped up straight after being in the Accrington side trounced 3-7 at Saltergate midway through the promotion season – a real snip at the £100 fee the hard-up Lancashire club accepted. He survived the war as a special constable in London and later made it to Wembley – as a groundsman.

Unrecognisable from the team that had been struggling in the League, Chesterfield scored again after eighteen minutes, Lee heading home from their first corner, taken by Austin. And, incredibly, in the 26th minute the gap widened still further. Bacon, whose six goals in a 7-3 defeat of Stoke in 1931 remain the Reading record, left four defenders sprawling helplessly on the sanded surface in a dribble from the halfway line before drilling a low shot into the net just out of Brown's reach. Pandemonium!

Of course, it was too good to last, and it did not. Chesterfield had a grim fight to hold out after having their lead halved by goals from Millership and Stephenson in the first fifteen minutes of the second half – especially when they were virtually reduced to ten men as Kidd played on in much pain from a thigh injury. But that was the end of the scoring, the traditional pitch invasion by exuberant home fans greeting the final whistle with the result as the Mayor of Chesterfield, Arthur Swale, had predicted: 4-2.

A visit to Darlington, who ended that season at the foot of the Third Division North held no terrors for Chesterfield in the fourth round, Austin and Lee scoring the goals that next paired them with Burnley at Turf Moor. That did not appear a formidable proposition either, for the Spireites had drawn there on the opening day of the season and then crushed those fellow Second Division strugglers 6-0 in the return game on New Year's Eve. But it was not to be. Burnley scored the only goal, and in the League they would also be the club that stayed up while Chesterfield went down.

The stirring knock-out of Wednesday so uplifted Saltergate spirits that McIntyre and his men climbed out of the relegation zone by going through their next five Second Division games unbeaten. After their Cup exit at Burnley, however, they sank back into it by going five more without a win. There were then only six more matches left, and when the last one came along, on 6 May 1933, hopes of avoiding the drop had as good as died. That final fixture just happened to be at home to the bottom club, Charlton Athletic, who, on 31 points, had already been relegated. Chesterfield were not only two points behind Burnley's 34, but also had the considerably inferior goals figures of 56-82 to their 66-79. The next club up the table, West Ham, were safe with 35 points.

Some outlandish results would therefore have been necessary for Chesterfield to have wriggled clear on goal-average by winning while Burnley lost. In the event, both won. Charlton, so soon to bounce back so emphatically that within three years they were in the First Division after two successive promotions, were duly dispatched 5-2. Burnley scored the only goal of their home game with Bury, who finished fourth. These were the final positions at the foot of the table:

Season 1932-33	P	W	D	L	F	A	Pts
19. Burnley	42	11	14	17	67	79	36
20. West Ham	42	13	9	20	75	93	35
21. Chesterfield	42	12	10	20	61	84	34
22. Charlton	42	12	7	23	60	91	31

Relegation did not cost manager Harvey his job. Faith in him was rewarded when, after the very near-miss of prompt promotion, Second Division status was regained in the 1935-36 season in which Charlton completed their record climb as runners-up to Manchester United. Bill Harvey (not to be confused with his namesake who managed Luton and Grimsby) stayed until the summer of 1938, when he took over at Gillingham, shortly after the Kent club had been voted out of the Football League, and saw them to third place in the Southern League's last full pre-war season.

Harvey, a Hampshire man, was with Birmingham as player and assistant manager before Chesterfield's directors decided he was the man to follow Teddy Davison in June 1932. He had been in charge of the Blues' reserve team that had won the Central League championship. Throughout his playing career as a right-winger he had remained an amateur – for Yorkshire Amateurs and the 2nd Battalion of the West Riding Regiment, and then in a century of Football League appearances shared between the Wednesday, Birmingham and Southend. He had won an England amateur cap against Ireland in 1920, and two more on that year's FA tour of South Africa.

George Ashmore and Johnny McIntyre, then in their mid-30s, both decided to give up playing after Chesterfield's relegation in 1933. Ashmore went back to Birmingham to take a job with the Midlands Electricity Board from which he retired in 1958, fifteen years before his death. McIntyre rejoined Derby County, first as the 'A' team's coach, then as assistant manager during the war, and finally as scout up to 1960. He was a few months from his 76th birthday when he died at Derby in 1974. Jack Lee and Arthur Bacon were among the others who also left after relegation. Lee moved to Aldershot, Bacon to Coventry (where his goals outnumbered his games, just, in another short stay before he went out of the Football League with Burton).

Chesterfield's new goalkeeper was Yorkshireman John Moody, a Manchester United ever-present in the past season after being Arsenal's fourth choice and then having spells with Bradford Park Avenue and Doncaster Rovers. In attack, considerable, if well advanced, experience was introduced with the return to his home county from Park Avenue of Calow-born Harry Bedford, who had been a product of Chesterfield junior football while working as a miner, but had started out from Grassmoor Ivanhoe with Nottingham Forest on the recommendation of Sam Hardy. Bedford had won two England caps while at Blackpool, and then been with McIntyre and Thornewell in Derby's promoted Second Division runners-up of 1925-26. Bedford's dozen or so goals in his one season at Saltergate before staying in Derbyshire as Heanor Town's trainer increased his League and Cup total to 326 in the 485 games of a career in which he also played for Newcastle and Sunderland. He announced himself at Chesterfield with a hat-trick in a 6-2 defeat of Gateshead, Colin Cook getting the home side's three other goals.

Chesterfield's other newcomers in 1933-34 included Harry Clifton, a prime Dormand discovery who was spotted playing at inside-forward for Scotswood by the club's North-East scout after failing to impress in trials with West Bromwich Albion. Clifton played rarely in the first team that season despite making a scoring debut, but his progress with the Reserves was rapid, and he began a regular run with the seniors on New Year's Day in 1935.

The season of 1933-34 was the one in which Chesterfield were cruelly denied an immediate return to Division Two. They topped the Third North table until the very last day, when they were overtaken, 62 points to 61, by Barnsley, who had themselves experienced bitter disappointment in being edged out of a rise to the First Division on a slender difference of goal-average several years earlier. It was small consolation for Chesterfield to know that the number of goals they conceded, 43, was the lowest in the entire League, most closely approached by the 47 of Arsenal, champions in the top flight for the second of what would be three consecutive seasons.

That 1933-34 season was also the first of the Third North Cup. It lasted for five more, then faded out with the war after only fourteen of the 22 clubs had taken part in its final season of 1938-39. Chesterfield never reached the final, but in the 1934-35 competition they gave their supporters something to shout about during a slide down to tenth in the table with an 8-1 knock-out of Mansfield Town. Five of the goals were scored by Ambrose Brown, the club's record for one match.

Clifton was a key figure in Chesterfield's surge to promotion in 1936, though outscored by Mick Dando's 29 goals in 27 games. They finished five points clear of runners-up Chester, who had to make do with defeating Darlington in the final of the Third North Cup, a trophy they retained against Southport the following season. Again Chesterfield had the League's best defensive record, the number of goals they conceded reduced still further to 39. The next lowest was the 43 of Manchester United's Second Division champions. For goals scored, the Spireites were eight goals short of Chester's 100. These were the final positions at the top of the Third North table:

Season 1935-36	P	W	D	L	F	A	Pts
1. Chesterfield	42	24	12	6	92	39	60
2. Chester	42	22	11	9	100	45	55
3. Tranmere	42	22	11	9	93	58	55
4. Lincoln	42	22	9	11	91	51	53

The year of 1936 was a memorable one for Derbyshire sport. In addition to Chesterfield's success, Derby County were runners-up in Division One, and Derbyshire claimed what has since become their only officially recognised county cricket championship (the other of 1874 was ruled out nearly 90 years later because they had not played enough matches). Chesterfield also splashed out with the expenditure of £14,000 on a new main stand.

Life back in the Second Division was a struggle for Chesterfield at first, but they improved from fifteenth in 1936-37 to eleventh the next season, and to sixth in the one after that, the last before the outbreak of another world war. Behind that steady climb lay the success of Clifton's link-up with another former Scotswood forward, Joe Spence, who had won one of his two England caps, in a 3-3 draw with Ireland in 1926, in the same team as his cousin George Brown, then a centre-forward with Huddersfield. Spence was an astute addition to Chesterfield's promotion-winning team from Bradford City after setting a Manchester United appearances record of 510 League and Cup games that stood for 40 years. His 58 games and ten goals for the Spireites, before switching to scouting for the club in his 40th year, 1938, took his career League totals to 614 and 195. His son, also Joe, followed him onto Chesterfield's books, but did not play in their first team before exceeding 100 appearances for York City. Whereas Joe Senior had three clubs in nineteen years, his son had three in eighteen months with Buxton intervening.

So greatly did Clifton benefit from playing alongside Spence, a penetrative winger capped twice by England, that he caught the attention of the national selectors as Chesterfield's top scorer with 26 goals in 1937-38, increasing his tally for the club to 67 in 121 League games. He also attracted Newcastle United, who in the January of that season had to fork out £8,000, the biggest fee Chesterfield had received up to that time when they could have had him for just the signing-on fee if they had not missed the potential that Harry Dormand spotted. Five months later, on 14 May 1938, Clifton was an England reserve for the match at which the players controversially had to give the Nazi salute before gaining a highly satisfying 6-3 victory over Germany in Berlin. He did get to play for England – just the once, in the first wartime international against Scotland at Newcastle, for which caps were not awarded, before going off for four years' Army service in the Middle East. Clifton did not score, but England won 2-1.

After demobilisation, Clifton twice did the hat-trick as a Newcastle regular in the transitional League North of 1945-46 before his transfer to Grimsby, on the second occasion leading a scoring spree of five goals in just over a quarter of an hour as Liverpool were beaten 6-2 in front of Newcastle's biggest crowd since pre-war days, just over 50,000. In three seasons with Grimsby, Clifton completed a century of League goals before the report of a knee specialist ended his playing career in his mid-30s in October 1949. He had been unable to turn out for Goole Town, who had signed him that summer, but the Midland League management committee ruled that the Yorkshire club must pay his wages until the end of the season because he had joined them in good faith. Goole softened the blow by appointing him to their backroom staff, but he soon returned to Chesterfield to work at the Tube Works, and then Arkwright Colliery. In 1968 he was also back at Saltergate as a steward, but he eventually settled again at Newcastle, where he died in 1998 at the age of 84.

Even if Clifton had played for England in that pre-war match in Germany, he would not have been the first to be capped while with Chesterfield. That distinction had already gone to Walter McMillen, a Belfast-born half-back, in Northern Ireland's 1-1 draw with Scotland at Aberdeen in November 1937, almost a year after his £2,000 transfer from Manchester United. McMillen, who also played for Millwall before returning home to join Glentoran, won the first three of his seven caps while with United – the second of them most notably back in Belfast, where a team reduced to ten men defeated the Scots by a 2-1 margin that McMillen did much to protect as stand-in goalkeeper for the injured Elisha Scott.

McMillen missed Northern Ireland's last match before the outbreak of war in 1939, when Chesterfield had another player, centre-forward Dudley Milligan, in the team beaten by Wales at Wrexham, but he turned out again for his country in their first three (uncapped) games after the war. Milligan's one Irish cap made him a two-country international, for he played three times for South Africa before breaking into British soccer with the Scottish club Clyde after failing to earn a contract with Dundee. Irish parentage was claimed for this son of a Johannesburg gold miner.

There have since been two other players who were capped by Northern Ireland while with Chesterfield: Gerry Armstrong and Mark Williams. Armstrong helped the Ulstermen to win the British Championship in 1980 (for the first time since 1914), and was voted the leading British player of the World Cup finals in Spain in 1982. His moves from Tottenham to Watford (both won promotion to the old First Division during his stay) and then to the Spanish club Real Mallorca involved fees totalling almost £500,000. Chesterfield obtained him on a free transfer from West Bromwich in January 1986, and after playing a dozen times for them that season he made his 63rd and final international appearance as a substitute in a first-round World Cup defeat by Brazil in Mexico. On his return he signed for Brighton and also had a spell on loan to Millwall.

Mark Williams, centre-half with Shrewsbury Town's Third Division champions of 1993-94, a couple of years before his move to Saltergate, made the first four of his 36 Northern Ireland appearances as a Chesterfield player. To just over 100 games for Shrewsbury he added nearly 170 for the Derbyshire club, among them a historic run to the FA Cup semi-finals (of which more later). He then went into the FA Carling Premiership with newly promoted Watford, but when they dropped straight back to the First Division of the League (the old Second Division) he went from one relegated club to another by joining Wimbledon. His last games for Wimbledon were under their new name of Milton Keynes Dons after relocating in 2004, and he saw out his playing career with Rushden & Diamonds towards the end of the penultimate season of their brief membership of the Football League.

4

Hardy, Middleton and Banks in a galaxy of goalkeepers

In August 1937 Chesterfield made another of their astute signings from the North-East by bringing in 17-year-old Ray Middleton as an amateur from Washington Church, a minor league side from near his Boldon birthplace in County Durham. He turned professional that October, and proceeded to claim a high place on the list of outstanding goalkeepers the Spireites have long been famed for producing. Not bad going for a £50 outlay.

On 3 September 1938, Middleton made his Second Division debut, displacing John Moody for a home match with Blackburn Rovers. His competent display in a 0-2 defeat by the coming champions launched him onto an unbroken sequence of 263 Football League and FA Cup-ties that he extended to 333 after his transfer to Derby County in June 1951. With the inclusion of the war years, during which he worked down the pit as a conscripted Bevin Boy and took the precaution of insuring his hands for £2,000, his first-team games for Chesterfield were not far off double that total. Not all those were consecutive, however, the first interruption occurring near the end of the 1939-40 season. Blackburn were also the opponents for the 500th, in 1948, when he played despite a broken bone in a wrist. The 600th came at Doncaster in November 1950.

In common with a number of others exceptionally proficient in the position, Middleton did not start out as a goalkeeper. He was a versatile player at school, mainly at centre-half, but just happened to impress in goal when chosen to play there for Sunderland Boys, with whom he gained an English Schools Shield medal. He was never coached, but benefited from closely studying the top goalkeepers. One from whom he particularly learned was his elder brother Matt, who played in the First Division for Sunderland and was also with Southport, Plymouth, Bradford City and York in making more than 250 League appearances.

But for being at his peak when England had a wealth of goalkeeping talent with clubs considered more 'fashionable', Middleton must surely have become a full international. He managed next best in playing four times for England 'B', once in a team that also included his Chesterfield clubmate Stan Milburn at full-back. Any chance of further honours for Middleton melted away, however, when he left Saltergate in the wake of relegation back to the Third North, only to be caught up in another decline that dispatched Derby in the same direction. Released by the Rams as their slump from First to Third within nine years of winning the FA Cup gathered momentum, he went into the Midland League as Boston United's player-manager, but soon returned to the Baseball Ground with five other former Derby players in a team that caused one of the biggest of all the Cup upsets by winning 6-1.

Middleton, who ran a grocer's shop at Old Whittington and became involved in local politics on behalf of the Labour party, was a footballing rarity as a Justice of the Peace and a lay preacher. He had a second spell with Boston after managing Hartlepool United – first as manager and then as secretary, a position he held until his death in 1977.

Of all the others in the imposing array of Chesterfield goalkeepers, Sam Hardy and Gordon Banks so obviously stand out for their extreme ability, but one of the earliest to be between the club's posts was in the news for very different reasons. In Charlie Bunyan's day goalkeepers were allowed to handle the ball anywhere in their own half, and the Spireites sacked him for too often being stranded upfield berating his forwards when a goal was conceded. Bunyan, who ran a public house near the club's ground, also ran foul of officialdom, suspended for altering a transfer form to show that Felix Davis had moved from Chesterfield Town to Derby County (another of Bunyan's clubs) instead of Brampton Works. It was alleged that Bunyan was paid every time the Rams signed a player on his recommendation.

As if all that was not enough, the colourful Charlie has been best remembered as the Hyde goalkeeper who was beaten a record 26 times in an FA Cup-tie with Preston North End in 1887. But on that occasion he was more of a hero than a villain. The score would have been even greater without his plucky resistance in the face of a constant barrage that left him so battered, bruised and exhausted that he collapsed in the dressing room after being carried off shoulder high by his team-mates. Preston's goalkeeper was also carried off, but that was because, having had so little to do on a bitterly cold day, he was seized with severe cramp that left him 'as stiff as any broomstick' according to one account.

Bunyan also showed courage during the 1914-18 war. On going back to England after being Standard Liege's coach in Belgium, he volunteered with his three sons for the Army, taking eight years off his age to be accepted. The fact that he was in his mid-40s came to light after he had been diagnosed with shell shock, and he was discharged in May 1916. The damage to his health resulted in his early death in 1922 back in Belgium, to which he had returned as coach with the Brussels club Anderlecht.

Sam Hardy, whose judgment and anticipation were uncanny, was the most famous England goalkeeper from 1905, the year in which, priced at £500, he left Chesterfield for Liverpool, to 1924, when he was forced into retirement at the age of 41 by an injury suffered while playing for Nottingham Forest against Newcastle. In between, he helped Liverpool to the First Division title in 1905-06, Aston Villa to the FA Cup in 1913 and 1920, and Forest to the Second Division championship in 1921-22. He also won 21 caps in an England career that lasted from 1907 to 1920 and played in two Victory internationals. His League and Cup appearances exceeded 600 – the first 77 of them with Chesterfield, for whom manager Jack Hoskin beat Derby County to it by signing him under the light of a lamp post at Newbold, a village to the north of Chesterfield in which he was born. Not, however, until the original offer of five shillings (25p) a week had been increased to eighteen (90p).

After serving in the Royal Navy in the 1914-18 war, Hardy first played for Forest as a guest in their Victory Shield defeat of Everton over the two legs of the 1919 final. During the next world war, when Middleton also guested for Forest in a Cup final (lost to WBA in 'sudden death'), Hardy was told he was too old when he answered a call for mineworkers to help increase coal production, but two days later he was in a 'heading', working the engine that hauled coal tubs up a steep gradient. Then nearing 60, he described himself as 'fitter than most men half my age'.

From football, Hardy turned to running public houses and billiard halls in the Chesterfield area right up to his death, aged 83, in October 1966, the year in which Gordon Banks joined the select band of England's World Cup winners. Banks, even better remembered for the spectacular one-handed 'save of the century' he made from Pele's header at the World Cup finals of 1970 in Mexico, rose from being a £2-a-match part-timer with Chesterfield to play 73 times for England, eight times as British champions (twice shared) in the Home Internationals, before losing the sight in his right eye when he pulled out to overtake a slow-moving lorry in his new Ford Granada and crashed head-on with a van on a bend just outside the Staffordshire village of Whitmore on the morning of Sunday, 22 October 1972. He was on his way home from Stoke City's ground, where he had been receiving treatment on a shoulder injured during defeat by Liverpool at Anfield the previous day in the 511th League match of his career (on which I reported for *The Daily Telegraph*).

Banks, the son of a Sheffield steelworker, began as a forward, but was a goalkeeper in colliery football when he jumped at the chance to join Chesterfield as an apprentice after not relishing his first jobs on leaving school, as a coal bagger and bricklayer. His progress through the youth and 'A' teams to the Reserves was broken by National Service with the Royal Signals in Germany, where he was in his regiment's Rhine Cup-winning team, but Teddy Davison offered him a full-time contract on his return, and he made his League debut at home to Colchester in the new Third Division in November 1958. There were to be only 22 more first-team games for him, however, before tightening purse strings compelled his £7,000 transfer to Leicester City in the summer of 1959 – originally as stand-in for Dave MacLaren, but very quickly as the firmly established first choice more than 350 times.

With Leicester, Banks played in two FA Cup finals (both lost) and two League Cup finals (one won, the other lost). With Stoke, he earned another League Cup winner's medal in 1972, when he was also emphatically voted Footballer of the Year by the Footballer Writers' Association – an honour, a well-deserved addition to his OBE, for which he had been runner-up and third in the previous two years. Stoke's manager, Tony Waddington, rated his £52,000 signing of Banks in April 1967 as the best he ever made (ahead, even, of that of Stanley Matthews, which he considered 'a publicity thing'), but it came about only because Peter Shilton, ten years younger than Banks, was growing restless in Leicester's Reserves. Shilton went on to succeed Banks as England's most-capped goalkeeper in completing the century of appearances Banks might well have also reached but for his serious injury, and he eventually followed him into the Stoke side too.

Hopes of a League comeback by Banks were inevitably dashed with his contract still having almost five years to run. He was given the go-ahead to resume full training early in 1973, ten weeks after the crash, and, although he had not then given up hope, he admitted he could 'only distinguish light objects from dark at close range' with his damaged eye. Late that month, watched by a crowd of 3,500, he scored a goal in his first game back – as a right-winger for an All-Stars team in a charity match at the village of Werrington, eight miles from Stoke's ground, in aid of the family of a local junior football official, Roger Lomas, who had died at the age of 32. It raised almost £1,000.

Banks came through his first real test when he kept goal in the first half of a friendly game in which Stoke defeated Olympiakos 3-0 in Athens that March, and soon afterwards he gave an almost flawless display in the Reserves' 1-0 home win against Forest Reserves. His handicap was too great, however, for him to continue at the top level, and his retirement was announced by Tony Waddington on 18 August 1973, before the Watney Cup final in which Stoke beat Hull 2-0. Even so, Banks was able to play in his testimonial match against Manchester United, who won 2-1, during December, when, despite incessant rain, receipts amounted to about £15,000 from a crowd of 21,308. It was not only the weather that threatened the match. 100 gallons of diesel fuel to power the generator for the floodlights mysteriously disappeared overnight, and emergency supplies had to be hurriedly brought in.

The United players travelled the 30 miles or so down the M6 for the match without asking for any payment – a grand gesture only ten days after Tottenham's Phil Beal had seen the entire profit from his sparsely attended benefit game wiped out by the £12,500 fee required by Bayern Munich. 'United aren't even asking for their travelling expenses,' said Waddington. The Portuguese international Eusebio, one of Stoke's star guests, opened the scoring (Bobby Charlton, against his own club, was the other) but United hit back with goals laid on by George Best for Tony Young and Lou Macari in the second half. Banks beat Alex Stepney, the United goalkeeper, 3-1 in a penalty-taking contest during the half-time interval.

Banks also took part in a testimonials for other players, one of them at Chesterfield. Nor was that all. After spells as a Stoke scout and manager with Telford United, he was voted Best Goalkeeper in the North American League when he spent part of two seasons with Fort Lauderdale Strikers. And he kept a clean sheet in one League of Ireland game for St Patrick's Athletic against Shamrock Rovers before briefly coaching with Port Vale.

Banks blamed player power for losing his job as Vale's first-team coach in November 1979. 'They didn't like the hard work,' he said when they complained about his methods. 'But I felt that if hard work had been good enough for me with 73 caps it was good enough for Fourth Division players.' Banks was demoted to reserve-team coach, but was also sacked from that post a month later at an emergency meeting called amid the upheaval caused by the resignations of manager Alan Bloor (only ten weeks after his appointment) and his assistant, Les Shannon.

In 2001, Banks made the difficult decision of putting his World Cup winner's medal up for auction because he wanted to save his children having to agree what to do with it after his death. The £124,750 it fetched was divided between them. His cap for that match was also auctioned, for £27,025. A year later, having, like Hardy, already become one of the Football League's 100 Legends, he, with Shilton, was among the first group of players inducted into the National Football Museum's Hall of Fame. Amazingly, Hardy's name has yet to be among those added annually to that list at the time of writing. In 2006 Banks was the first to have a plaque bearing his name installed on the pavement in the Walk of Fame in front of Sheffield's Town Hall, and in 2011 he entered Stoke's Hall of Fame.

The next big name in this parade of Chesterfield's goalkeeping greats is Ron Powell, on the strength of his 471 League appearances (508 in all) that took the club's record from Horace Wass. He was signed in the summer of 1952 to fill the gap left by Middleton, after playing in only a dozen senior games between the careers of Frank Swift and Bert Trautmann during his four years with Manchester City. At Saltergate he spent twelve years, his consistency underlined in a sequence of 284 League games broken by Banks. Like Banks, he was forced out of top soccer by injuries suffered in a car crash. It occurred in December 1964, while he was returning from watching a match at Peterborough with his clubmates Ralph Hunt, Peter Stringfellow and Doug Wragg. Hunt, scorer of 186 League goals for his nine clubs, and brother of Stringfellow's former Gillingham team-mate Dennis Hunt, died from his injuries. Stringfellow, an inside-forward who had joined Chesterfield from Gillingham in exchange for Charlie Rackstraw, a Sheffield-born striker, was not, as driver, blamed for the accident, but he lost form so badly that he was released at the end of that season and emigrated to Australia.

Towards the end of Powell's reign as a first-team regular, Chesterfield signed a goalkeeper who was nicknamed the 'Brain of Football' for the exceptional general knowledge he showed during the BBC's televised *Quizball* series. This was John Osborne, also known as the 'bionic goalkeeper' after having a plastic joint inserted in an arthritic finger on his left hand.

Osborne was born in Derbyshire, at Barlborough, a village near Worksop, but after playing in schools football at town, county and international levels, he was with Bolton Wanderers as an amateur before becoming a product of Saltergate's famous goalkeeping 'academy'. He was another who found his true position after beginning as an outfield player, and he made one of his 110 League appearances for Chesterfield at centre-forward before his £9,250 transfer to West Bromwich in January 1967.

With Albion, Osborne gained an FA Cup winner's medal in 1968, against Everton after extra-time, was a runner-up to Manchester City in the 1970 League Cup final, and did not miss a match when promotion from the Second Division was won in 1976. He was the club's first choice in 312 matches, but with two breaks in the early 1970s when he left complaining that 'the heart has gone out of the game'. He went into partnership in a sports good business with fellow goalkeeper Jim Cumbes, and 'traded the peaks and caverns of professional football for the nice evenly balanced life of a man in the street.'

Towards the end of 1972 Osborne spent his 32nd birthday covering an Aston Villa match for a local radio station, but, after absences for the best part of four seasons, it was not until 1978 that he finally left Albion – with a testimonial that realised £32,000, then a record for a Midlands player. Later that year, he was back in action for Shamrock Rovers, whose player-manager, Johnny Giles, the former Leeds and Eire playmaker who had also been player-manager with WBA before returning to the Republic, urgently needed a replacement for Alan O'Neill, who had been injured on a pre-season tour of Spain.

Osborne recalled that: 'Giles rang me and said "What are you doing a week next Wednesday? Nothing? Right, you're playing in the Cup-winners' Cup." He gave me the benefit of a warm-up in a league game against Dundalk, which we lost 2-1, and then I was in for the first leg against Apoel. I stood there soaked, telling myself that I must be crackers. I should have been at home in Sutton Coldfield, watching the telly with a fag and a pint.' Osborne, who was also persuaded to give up some of his next year's holiday to join Shamrock in Cyprus, added: 'I certainly didn't do it for the money. It was expenses only. I did it simply because I owe a lot to Johnny Giles. At Albion he gave me two extra years on a good contract.'

Even then Osborne was not finished with football. He was working in the promotions department of the *Sandwell and Birmingham Evening Mail* when, at 41, he was signed by Walsall as cover for Ron Green because Mick Kearns, the reserve goalkeeper, had broken a finger. He was on stand-by for an FA Cup-tie against Birmingham in January 1983, but was not needed. Green played in the goalless draw, and in the replay Walsall lost after extra-time.

Osborne, who also had a keen interest in cricket (he became commercial manager with Worcestershire CCC), was followed as a 'home-grown' Chesterfield goalkeeper by Staveley-born Alan Stevenson, who was an amateur, aged eighteen, when he made his League debut at home to Scunthorpe in October 1969 as an emergency replacement for the injured Alan Humphreys. From then until his £55,000 transfer to Burnley in January 1972 Stevenson played in all 115 of Chesterfield's senior games and helped them out of Division Four. Humphreys, one of the best goalkeepers in the lower divisions after being a star centre-half at school in Chester, dropped out of League football, in which he had also played for Shrewsbury, Leeds and Mansfield, and, as with Osborne, became commercial manager of a first-class cricket club – Derbyshire.

Stevenson's move to Turf Moor, with Peter Mellor (soon afterwards transferred to Fulham) joining Chesterfield on a month's loan as part of the deal, made him England's most expensive goalkeeper up to that time. 'I suppose I wanted to play in a higher grade of football,' he said, 'but I had no driving ambition to leave Chesterfield. I know they are a small club, but I always enjoyed my football with them. As far as I know, it was only the bank overdraft which forced them to sell me.' He had then been a professional for just 2½ years, and admitted that, although already an Under-23 cap, he still had 'an awful lot to learn'. A full cap never came his way, but over the next eleven years he amassed 543 appearances for Burnley, falling only two games short of a post-war record for the club when surprisingly given a free transfer in the summer of 1983. He was an ever-present when they won the Second Division championship in 1972-73, and, remarkably, again when they took the Third Division title in 1981-82.

Rotherham and Hartlepool United (on loan to replace the injured Eddie Blackburn) were Stevenson's last League clubs. He combined playing for Hartlepool with being their commercial manager, a role to which he was also appointed at Middlesbrough and West Bromwich. He continued to live at Chesterfield and train at Rotherham while out on loan, and saw the Hartlepool players for only a few hours on match days. 'People said I must be mad going up to Hartlepool,' he said. 'To them it was the end of the world, but it meant first-team football for me. After fifteen years of that, it was hard being stuck in the Reserves at Rotherham. Because of the travelling, I don't see the players before two o'clock at a home match, and I sometimes have a job remembering names. Two of our defenders look the same from the back, and I often find I'm shouting at the wrong one during a game.'

After Stevenson, goalkeepers off the production line at Saltergate included Phil Tingay, Chris Marples, who were both born at Chesterfield, and Steve Hardwick, who came from Mansfield. Tingay, signed from Chesterfield Tube Works, totalled 181 appearances over ten years before leaving for Kettering Town in 1981. Marples, who kept wicket for Derbyshire (he was one of their Asda Challenge Trophy winners in 1985), played almost 150 times for the Spireites in two spells, arriving first from Goole and then from Scunthorpe after also assisting Stockport and York. Hardwick, an England Youth international, was swiftly snapped up by Newcastle for £80,000, but he was driven away from the North-East by barracking, and when he returned there with Oxford United for a Milk Cup-tie in 1983 he was pelted with coins.

Other goalkeepers who graduated from Chesterfield will crop up in their proper turn, but we cannot leave this chapter without recalling two of those who most notably slipped through the Saltergate net: Jovan (but known as John) Lukic and Bob Wilson.

Lukic went straight from Derbyshire schools football to Leeds United, and on ousting Scottish international David Harvey in December 1979 he embarked on a club record of 146 consecutive League appearances that ended only when he asked for a transfer and was promptly dropped. The international recognition he sought with his £75,000 move to Arsenal never extended beyond the Youth and Under-21 level he had reached with Leeds, thus saving the Londoners the £25,000 they had promised to add to their initial £75,000 (plus another £50,000 they paid after his first fifteen senior games) if he won two full caps. However, in exceeding 200 games for the Gunners he helped them to win the Littlewoods Cup in 1987 and the First Division title in 1988-89 (dramatically snatched from Liverpool at Anfield in the last minute of their last match) before Leeds made him their first £1m player by taking him back to Elland Road in May 1990. He was also in the Arsenal side that again reached the Littlewoods Cup final in 1988, but lost to Luton in the last minute. No wonder the trophy broke in two at the neck during the evening's celebrations.

An ever-present when Leeds became inaugural members of the FA Premiership as the last champions of the old Division One in 1991-92, Lukic chalked up another 200-plus games for the Yorkshire club, picking up a League Cup runners-up medal on the way. He then took his overall total to 668 after also returning to Arsenal, and, although no longer a first choice, he was again a medal winner, if a losing one, when he was on the bench for the UEFA Cup final in which Galatasaray defeated the Gunners on penalties at Copenhagen in 2000. He shares his distinction of playing League football in England across four decades with Stanley Matthews, Peter Shilton, and another of the goalkeepers Chesterfield gave to the game, the 6ft 4½in tall Steve Ogrizovic.

'Oggy' played only a few first-team matches for the Spireites, and even fewer for Liverpool, though he gained European Cup-winners' medals with the Merseysiders as an unused sub. He then established himself with Shrewsbury before being in Coventry's first FA Cup-winning team and raising their appearances record beyond 500 (including another club best of 241 in succession ended by injury). To get the final contract of a career that spanned 23 years he accepted City's ultimatum by smoking his last cigarette. Not until May 2000, at the age of 42, did he finally step down as a player – and then it was to continue with the Sky Blues as goalkeeping coach.

Lukic had Yugoslavian parents. Ogrizovic was born at Mansfield of Serbian stock. Bob Wilson first saw light at Chesterfield, but his parents were Scots, and that enabled him to fulfil the ambition his father had for him by winning his international caps with Scotland (after playing in the England Under-15 team). He and Hibernian's Alex Cropley, who came into this world at Aldershot, were the first English-born players to do so since the Scottish FA's formation in 1873, soon followed by Derby's Bruce Rioch, after the rules were changed in 1970 so that 'foreigners' could turn out for the country of their parents' birth if they had not already played for their own country in a full international. Sadly, Wilson's father did not live to see him make his international debut, with Cropley, in a 2-1 defeat of Portugal at Hampden Park in October 1971. Nor, because of illness, did he see him play in the FA Cup final at Wembley earlier in that year of Arsenal's League and Cup double.

Wilson, who also helped the Gunners to win the Inter-Cities Fairs Cup, was denied more than his two caps partly by injury, but also because Tommy Docherty, the man who had selected him, was soon afterwards lured to Manchester United and followed as Scotland's manager by Willie Ormond, who preferred to revert to a Scottish-born goalkeeper, Aberdeen's Bobby Clark.

The youngest of five brothers who all attended Chesterfield Grammar School, Bob Wilson was a fine all-rounder, 6ft tall when only fifteen. An accomplished wicketkeeper, he captained the Derbyshire junior cricket team, and also ran the 400 metres in the national schools championships.

As a goalkeeper, he was in the British Universities team, and in the amateur and Olympic squads, but it was with Chesterfield and England Boys during the 1956-57 season that he caught Manchester United's interest. John Osborne, then a left-half, captained the town's schools team in which Wilson played. Although training at Old Trafford, Wilson rejected the chance to sign for United on the advice of his father, who first wanted him to have a career outside football. That took him to Loughborough College, where he studied history and physical education for three years and completed his teacher training course. During that time he was an amateur with Wolves, but it was to Arsenal that he turned after being shown round Highbury by Billy Wright, the former Wolves and England captain who was then the Gunners' manager. The London club got onto his trail through Bertie Mee, who was the British Universities' physiotherapist as well as Arsenal's before succeeding Wright as manager. In his book *Life In The Beautiful Game*, Wilson revealed that he was the only amateur footballer for whom a transfer fee was paid.

When Wolves challenged his registration with Arsenal, the Gunners avoided a legal wrangle that could have dragged on for months by paying the Wanderers £6,500.

Wilson was a few days from his 22nd birthday when given his first League opportunity by Arsenal in October 1963, but was 26 before he became a regular choice for over 300 games up to his playing retirement in May 1974, at the age of 32. A dislocated elbow and broken ankle were among the obstacles he had to overcome. He afterwards enjoyed further success in television as a presenter of football programmes for both the BBC and ITV. He also kept in close touch with the game, and for 28 more years with Arsenal, as a qualified FA coach, giving valuable assistance to some experienced as well as aspiring goalkeepers.

5

'Legs' Linacre and the famous Milburn family

Bury's refusal to give manager Norman Bullock, their former England centre-forward, complete control of the team caused the resignation that made him conveniently available to succeed Bill Harvey as Chesterfield's manager in the summer of 1938, even though he was also not exactly free from interference by the directors at Saltergate. He had the satisfaction of promptly seeing the Derbyshire club to their highest final position up to that time, sixth in the Second Division, but because of the outbreak of war that would be his only Football League season with the Spireites. He rejoined Bury in July 1945, when, most remarkably considering that they had then been in existence for 60 years, he became their first manager to be given the responsibility of picking the team.

Bullock, a Lancastrian, began his association with Bury in September 1920, when he gave up his work as an analytical chemist and left Sedgeley Park, a Manchester amateur side, to join the Gigg Lane club for just the £10 signing-on fee after graduating from the Salford Boys team to Broughton St John's and Prestwich Amateurs. Less than three years later he won the first of his three international caps, scoring in the 6-1 defeat of Belgium at Arsenal's ground. In the season after that, 1923-24, he led Bury back to the First Division as runners-up to Leeds, nudging Chesterfield's Derby neighbours into third place by 0.015 of a goal.

Towards the end of his playing days Bullock dropped back from the attack in an emergency to prove equally reliable at centre-half, and he had nearly 550 games and 130 goals for Bury behind him when he first became the club's manager in June 1934. His 506 League appearances are still the most made by a Bury player. At first his authority as manager was restricted by the directors' insistence of continuing to have the final say on team matters, but he was allowed a little more control when disappointing results provoked criticism from supporters, and in 1936-37 Bury rose to third in Division Two. Then, however, came the difference with the board that took him to Saltergate, where he took over a team in which Ray Middleton had become well established in goal and such experienced players as George Milburn, Joe Devine and Peter Ramage had also recently been introduced.

Milburn, Billy Kidd's new partner at full-back, was a rugged, stockily built member of a famous footballing family that most notably included his cousin Jackie Milburn, a folk hero with Newcastle United, and his nephews Jack and Bobby Charlton, World Cup winners along with Gordon Banks. There were also three other Milburns who were George's brothers – Jack and Jim, who were with him at Leeds before the Second World War, and Stan, a clubmate at Chesterfield after it. During his school holidays the young Bobby Charlton used to visit his uncles George and Stan Milburn, and he went to Saltergate to watch them in training. All the Milburns were born at the Northumberland coal-mining town of Ashington. The three Milburns with Leeds provided the only case of three brothers each making the maximum number of Football League appearances in a season with the same club. They were also the only three brothers who each received two benefits from the same club.

George Milburn was a centre-half with Ashington Colliery Welfare when Leeds United signed him in 1928 at the age of seventeen, but he was soon converted into a full-back and he partnered Jack in more than 150 League and Cup games before captaining the Reserves to their first Central League title in 1936-37. The £1,500 Chesterfield invested in him in May 1937 proved to be money very well spent. His playing career at Saltergate stretched across 102 Second Division matches and 221 games during the war (his employment at the local tube work kept him out of the armed forces), and when it ended in 1948 he continued on the club's coaching staff for just over a dozen more years. Although primarily a defender, he appeared occasionally in attack and retired from playing as one of the few to have scored a hat-trick of penalties – against Sheffield Wednesday on the last day of the 1946-47 season, which was extended into June because the many postponements during a winter of extremely icy weather.

Joe Devine, a nephew of Joe Cassidy, a former Glasgow Celtic and Scotland forward, joined Chesterfield from Birmingham, also in 1937, after entering English football with Burnley from Motherwell and also playing for Newcastle, Sunderland and Queens Park Rangers. A slightly built but tricky inside-forward or wing-half, he was prematurely forced to give up playing after breaking a leg in a League match at Tottenham in 1938, but he, too, gave further service as a coach, on both sides of the Second World War. It was from him that George Milburn took over as trainer to Chesterfield's Central League side. Devine died back home in Scotland in 1980 (the same year as George Milburn) after ending his connection with football as a referee in the Highland League.

The Chesterfield head trainer with whom Devine and Milburn worked was Olly Thompson, whose five years with the club as a player began at left-half in the Third Division North's inaugural season of 1921-22. He returned to Saltergate as trainer in 1935 after also playing for QPR, York and Halifax, and early in 1959 he completed the full set of the then 92 Football League grounds when he trundled the team's skip into Layer Road, Colchester. The day he looked back on as his most memorable as a player came at St James' Park, only twenty minutes from the house in which he had lived, against a Newcastle side that included Hughie Gallacher, Jackie Milburn's predecessor as the footballing idol of the North-East.

Tottenham were especially familiar opponents for Chesterfield around the time of Joe Devine's career-ending injury. The clubs met four times during the 1937-38 season, twice in the Cup between the two League games from which the Spireites gleaned just the one point from a 2-2 home draw at the end of October. The attendance for that match was little more than 16,000. When Spurs revisited Saltergate in the fifth round of the Cup the score was the same, but the gate swelled to a new record for the ground, 30,561. The replay resulted in a hard-earned 2-1 win for Tottenham, but out they immediately went to a lone Sunderland goal in a quarter-final watched by a crowd of 75,038, still the biggest at White Hart Lane.

It was against Sunderland, and also before a record crowd, 75,118 (with thousands more locked out), that Peter Ramage reached the high point of his career. This often underrated Scot, signed by Chesterfield from Derby County at about the same time as the arrival of Milburn and Devine, was a schemer rather than a scorer, but he was best remembered by Rams fans, many of whom failed fully to appreciate his true value, for the winning goal he so spectacularly headed in a quarter-final replay at Roker Park in 1933. After more than 250 games for Derby, who were twice First Division runners-up while he was with them, he gave Chesterfield further unselfish service before ending an English career he had begun with Coventry City by moving to Heanor Town as the clouds of another world war were gathering. His last games were played for Atherstone Town with peace restored.

Another Scot brought into Chesterfield's attack soon after Ramage was Tommy Lyon, scorer of four goals against Southampton on the first Saturday of December in 1938. He was born in Glasgow, first taken South by Blackpool, but his brother Willie, a centre-half with Glasgow Celtic, was an Englishman, born at Birkenhead. Tommy was transferred to New Brighton, then a Third North club, after a war-interrupted ten-year stay at Saltergate. Willie became Dundee's assistant manager at about the same time.

In 1940, Chesterfield were champions of the wartime East Midlands Regional League. In 1941, they were runners-up in the League North. In the 1941-42 season, two players who were to make their mark in post-war football, winger Billy Linacre and centre-half Bill Whitaker, graduated from the Reserves.

Linacre, lithe and leggy, was nicknamed 'Legs' – ironically so because he broke his right leg three times. That first happened in a match with Grimsby in November 1945, and occurred again only ten months later, when, against Manchester City at Maine Road in September 1946, he began the most unusual and unwelcome experience of breaking a leg in two of the three away games he played for different clubs in the same city, and being ordered off in the other.

His dismissal by referee Arthur Ellis, along with that of Henry Cockburn, Manchester United's England wing-half, came in the local derby of September 1949, after Linacre's transfer to Manchester City. United were the home club because they were sharing City's ground while their own war-damaged Old Trafford stadium was being repaired. Linacre was with Middlesbrough when he broke the leg for the third time back at Maine Road in February 1950.

Linacre, the son of a noted local sprinter, was spotted by Chesterfield playing for Derbyshire Boys. He made his first-team debut at the age of 16½, at centre-forward against Rotherham United in December 1941, and went on to complete exactly 100 further wartime appearances, scoring 40 goals. He had expected to follow his brother into the RAF, but he became available to his home club because he was drafted to Bolsover Colliery as one of the Bevin Boys named after Ernest Bevin, then the Minister of Labour and National Service. Linacre turned semi-professional in February 1944, and became a full-timer at the end of the war. Skill and speed of thought were his greatest assets. Olly Thompson reckoned 'he could do anything with the ball except make it talk', and but for his injuries he might well have borne out the forecast of those who saw him as the natural successor to Stanley Matthews in the England side.

Indeed, Linacre could also have followed Matthews into the Stoke City team. While he was with Manchester City, who beat several other clubs for his transfer by finally breaking down Chesterfield's resistance in October 1947, he was sought by Stoke in exchange for inside-forward Frank Bowyer, then the Potters' leading scorer, and a cash adjustment. Linacre, however, refused the move, and the Manchester officials who had been preparing to visit Stoke to seal the two-way deal, were also thwarted when they countered with a straight offer for either Bowyer or Syd Peppitt, a former winger turned inside-right who had attended the same school as Matthews. Stoke were prepared to part with either player only on an exchange basis.

It was an exchange transfer that took Linacre from Chesterfield to Manchester City after he had enhanced his reputation in only 22 peace-time games, scoring just three goals. To make up for his loss, the Spireites received £8,000 and two players, Tommy Capel, an inside-forward, and wing-half Peter Robinson. This pair, team-mates with Manchester Boys, had signed amateur forms for City on the same day, had joined up on the same day (Capel in the Royal Marines, Robinson in the Army), and been demobilised on the same day, but they would be on opposite sides when they later got to Nottingham, Capel with Forest, Robinson with County.

Linacre was comparatively clear from injury with Manchester City, showing his versatility in all but inside-right of the five forward positions of those days, and he made almost 80 Cup and League appearances for them (but failed to get into double figures for goals) before his £12,000 move to Middlesbrough in September 1949. The last dozen of his 35 games for Boro were made after the breaking of his leg for the third time had kept him out of action for just over a year. This injury was the most serious, also involving muscle damage, and he was released in the 1952 close season, shortly after being among thirteen players placed on the transfer list. Following a season out of the League with Goole Town, he returned to it with Hartlepools United, for whom his sons John and Phil also played (Whitby received a set of club strips as John's 'transfer fee'), and he totted up another century of games before his move to Mansfield gave Middlesbrough, not Hartlepools, the fee in accordance with the con-ditions agreed when he left Boro. After ending his playing days with Mansfield, Linacre settled in the Middlesbrough area, working in the con-struction and onshore oil industries.

Bill Whitaker, who was also conscripted as a Bevin Boy during the war, left Chesterfield for Middlesbrough by the direct route, preceding Linacre to Ayresome Park by more than two years with his £9,500 trans-fer in June 1947. He signed amateur forms for Chesterfield in April 1942, turned professional that summer, and gained his first senior experience in the wartime regional leagues. He played only thirteen times in the Second Division for Chesterfield in the first post-war League season, but went straight into Boro's First Division side and was their first-choice central defender for most of the next two seasons. He then lost his place to Tom Blenkinsopp, but not only regained it before there could be any develop-ments from his transfer request but also rose to the captaincy and won selection for the Football League in a team (also including Chesterfield's Stan Milburn) that defeated the Irish League in Belfast.

Knee trouble dogged Whitaker throughout his career, however. He dropped out of the first team again with damaged ligaments, and a cartilage problem ended his playing days in 1954 after 184 appearances for Boro, 177 of them in the League. He went back to working down the mine.

Albert Collins, a tricky little forward later with Halifax Town, Carlisle, Barrow, Bournemouth and Shrewsbury, was another prominent member of the Chesterfield side during the war, but there was one player the club were made to regret letting slip from their clutches when he became an FA Cup winner in the first post-war final. This was Jim Bullions, a wing-half who was at Saltergate as an amateur, but refused the chance to continue with the club after being unfeelingly replaced in the team by a guest player at very short notice. He also turned down an offer from Blackpool before signing professional forms for Derby County, with whom, at 22, he was the youngest on either side in their extra-time defeat of Charlton Athletic at Wembley in 1946.

Wartime football for Chesterfield ended on a promising note with progress to a War League Cup semi-final in 1945, when they knocked out Liverpool before losing to Manchester United, and a creditable seventh place in the League North of the transitional 1945-46 season. But their financial situation was not so bright, small attendances (only 300 turned up for one visit by Rotherham early in the war) increasing a debt the club sought to remedy by the issue of debenture shares to the value of £42,500 after the especially hard-up season of 1943-44.

As in the 1914-18 war, casualties among Chesterfield players also mounted. One of the first to fall in that earlier conflict was Charles Newcombe, a former head boy at Chesterfield Grammar School who was in the Town sides of 1911 and 1912. Newcombe, who also played cricket for Derbyshire, was serving with the King's Own Yorkshire Light Infantry when he was killed in action at Fleuraix just after Christmas in 1915. Gerald Graham, another member of the old Town team, in the Midland League of 1910-11, lost his life during the Battle of Valenciennes in November 1918, only a few days before peace was declared He had returned to France with the 21st West Yorkshire Regiment after recuperating at home from three wounds suffered within ten days the year before.

Jimmy Revill, a Sheffield United player who was a wartime guest for Chesterfield Town before being posted to the Royal Engineers' 104th Field Company, was killed on the first day of the Arras offensive at the Battle of the Scarpe in April 1917, and was among some three thousand British soldiers buried at Bethune. His namesake Arthur Revill, who was born at Chesterfield, was called back into the Grenadier Guards with which he had served before the war. Just over a year later he died of wounds suffered at Loos.

Centre-half Joe Smith became a sergeant-major in the 17th Battalion of the Middlesex Regiment – the famous 'Footballers' Battalion' under the leadership of Major Frank Buckley, a prominent figure in football as both player and manager – after joining up midway through the 1914-15 season with his pals in Chesterfield's half-back line. He was mentioned in dispatches for bravery, continuing to rush into battle despite being shot, after his death at Serre during the last action of the Battle of the Somme in November 1916. Billy Gerrish, whose career with Chesterfield Town was curtailed by a broken leg, was also killed with that battalion on the Somme.

Two other Chesterfield players who failed to survive that war were with the Sherwood Foresters. Jimmy Knowles, a Brampton-born forward who played a few times for the first team in 1914-15 and scored regularly for the Reserves, did duty with the 5th Battalion in Ireland before being posted to France. He died at Boulogne on the first day of May in 1917 from wounds inflicted during the advance to the Hindenburg Line. Vernon Bowmer, a lieutenant in the 16th Battalion, won the Military Cross in 1917 for conspicuous gallantry in action, but was seriously wounded near the end of the war and died in a military hospital at Bath in October 1919. He had made one appearance in the Town team.

Another former Town player, wing-half Albert Tye, left his job outside football as a painter and decorator to join the 4th Battalion of the North Staffordshires and was sent to Mesopotamia (the modern-day Iraq) in 1916. He lost his life at the battle for the Hai salient, near Kut, in January 1917.

In the Second World War, the biggest name among the Chesterfield club's fatal casualties was Allan Sliman. Having enlisted in the RAF in 1943, he was with the 75th New Zealand squadron that caused the widespread destruction of Hamburg and made the famous raid on factories at which V1 rockets were made. He was mortally wounded on a mission to bomb the U-boat yards at Kiel in April 1945, and was buried at Chelmsford.

Three other Chesterfield footballers, Bob Wrigglesworth, Albert Bonass and Fred Fisher, also perished on RAF service. Yorkshireman Wrigglesworth, whose elder brother Billy played for Manchester United, was an outside-left from Frickley Colliery who won rapid promotion from the 'A' team through the Reserves to the senior side in the relegation season of 1932-33. An air gunner with the rank of flight-sergeant, he was buried at the military cemetery near Athens after perishing when his Wellington bomber, flying out of Egypt, was shot down over Greece in January 1943. Bonass, also a left-winger, was with York City (his home club), Darlington and Hartlepools United before falling only two games short of 100 appearances for Chesterfield. On leaving for QPR, he had time only to play in their three Third South matches of the aborted 1939-40 season, then returned North and played again for York as a guest after joining the RAF as a wireless operator. He had been named in their team for a match at Halifax in October 1945 when his aircraft crashed at Tockwith, near York, while on a training flight. Fisher, another winger, died when the Lancaster in which he was serving with the 166th squadron came down near Aubigny in France.

Alec Campbell, who had so briefly been Chesterfield's manager in the 1920s, served in both wars. He was in the Royal Artillery, with the rank of lieutenant, when, as already recalled, he was taken fatally ill in June 1943.

6

The Toff leads Spireites to highest final League position

Norman Bullock's achievement of guiding Chesterfield to their highest final Football League position in his first season as their manager (sixth in 1938-39, the last pre-war) was emulated by his successor, Bob Brocklebank, who saw his new charges to fourth position in the Second Division in his first League season with the club of 1946-47 (the first post-war).

Brocklebank actually took over at Saltergate in September 1945. It was his first managerial appointment, after a senior playing career as a stylish inside or centre-forward that started with Aston Villa in 1929 but did not take off until after his transfer to Burnley in March 1936. From then until the last day of the 1944-45 season his was a familiar name on the Turf Moor club's teamsheet. He played in 121 Division Two games and seven FA Cup-ties, scoring 38 goals, and during the war made 191 more appearances, scoring 77 goals. His gentlemanly approach to life and football, always immaculately turned out, earned him the nickname The Toff.

One of eight brothers, Robert Edward Brocklebank was born at Barnet in 1908 and played for Finchley District Boys before joining the Finchley club as an amateur in the London League. After only twenty First Division games, and two goals, in his six years with Villa, who were heading for relegation when he left, he made his debut for Burnley the week before a 16-year-old centre-forward named Tommy Lawton was brought into the team alongside him. When Lawton soon afterwards departed for fame, if not fortune, with Everton and England, Brocklebank succeeded him as the club's top scorer with sixteen goals in the 1937-38 season. The Toff obtained most of his goals in singles or doubles, but had a rush of blood with four against Blackburn in a 1944 War Cup qualifying tie.

Within days of Brocklebank's arrival at Saltergate, Chesterfield moved to the top of the League North by beating Sunderland 3-0, and a week later they went three points clear as Billy Linacre scored three of their five goals, with none again conceded, in the return game at Roker Park. On the last Saturday of October Linacre did the hat-trick again, with the aid of a penalty, in a 4-0 victory at Middlesbrough. Not until late November, when they drew 3-3 at Grimsby, were Chesterfield dislodged from the leadership, and, shrugging off the loss of the injured Linacre, they promptly regained it in the grand manner by defeating the club that had replaced them – Blackpool, and on their own ground too. This time there was only one goal, scored in the second half by Bob Sinclair, but it was quite a feat for the defence to keep quiet an attack containing two of the most prolific forwards of the time, Jock Dodds and Stan Mortensen. The burly Dodds scored more than 200 goals in his six years with Blackpool, 65 of them in the 1941-42 season alone; Mortensen, then a coming England sharpshooter, was the Seasiders' leading scorer in 1945-46 with 39 goals, and he exceeded a double century for the club in also heading their scoring list in each of the first nine seasons after the war.

Blackpool gained 3-0 revenge at Saltergate the Saturday after their defeat by Chesterfield at Bloomfield Road (two for Mortensen, the other a Whitaker own-goal), but the Spireites bounced back to the top by beating Bury on Boxing Day with goals from Johnnie Wilson, George Milburn and Harold Roberts.

Winger Wilson, signed from Glasgow Celtic shortly before the war, had only recently returned to Chesterfield after guesting back home for Dunfermline, Hamilton, Berwick and Cowdenbeath. He moved to Oldham during the first League season after the war, and ended his career with Accrington Stanley.

Roberts, a Liverpudlian who had been on Everton's books as a youngster before joining Chesterfield shortly before the outbreak of war, was showing excellent form on the left wing after also being newly back in the fold. He was a Commando in the war, and had spent just over three years as a prisoner at a camp in Bremen after being captured during the raid on the French port of St Nazaire in 1942. Wounded in the legs, he owed his ability to continue playing football first to the skill of a German surgeon, and then to Joe Spence, with whom he lodged on his return. Spence, then coach at Saltergate, played a major part in Roberts' recovery through the work he put in with him.

After almost 100 games for Chesterfield, the skilful and speedy Roberts raised the record fee received by the club to £10,600 with his transfer to Birmingham City in November 1948. Injuries restricted his appearances for the Blues, but he played regularly in two seasons with Shrewsbury Town before ending his League career with Scunthorpe. He was afterwards with Matlock Town, Gresley Rovers and Burton Albion, helping with the coaching of the Matlock reserve team that won the Central Alliance Second Division title and League Cup in the 1959-60 season. He subsequently started a football team during his eight years at Staveley Chantry Youth Club before going back to Chesterfield, initially as an assistant youth coach. He remained at Saltergate until he was among several members of staff dismissed by a new board of directors in 1983.

Roberts, who was 87 when he died in hospital in Chesterfield in 2007, and his wife Dorothy had two sons, one of whom, Peter, also a winger, made a couple of League appearances for Chesterfield before joining the Nottinghamshire club Eastwood Town.

While neighbours Derby were starting out in January 1946 on the path to their first FA Cup final win, Chesterfield went straight out of the competition, beaten 2-3 at York in extra-time after a draw in the first leg. York were two goals ahead after an hour, one of them an own-goal, but within five minutes the scores were level again. The extra period was then confined to ten minutes each way in gathering gloom, and the decider against the then League North leaders was snatched by Ian Winters, the York centre-forward, following a penetrating run by Harry Thompson, who had been signed from Sunderland just in time to qualify for the Cup's third round after being a City guest for three seasons.

Chesterfield's team for those Cup-ties included the only two players, Sinclair and Alan Pringle, a versatile defender, whose first-class careers with the club were otherwise confined to the 1939-40 season that did not count because it had to be aborted when war was declared. They also appeared, however, in the guest-ridden wartime competitions – as did two other players, left-half Les Hobson and inside-left George Dooley, whose only peacetime first-team appearances for the club were made in the Cup exit against York.

One valuable player Chesterfield lost for that third round of 1946 was Jock Davie, who, as a guest, was ineligible. He returned to his own club, Brighton, for their first-round ties with Romford's amateurs, travelling down from his Army unit at Newcastle. On arrival in the early hours of the morning, he was unable to find accommodation at a hotel and spent the rest of the night in a police cell. None the worse for such an unusual experience, he scored twice in Brighton's victory that afternoon, but the Sussex club were later one of those Derby defeated on their way to Wembley.

Less than a fortnight after going out of the Cup, Chesterfield's hold on first place in League North was also finally broken when Manchester City defeated then by an only goal for the second time, but, despite then falling away to finish seventh, they had other big wins against clubs of First Division status to relish. Blackburn Rovers, Division Two champions of the last pre-war season, were beaten 7-0 and 4-0, and Manchester United (admittedly not then the power they were so soon to become) by 2-0 at borrowed Maine Road. Liverpool were twice held to a draw.

Against that there was one big blemish. At Stoke they let in six goals, the first of them an early penalty converted by Matthews after Whitaker had handled.

Stoke were just above the dividing line, and Derby just below it, that split clubs from the Football League's First and Second divisions into the North and South sections of that transitional season. Those of Third status were in four smaller groups: North (West), North (East), and, most incongruously, South (South) and South (North)

The players Bob Brocklebank brought into the team for the resumption of the Football League programme in 1946, with fixtures the same as those arranged for the abandoned season of seven years before, included Syd Goodfellow, an inside-forward who, with Ray Middleton, was an ever-present in the first post-war Second Division campaign. Chesterfield were the third of the ten clubs for which Goodfellow played after being with the Hanley and Silverdale youth teams in his home county of Staffordshire – he was born at Wolstanton, a district of Newcastle-under-Lyme – and the one for which he made most appearances (80 in a total of just over 300). He entered the League with Port Vale in the Third North in 1936, and also assisted Glentoran and Rochdale before the war. His path after Chesterfield led from Doncaster to Oswestry Town via Oldham, Accrington, Wellington Town and Stafford Rangers.

The other most regular members of Chesterfield's team on the resumption of League football, each in more than 30 of the 42 games, were Sid Ottewell, Tom Swinscoe, Billy Kidd, Harold Roberts and Dick Cushlow.

Ottewell, who hailed from Horsley, a Derbyshire village near Ripley, was another man of many clubs – their number well into the teens including those for which he guested during the war while a physical training instructor in the RAF. He was also one of the game's great characters, and among its most versatile. His senior playing career stretched from 1936, when he joined Chesterfield from Holbrook Colliery Welfare, to 1953, when he left Scunthorpe and moved into player-management with Spalding United. After that he was Lockheed Leamington's manager for most of the 1960s, leading them to the championships of the Birmingham and District League and the Midland League, plus the Birmingham Senior Cup. He celebrated his 90th birthday in October 2009.

The dozen goals Ottewell scored in the 1946-47 season, after which he departed to Birmingham City, put him only one behind Chesterfield's leading scorer, Swinscoe, a centre-forward discovered at the age of 26 while playing in wartime Services football in Italy. Swinscoe, who had previously been with a Shirebrook team, also left Saltergate soon after-wards – for Stockport, from where he moved to Peterborough. Cushlow, a centre-half from the Murton Colliery team, did not stay long either. He was transferred to Sheffield United, then Derby and Crystal Palace.

Ken Booker, an elegant-looking Sheffield-born half-back with a pow-erful long throw, and his fellow Yorkshireman Bill Watson, Kidd's most regular partner at full-back after arriving from Lincoln City, were other key members of the side for the resumption of Second Division football. Booker was switched to succeed Cushlow in the centre of defence so efficiently that he got close to a double-century of League appearances before his transfer to Shrewsbury in July 1952, just one season after rel-egation. Less his five years away in the Royal Navy during the war, Booker had been at Saltergate since 1934. Having represented Yorkshire Boys and been a reserve for England against Wales in a schools international at Chesterfield's ground, he was first signed as an amateur, then turned professional shortly after his eighteenth birthday.

Booker's League debut was marred by a 0-5 defeat by Luton Town, but according to contemporary accounts he acquitted himself far better than was indicated by the fact that four of the goals were scored by the man he was marking, Hugh Billington. Even so, he had made just over 30 League appearances when he was awarded a £750 benefit in 1947, a rather unusual statistic. Some thought that he was such a gentlemanly type, off the field as well as on, that he could have made the grade with a bigger club if there had been a sharper edge to his game. As it was, he made up most impressively for so much of the time lost during his eight-een years as a Spireite.

An intriguing addition to the playing strength in the autumn of 1946 was Jackie Hudson, who came from the County Durham club West Stanley after Newcastle had very rarely used him in their first team throughout the war. Intriguing, because he was a natural right-winger, and therefore appeared to be just the man to fill the gap left by the second breaking of Linacre's right leg in only the second match of the season. But no. Instead, Chesterfield mainly employed him in other forward posi-tions, and, although he was their leading scorer with a dozen goals in 1948-49, it could reasonably be argued that he might have best served them if he had not been so exploited by team tinkering.

Hudson became further disillusioned after relegation in 1951, espe-cially when he was transfer-listed at the end of the following season with such an over-inflated price tag that he was forced to go out of the League with Bangor City to carry on finding a living. Shrewsbury brought him back a year later, buying his registration from Chesterfield for £500. He did well for them in his then settled role as a central striker, but two years later was allowed to join Buxton in the Cheshire League to avoid the travelling to and from Gay Meadow that had become too tiring. In two more years with Buxton he scored 46 goals in 55 games, then ended his playing career with a season at Burton Albion. For some fourteen years after that he worked in a rolling mill at a Chesterfield foundry, and finally retired in 1988 after sixteen years at the Lamp Caps factory in the town.

Stan Milburn's name first appeared in the Chesterfield line-up during the first League season after the war. Thanks to the tip-off from his brother George, he came to the Derbyshire club's attention while playing for Ashington, and was signed from under Newcastle's noses towards the end of 1946, shortly after his twentieth birthday. He became a regular choice the following season, forming a full-back partnership with George on several occasions, and he took his total of League and Cup games close to 200 before his £10,000 transfer to Leicester City, then managed by Norman Bullock, early in 1952. While at Saltergate he gained an England 'B' cap, joining clubmate Ray Middleton in the team that defeated Holland 1-0 at Newcastle in 1950, and in the same year he helped the Football League to a 3-1 win against the Irish League in Belfast, besides touring Canada with an FA party.

With Leicester, Milburn got near another double-century of appearances, keeping Irish international Willie Cunningham out of the side for lengthy spells. He was in City teams that carried off the Second Division championship in 1953-54 and, as an ever-present, in 1956-57. Most memorably of all, however, he shared a unique moment in soccer history with his team-mate Jack Froggatt, who also made a name for himself by enjoying a second career as an England centre-half after first being capped at outside-left. At Stamford Bridge on 18 December 1954, their misunderstanding resulted in both making contact with the ball at precisely the same time in attempting to clear a Chelsea attack, and it was deflected into the net for the only joint own-goal on record. That freak 'double feet' helped the London club to a 3-1 win on their way to their first League title in their Golden Jubilee year.

Stan Milburn did something else out of the ordinary in having a testimonial with three clubs. After Leicester he was with Rochdale, for whom he made more than 200 appearances in reaching a career total of around 600. These included the 1962 League Cup final, in which Rochdale, a mid-table team in Division Four, lost to Second Division Norwich over two legs after knocking out Blackburn, a First Division side, in the semi-finals. Milburn was almost into his 40th year when he left League football at the end of the 1964-65 season, and, on becoming a warehouseman after settling in the Rochdale area, he played for his company's side until his late 50s. When he died in July 2010, at the age of 83, his England 'B' cap was placed on his coffin at his funeral at Rochdale crematorium.

Another player whose first few games for Chesterfield were in the first post-war season was Hugh McJarrow, a Motherwell-born centre-forward from the Maryhill club. He was soon off the mark in a 3-1 home win over West Ham that began an unbeaten sequence of six games in which only one point was dropped, after only one had been gained in the first three matches, but his opportunities that season and also the next two were restricted in face of competition from more experienced players. When he was used more often in 1949-50 he top-scored with Jackie Hudson (if with only nine goals), and was promptly successfully sought by Sheffield Wednesday.

With the Owls he was again a top scorer, his fourteen League goals in 1950-51 putting him level with Redfern Froggatt and Dennis Woodhead, a winger who later played for Chesterfield, but Wednesday were relegated and McJarrow featured rarely in the team that went straight back up. Off he went to Luton Town, then took his total of senior games into three figures with Plymouth Argyle before going into the Midland League with Peterborough United.

Chesterfield were never out of the top eight after the first few settling-in games of the 1946-47 season, catching most attention before the crucial closing weeks with a 4-3 win at Tottenham, who began the game in third place, a 1-0 defeat of Newcastle, another of the promotion contenders, and a 5-0 swamping of Southampton. In the Cup, a prized scalp was also claimed at home to Sunderland, though they lost by the same score, 1-2, in the next round to other North-East opposition of First Division standard at Middlesbrough.

Straight after that exit came the Big Freeze, in which Chesterfield were caught up with the postponement of all but two (both drawn) of their next seven matches. The hold-ups really began to bite in early February when the number of games off, 22 in England and Scotland, was the highest since the corresponding stage of the season in 1940, when Plymouth won 10-3 at home to Bristol City in the only game played. Chesterfield were able to fulfil their goalless fixture at Birmingham when 23 of 44 Football League matches had to be called off a fortnight later, equalling the worst of February 1933, but they were again idle as the postponements rose to 27 two more weeks after that.

Not until the penultimate Saturday of March was a full League programme completed for the first time since the middle of January.

Chesterfield entered that bleak weather-hit period smarting from their heaviest defeat of the season, inflicted by five goals at West Ham between their two Cup-ties, and they came out of it with a shock 0-3 loss at bottom-of-the-table Newport. It was only the sixth victory in 30 matches for the Welsh club, whose 22 defeats up to that time had included a 0-13 thrashing at Newcastle (six for Len Shackleton on his debut).

It said much for the character and ability of Brocklebank's men that they recovered from that spell of inactivity and those two severe setbacks so promptly and effectively that they lost only three of their remaining fourteen games, each by only the odd goal, despite having to cram them into a run-in made hectic by the postponements. They won eight of those matches, culminating in the 4-2 home success against Sheffield Wednesday in which George Milburn did his penalty hat-trick. All three of those spot-kicks were belted past goalkeeper Roy Smith in the space of 22 second-half minutes, the first two of them after Billy Linacre, newly back in the side, had twice been brought down within six minutes. The other penalty was awarded when a defender handled.

At a quarter past five on that sweltering afternoon of Saturday, 14 June 1947, Charlie Buchan, the former Sunderland, Arsenal and England forward who was then the *News Chronicle*'s football correspondent and editor of his *Football Monthly*, walked into the home dressing room at Saltergate and told the Chesterfield players wallowing in the communal bath that Newport had avenged their mauling at Newcastle by winning the return game, also by 4-2. He recalled that this news 'brought a cheer which burst through the steamy atmosphere, for it meant that Chesterfield had finished fourth in the Second Division and earned talent money'. Not that such remuneration was all that munificent in those days when the maximum weekly wage was £12 in the season and £10 out of it, with the respective minimums of £7 and £5 for full-time players aged twenty or over.

Increases in talent money were sanctioned as follows at the League's annual meeting that year: from £275 to £550 for the championship club in Divisions One and Two; from £220 to £440 for the second club; from £165 to £330 for the third club; from £110 to £220 for the fourth. In each of the Third Division sections, the increase for the champions was from £220 to £275, for the second club from £165 to £220, and from £110 to £165 for the third.

Chesterfield were not to get as far as the FA Cup semi-finals for another 50 years, but it is also interesting to recall that in that competition the winners, runner-up, beaten semi-finalists and losers in round six then received the same rates of doubled talent money as the leading four

First Division clubs. A win in the final brought players £20 each instead of £12, and in the semi-finals £15 instead of £10.

Chesterfield were sixth in the Second Division table right through the month of May in 1947 until the very last day, when a 3-1 home win over Bury lifted them to fifth, one of three clubs on 48 points. They were sandwiched on goal-average between Newcastle, who had no match that afternoon, and West Bromwich Albion, who completed their programme with victory by the same margin against Manchester City, the already assured champions. At the same time, Burnley clinched the other promotion place, their five goals without reply from West Ham at Upton Park hoisting them above Birmingham City, who had played their last game the previous weekend. Chesterfield's concluding defeat of Wednesday then combined with Newcastle's shock defeat in South Wales to take the Derbyshire club two points clear of the costlier North-Easterners, Spurs and Albion in these final leading positions:

Season 1946-47	P	W	D	L	F	A	Pts
1. Manchester C	42	26	10	6	78	35	62
2. Burnley	42	22	14	6	65	29	58
3. Birmingham	42	25	5	12	74	33	55
4. Chesterfield	42	18	14	10	58	44	50
5. Newcastle	42	19	10	13	95	62	48
6. Tottenham	42	17	14	11	65	53	48
7. West Bromwich	42	20	8	14	88	75	48

In his *Football Monthly*, Buchan wrote: 'That evening, those closely connected with Chesterfield thought in terms of a First Division future. They had a fine stand and offices which had gone up in the 1930s; there were plans to erect cover behind one of the goals at the town end, and the set-up, while not large was trim and good. The top 22 did not seem like something on another planet as we toasted a season of success just ended and looked forward to the next.'

But things were not to work out so rosily. Those of a superstitious turn of mind might well have regarded it as an ominous omen when ambitious plans for a tour of Brazil were thwarted by FA objections. At any rate, Chesterfield were relegated four years later, and ten after that they were in Division Four.

7

Brisk transfer business with Manchester City

Transfer business was particularly brisk between Chesterfield and Manchester City during the first few seasons after the Second World War. So much so that there were even rumours of some sort of 'special arrangement'. It began in the autumn of 1947 with the deal that took Billy Linacre to Maine Road in exchange for Tommy Capel and Peter Robinson, then touched its peak for profitability as far as Chesterfield were concerned with the signing of Ron Powell, their appearance record-breaker (until Dave Blakey took that distinction from him), and George Smith, the first to follow Herbert Munday to 100 goals for the club.

Saltergate was where Tommy Capel coincidentally made his League debut, in a victory Manchester City gained four days into 1947. He did not score that game's only goal, but he bagged one of the three with which Chesterfield won at Barnsley when he first played for them on the last Saturday of the following October. In between he netted twice in his eight other League appearances for City, acquiring a little First Division experience after their promotion as Division Two champions, and twice more in an FA Cup run that ended in a heavy fifth-round defeat at Birmingham.

Robinson, his friend from schooldays, had only two first-team opportunities while with City, but, by another coincidence, he and Capel both went on to turn out 64 times in Chesterfield's senior side.

Capel also scored on his home debut for the Spireites, in a 1-1 draw with Plymouth Argyle, the club for which he had guested during the war. Chesterfield were anxiously hovering immediately above the two relegation places when he and Robinson arrived, having gleaned only eight points, all away from home, from a dozen matches. By early in the New Year they were up to eighth, and, although they were unable to sustain that improvement, they ended ten points clear of the relegated pair, Doncaster and Millwall. Capel was again on target when a home victory was at last claimed at the seventh attempt, getting one of the four goals against the then bottom club, Brentford, which doubled the number Chesterfield had previously scored at Saltergate that season. Manager Brocklebank attributed the revival in form to the fact that the players now had lunch together in the town before home matches.

The sixteen goals Capel added to the one he had scored for Manchester City in the First Division made him Chesterfield's leading marksman in 1947-48. His output was down the following season, one behind Jackie Hudson with eleven goals. During the summer of 1949 he was transferred to Birmingham City for £10,000 – signed for the second time by Bob Brocklebank, who had left Chesterfield early that year to fill the managerial vacancy at St Andrew's caused by Harry Storer's return to Coventry. Capel left behind him at Saltergate his younger brother Fred, a full-back recruited on his recommendation. Their only game together with Chesterfield was in the reserve side, but once Fred got into the first team he firmly established himself with about 300 appearances over eight years before going to Buxton. The brothers were later reunited with another Derbyshire club, Heanor Town, after which Fred was with Sutton Town as player-manager.

The move to Birmingham did not work out well for Tommy Capel, nor for Brocklebank initially. After only eight League games and one goal for the Blues, Capel was transferred to Nottingham Forest, his value increased to £14,000, but it was there that he enjoyed the most success-ful phase of his career.

Things also looked up for Brocklebank after his first full season with Birmingham had ended in relegation back to Division Two, even though he resigned, very reluctantly, in October 1954 after being summoned from his sick bed (he had been away for two days with a heavy cold) to an interview with the club's chairman, Harry Morris. Birmingham were then in mid-table, but Brocklebank had rebuilt the team so soundly that within six months they were promoted – and two years after that they were in the FA Cup final.

The next club that 'Gentleman Bob' managed, Hull City, were also rel-egated in his first full season, and although he succeeded in guiding them back up again three years later from the newly formed Division Three, he again resigned as his relationship with the directors deteriorated in the wake of another relegation. He was finally with Bradford City, who had to apply for re-election between two pushes for promotion while he was in charge, and he once more resigned in 1964, disillusioned by another poor start. He retired to Brixham, where he died in September 1981, aged 73.

Nottingham Forest, newly relegated to the Third Division for the first time, signed Tommy Capel a few months after manager Billy Walker's team strengthening had brought in centre-forward Wally Ardron from Rotherham, and it was these two who did most of the scoring when the climb back was completed at the second attempt in 1950-51. Ardron

responded with a club record 36 goals; Capel collected 23, plus another
in the Cup. I was then reporting on Forest matches for the *Derby Evening
Telegraph*, having moved on from covering Chesterfield games, and I still
have clear memories of the lanky Capel's party trick of leaving an oppo-
nent standing with the sudden lengthening of his already considerable
stride, and of the power he packed into his left boot (but not, unfortunately, into his right). Four of his goals, and three for Ardron, came in
Forest's highest-scoring game of that promotion season, a 9-2 home
romp against Gillingham.

After totalling 72 goals in his 162 appearances for Forest, Capel was
transferred with his wing partner Colin Collindridge to Coventry City in
the 1954 close season. From there he rounded off his League and Cup
career of 294 games and 129 goals with a short stay at Halifax that gave
him the full set as a player in the League's four divisions of the time. Next
came the 1956-57 season in which Capel helped Heanor Town to the
Central Alliance North title, a success he sealed by scoring all five goals
in their final game against Sutton Town. One of them was from the
penalty-spot, struck with his unfavoured right foot.

Peter Robinson's career after Chesterfield took him first to Buxton,
then back into the Football League with Notts County – too late to play
more than just once in the side that won promotion from the Third
South the season before Forest, but as an influential wing-half in each of
the first two back in the Second. His senior appearances reached a neat
150 before he went out of the League again with King's Lynn.

George Smith was in Manchester City's forward line, at either inside-
right or inside-left, in each of the thirteen League and Cup games Tommy
Capel played for the club. Smith, born at Fleetwood, was signed by City
from the Adelphi Lads Club at Salford in May 1938, but, with internationals Alex Herd and Peter Doherty firmly in possession of the inside-
forward positions, and then the intervention of war, he had to wait until
the last day of August in 1946 for his League debut. And even then, in a
3-0 win at Leicester, he was out on the left wing to accommodate Herd's
fellow Scottish cap Andy Black, a recent recruit from Hearts, as his partner. Smith, however, had already played in not far off 100 first-team
games for City, during the war and in the League North of the transitional season that came straight after it. He did not score in the first of
them, a remarkable home draw with Stockport in which Jimmy Heale hit
five of City's six goals, but he did the hat-trick in a 4-1 win against
Tranmere and went one better by doing all City's scoring when a match
with their United neighbours had the same result. He was near a half-century for goals before the resumption of League football.

George Smith also played for the Army and FA representative sides during the war, but at one period his service took him to East Africa. It was out there, as a sergeant on secondment to the King's African Rifles, that his right hand and arm were badly injured in a 'friendly fire' incident while on a training exercise. A bullet from a machine gun fired by a South African airman went through his elbow, down his forearm, and out through his hand. 'Sorry,' he was told by an officer, 'you were in the wrong place at the wrong time.' When Smith, City's oldest former player, celebrated his 90th birthday on 7 February 2011, Peter Spencer, a supporter of the club since schooldays, recalled that 'those of us who watched George after the war will never forget the way that stiff arm hung in a sky blue sleeve as he glided round the field like a ghost'.

The damaged limb at first caused City such doubts about Smith's ability to continue playing football that, as his son Ian later explained, he had to prove he could still perform at the top level before his contract was renewed at all of £2 10s (£2.50p) a week. Those doubts were swiftly swept aside as he scored 42 goals in the last two seasons before the Football League got under way again, then top-scored with 23 in 38 games in the first post-war Second Division season of 1946-47. He most suitably rounded off City's promotion as champions with all five in a last-day defeat of relegated Newport County.

Having missed much of the 1949-50 season in which City were again relegated, Smith was a mainstay of the side that went straight back up. Of the 21 goals he contributed to that rise, three put City into an apparently unassailable interval lead at Doncaster, only for their unbeaten start of ten games to be brought to an abrupt halt by a remarkable Rovers revival. And two of the four goals with which the home side hit back in eight second-half minutes were scored by player-manager Peter Doherty, the former Maine Road favourite.

By the time of Smith's £5,000 move to Chesterfield in October 1951 he had 80 goals to his name in 166 League and thirteen FA Cup matches, and if City thought he was then well past his best in his 30th year they were very much mistaken. In seven Third North seasons with the Spireites he totted up 96 more goals in 251 games, getting to exactly 100 with four in the Cup. In five of those seasons, successively, he never failed to score at least fifteen times, with a best of twenty in 1953-54. Sadly, his efforts were not rewarded with promotion, but he earned selection for the Third North representative team against the Third South.

Ian Wilson, a Scot from Leicester City, was signed on the same day as Smith, and formed a penetrative left-wing partnership with him in some 80 games before making Rotherham his fifth English club and exceeding

200 League appearances in all. After him, Smith linked up to similar effect with Pat Keating, an Irishman from Wisbech Town who made up for limited opportunities with Sheffield United and Bradford Park Avenue by playing for the Spireites in all but five of his 100 League games.

Smith returned to Manchester when he left Chesterfield in 1958. He played for Mossley in the following season, and afterwards for Hyde United and Prestwich Heys. Away from football, he worked until retirement in one of the tyre departments of the Kenning Motor Group, which began as a hardware business at Clay Cross in 1878

Ron Powell, a Welshman who played for his home club, Knighton Town, before joining Manchester City towards the end of 1948, took the path from Maine Road to Saltergate eight months after Smith, on 12 June 1952. With him went Dennis Westcott, a centre-forward who had scored a stack of goals for Wolves, Blackburn and City – not far off 300 including wartime. Yet Westcott never won an England cap, unfortunate in that respect to have the peak years of his career coincide with Tommy Lawton's. His only appearances for his country were made during the war. He failed to score in a defeat by Wales at Wembley in 1940, but netted once in each of his three other games in 1943 (a win and draw against Wales and a win in Glasgow over Scotland). His other representative appearance was made for the Football League against the Scottish League at Hampden Park in 1947, when he got one of the goals in a 3-1 victory.

At club level, too, Westcott missed major honours, having to be satisfied with Wolves' League War Cup final defeat of Sunderland, in which he scored three times over the two legs during the 1941-42 season, and Manchester City's promotion from the Second Division in 1950-51. Wolves finished just one point behind Arsenal's champions in 1938, but the bitterest disappointment for Westcott and his team-mates came the following year. They were not only again First Division runners-up, four points adrift of Lawton-inspired Everton, but also, as the hottest favourites for years, well beaten by Portsmouth's outsiders in the FA Cup final.

The Wallasey-born Westcott became an England schoolboy international while with New Brighton, then a lowly Third Division North club which he joined as a 15-year-old in the 1932-33 season. He moved to Wolverhampton in July 1936 after West Ham had made the big error of rejecting him, and in the following February scored in the seventh minute of his senior debut as a right-winger in a 6-2 defeat of Grimsby Town in a fifth-round FA Cup replay before a Molineux crowd of more than 56,000. The first of his career total of 303 League games came when he also played on the wing against Manchester City a few days later, but it was not until after Gordon Clayton's transfer to Aston Villa the following autumn that he was able the make the centre-forward position his own. And how! On Good Friday that season he scored four times in Wolves' record 10-1 League win against Leicester, and just under a year later another four-goal blast in a Cup semi-final defeat of Grimsby at Old Trafford was among the five other hat-tricks he completed before the war. In 1938-39 he achieved a personal best of 43 goals, eleven of them in the Cup run to Wembley.

Westcott scored three or more goals in ten matches for Wolves while the League was in limbo, including six of the seven against Nottingham Forest and another four into Northampton's net. During those war years he also played for Services teams in Iceland and Germany, and for the BAOR (British Army of the Rhine) side. And when the First Division got going again in 1946-47 he broke Wolves' individual record for one League season with 38 goals in 35 games Eight came on successive Saturdays in December — four in a 5-1 win over Liverpool at Anfield, where he did the hat-trick inside eight minutes, and four more in a 5-0 home win over Bolton. His output was down to fourteen goals the next season, among them his last hat-trick for the club in a 4-2 win at Middlesbrough on New Year's Day, but it was still a surprise when he was off-loaded to Second Division strugglers Blackburn Rovers during the spring of 1948. In 66 appearances for the Lancashire club he did what he was also to do in 75 for Manchester City, score 37 goals.

The match at Maine Road in which Billy Linacre broke his right leg for the third time was also the one in which Westcott first played for City after his £12,500 transfer from Blackburn on 14 February 1950. Middlesbrough's victory by a lone goal kept City firmly anchored in the relegation zone, and there was to be no escape. Westcott's winner against Burnley was his only goal in his dozen other games for the club that season, but he was top scorer with 25 in his attacking partnership with George Smith as they bounced straight back as runners-up to Preston in 1951. Chesterfield ended that season at the opposite end of the table, returned to the Third North with Grimsby Town.

So it was first to Smith, and eight months afterwards to Westcott, that the Spireites turned in their quest for an early rise. For Chesterfield fans of the 1930s, the signing of Westcott stirred memories of Reg Weaver, another former Wolves striker who had made his way to Saltergate from Bradford City and then returned to his first League club, Newport County. Weaver, a son of Somerset, was a noted athlete, winner of the Welsh Powderhall sprint at Caerphilly in 1931.

Chesterfield finished Westcott's only season with them, 1952-53, in mid-table, joint twelfth with Tranmere Rovers, level on goals figures, 65-63, as well as points (the only time this has happened in the League's history), but his renewed link-up with Smith proved profitable. Of the 37 goals they shared, 21 went to Westcott, who made a most impressive start by scoring all four with which Mansfield Town were beaten at Saltergate on the opening day. Just over a month later, on the first evening of October, Westcott scored his 200th goal in League and Cup, the equaliser in the semi-darkness of a home Third North match with Barrow.

Westcott altogether notched 23 goals in 43 games for Chesterfield, taking his overall League and Cup totals to 221 in 328. With the inclusion of his wartime appearances for Wolves, those figures expanded to 311 in 398, and then there were those other Services games. From Saltergate he went into the Cheshire League with Stafford Rangers, finally giving up playing in 1957 as his 40th birthday neared. He then became a licensee at Stafford, but his life was cruelly cut short by leukaemia on 13 July 1960. He had turned 43 only eleven days earlier.

The next player involved in a deal between Chesterfield and Manchester City after Westcott was Bill Leivers, a resolute defender who moved to Maine Road for £10,500 in November 1953 after only 27 appearances for the Spireites. The Bolsover-born Leivers, who stood 6ft 2in, joined Chesterfield as an amateur from Clay Lane Sports Club in 1948 and turned professional early in 1950. His skill and commitment soon attracted the attention of other clubs besides City, but his League debut for the Maine Road club against Preston on the first day of the 1954-55 season was an unhappy one. He was not only injured – he was a most unlucky frequent casualty while with the club, including breaking his nose five times – but also saw City tumble to a 0-5 defeat as a try-out for the Revie Plan, named after the club's deep-lying centre-forward in an adaptation of Hungarian tactics, misguidedly misfired.

Less than two years later, however, Leivers, again at right-back after reverting from centre-half, was the outstanding member of the team that defeated Birmingham in the FA Cup final, despite again not being fully fit. Don Revie, as king-pin of the plan which that day worked a treat, and goalkeeper Bert Trautmann, who played on not knowing that he had broken a bone in his neck, cornered all the publicity afterwards, but Revie himself picked out Leivers as the main man – as did other team-mates who voted him the most influential player afield.

Revie, who, ironically, was back in the side at Wembley only because right-winger Bill Spurdle dropped out on the eve of the game with an infected swelling of the right arm he had skinned in a League game at

Luton, told journalists: 'Bill had two pain-killing injections on his sprained ankle, yet he played the game of his life. Many of our attacking moves stemmed from his intelligent passing, which switched defence to attack.' One of those passes began the move that led to City's opening goal in their 3-1 win as early as the third minute. For Leivers the last three minutes were contrastingly painful. He landed awkwardly on his tightly strapped ankle and ricked it slightly.

For all his absences through injury – especially in the 1960-61 season, when he played in only a dozen games – Leivers still made 250 League appearances for City, plus 31 in FA Cup and League Cup. He deserved more than just the one representative honour he gained with an FA XI against the Army. His stay of more than ten years at Maine Road ended with a free transfer to Doncaster, where he was player-manager from July 1964 until February 1966, when he resigned amid talk of a difference with the directors after guiding Rovers to the top of the old Division Four.

Following a spell as manager of Workington, Leivers was in charge at Cambridge United when they won the Southern League championship by one point in successive seasons, 1968-70, gaining entry into the Football League on the second occasion. Promotion was achieved three years later, but he was dismissed as the team continued to struggle after an immediate return to Division Four. Though noted for being scrupulously fair, Leivers was also tough-talking, and there was a pre-season friendly with Colchester in which he was so incensed by a goal awarded against Cambridge early in the second half ('Two Colchester players were yards offside') that he took the extreme step of ordering his players off the field. Play was resumed after a two-minute stoppage, during which the Cambridge players clustered uneasily in the tunnel. Leivers, persuaded by referee Alan Harrington and Jim Smith, the Colchester manager, then decided that the game should be completed for the crowd's sake.

Leivers returned to management with Chelmsford City before going back to Cambridge to join the other club there, City – first as manager, then as general manager, a post he held until his retirement in 1999. He moved to live in Cornwall at St Austell, and accepted an invitation to become president of the south-west branch of the Manchester City Supporters' Club.

Chesterfield's next import from Manchester City after Dennis Westcott was Billy Sowden, also a centre-forward. Sowden, who was born in the Gorton district of Manchester, was mainly a reserve in his five years with City, whom he joined from his local side Greenwood Victoria in 1949, but, according to the obituary published in the *Stockport Express* after his death at 79 in November 2010, he was one of the club's first players to own a car, and he often used to give a lift to fans he saw on his way to matches.

Sowden played in only eleven League games for City, scoring his two goals at that First Division level in a 3-3 draw at Tottenham two days after making his debut in a 2-1 home win against Manchester United, but Chesterfield had good enough reports about him in the Central League to encourage a £1,500 investment in November 1954. He repaid it with 59 goals in 97 Third North matches, plus three in six FA Cup-ties before leaving for Stockport in the summer of 1957. His best season for Chesterfield was that of 1955-56, in which he top-scored with 32 goals in 45 League games, plus another in the Cup and two more in a 3-2 defeat of Leeds United in Fred Capel's benefit match. Sowden did the hat-trick in a 5-0 win at Bradford Park Avenue, and in an 8-0 home victory over Crewe, but enjoyed his biggest success in one game late the previous season with four of the six goals Accrington Stanley conceded at Saltergate.

Accrington were runners-up that year, 1955, four points behind promoted Barnsley, but Chesterfield could do no better than finish sixth in each of the three seasons Sowden spent with them despite his productive partnership with George Smith. After a season with Stockport, Sowden joined Macclesfield Town as player-coach, then moved from Moss Rose to Moss Lane by playing for Altrincham in their last eight games of 1960-61. On giving up playing he took over the bakery business in which he had helped his father while still a professional footballer, and spent the rest of his days in the Heaton Chapel district of Manchester.

Sowden's stay at Saltergate slightly overlapped that of Keith Marsden, a Derbyshire lad from Darley Dale who joined Chesterfield from Youlgreave Boys' Club. Like Leivers, Marsden did not play very often in the Spireites' first team, but he scored fifteen goals in his 22 League games and was regarded as such an excellent centre-forward prospect that his sale to Manchester City for £6,250 in July 1955 stirred up strong protests among fans who were losing him. Yet he failed to make his mark at Maine Road in a big way – just fourteen League outings (none of them as an orthodox centre-forward) and only one goal, scored on his debut in a defeat at Chelsea, before he was off-loaded to Accrington Stanley four years later.

The explanation was that he fell foul of another of manager Les McDowall's plans. The Marsden Plan was never anywhere near emulating the eventual success of the Revie Plan. It was tried in September 1957, when Marsden, nominally No 10, the inside-left of the time-honoured 2-3-5 formation, dropped back to operate as a twin centre-half either alongside or behind Dave Ewing in a 4-2-4 system, but it was abruptly jettisoned, along with Marsden, during a 2-9 eclipse at West Bromwich that came three days after a 1-6 mauling at Preston. This Plan was negative in the extreme, with four forwards making little impression against five defenders, and lack of cover in defence compelled the reversion to the customary line-up.

Marsden did not appear in City's first team again. A week later he was back at the Hawthorns with the Reserves for a Central League game, and fate struck him another cruel blow when he broke a leg in another defeat, this time by only one goal. It was because of this injury that Accrington at first refused to consider signing him. And after they had done so he did not play in their League side. He took over the running of a nightclub at Stockport in December 1968. Eighteen years later he was killed in a road accident in Africa.

There was also a managerial connection between Chesterfield and Manchester City in the early post-war years. The successor to the departed Bob Brocklebank in February 1949 was Bob Marshall, who had been both an FA Cup winner and First Division champion with City in the 1930s.

8

Relegated back to the Third Division North

Bob Marshall, a Nottinghamshire man born at Hucknall on 3 April 1903, had two careers as a player. In the first one with Sunderland, whom he joined from Hucknall Olympics at the age of seventeen in May 1920, he scored 73 goals in 205 games as an inside-forward. In the second one with Manchester City, to whom he was transferred in March 1928, he continued mainly in attack, scoring 80 goals in just over 250 games, before establishing himself at centre-half, a position in which he had previously played in an emergency, for his last two seasons with the club, 1936-38.

As a clever ball-playing forward, Marshall helped Sunderland to finish second once and three times third in the First Division, and Manchester City to reach two successive FA Cup finals – the first lost to Everton in 1933, the other won against Portsmouth after being behind. He was also a promotion winner with City within two months of his transfer in 1928, and in their team that ended third in Division One two years later. As a centre-half, he missed only four matches when City were League champions for the first time in 1936-37. His appearances for the Maine Road club altogether totalled 355, after which he entered management with Stockport County in March 1939.

Following wartime service as a physical training instructor, Marshall guided Stockport to fourth place in the Northern Section of the Third Division in 1946-47, and they were again doing reasonably well when Chesterfield came calling in February 1949, the month after Bob Brocklebank's departure. Marshall took over when the Spireites were comfortably inside the top half of the Sdeductedecond Division, and they ended that season in a creditable sixth place, having suffered only ten defeats in their 42 games.

On the first anniversary of Marshall's appointment, Chesterfield enjoyed more prosperity by reaching the fifth round of the FA Cup for only the second time in their history. After beating Yeovil's giant-killers from the Southern League, and First Division Middlesbrough, they were again drawn at home and held another club from the top flight, Chelsea, to a draw before a crowd of 27,500, Saltergate's biggest of the season. Jackie Thompson, a forward from Doncaster, scored their second-half equaliser. Three goals were conceded without reply in the replay, watched by 60,000, but extra-time at least looked likely until a quarter of an hour from the end, when Roy Bentley, soon to win the second of his dozen England caps, broke the deadlock by netting twice in three minutes.

In the League, however, there were ominous signs that all was not well. Chesterfield rose as high as fourth in the Second Division after beating Blackburn at the end of September, and they were again in the top six two months later, but they then fell away to finish fourteenth, suffering a dozen of their eighteen defeats during that period. The next season, 1950-51, the rot really set in, with only nine League wins against 21 defeats and an immediate exit from the Cup at the hands of Brighton, a mid-table Third South side.

After the deceptive start of losing only one of their first five games, by the odd goal at home to Barnsley, Chesterfield conceded nine goals in four days in beatings by Preston and Manchester City, the clubs that would go on to win promotion. Hopes revived with just two, narrow, defeats in the next six games, but from that point it was downhill all the way back to the Northern Section of the Third Division. To doubts about a defence that had hitherto been so reliable were added worries about an attack whose shortcomings were underlined when, in mid-September, Fred Capel was the only full-back in the whole League who was his team's leading scorer (with four goals, two of them penalties). He did not add to that total, which would be a quarter of his career output, but only three players were ahead of him in the club's scoring list at the season's end – Chris Marron, a former South Shields centre-forward, with eleven goals, and Jackie Hudson and Dave Massart, both with five. Down Chesterfield went with 30 points, their smallest number in a season of 42 matches. This was how they finished at the foot of the table:

Season 1950-51	P	W	D	L	F	A	Pts
19. Luton	42	9	14	19	57	70	32
20. Bury	42	12	8	22	60	86	32
21. Chesterfield	42	9	12	21	44	69	30
22. Grimsby	42	8	12	22	61	95	28

It was during this relegation season, on Boxing Day 1950, that Dennis Thompson, a winger, became the youngest to play in Chesterfield's first team at sixteen years, 159 days. Sadly, it did not coincide with a victory, though it was only with a penalty that Notts County took both points at Meadow Lane. Thompson made one further appearance that season, and two dozen in all before moving to Scunthorpe United in 1953.

A final position of thirteenth back in the Third North was indeed unlucky for Bob Marshall. In July 1952 he left not only Chesterfield but football too, opening the way for Teddy Davison's second coming. Marshall resigned along with secretary Eric Willey after differences with the directors over club policy, and in the same month the long-serving Billy Kidd also quit as third-team trainer. Not the most ideal of circumstances for Davison's return. Marshall became licensee of the Glapwell Hotel, and there he stayed until his death in 1966.

As manager, Marshall obviously had to shoulder some of the blame for the decline that ended eight seasons (less the war years) of Second Division membership dating back to 1936. But he was far from being given a free hand. The directors interfered in team selection, even disagreeing among themselves about whom to play, and where. This, however, was nothing new. Complete control had been denied ever since the club had first made someone responsible for team affairs as far back as the early 1870s, even enough their earliest secretaries had been said to have 'full powers of management' on match days (possibly the first reference to management in football history). Not until at least the late 1950s did Chesterfield's directors begin to trust the club's managers to do their job properly, allowing them the decision-making right down to the choice of the team.

Bob Marshall's task was made all the more difficult because the board also sold key players without properly consulting him. And, as that was a result of the club's desperate financial situation, there was insufficient money with which to obtain suitable replacements – with one big exception: George Smith. As a former Manchester City man, Marshall might well have been seen as the major influence on the spate of transfers between City and Chesterfield, but Smith figured in the only significant deal of that kind while Marshall was the manager at Saltergate.

In his quest for new blood, Marshall was also handicapped by the fact that Chesterfield's share of receipts from the Cup run was diverted for other purposes. Furthermore, the dwindling of attendances at some home League games into four figures added to the debt that had been manageable before the war but had since become a millstone of alarming proportions. With the pressing need to have new terracing installed in 1950 worsening the problem, there was some tentative consideration of a ground move as several options were explored. That, however, was a radical decision which would not be made until almost 40 years after the debt was eventually cleared during the 1970s.

As 'Wingerworth,' the *nom de plume* (borrowed from the name of a village a few miles south of the town) given to those who reported on

Chesterfield FC for the *Derby Evening Telegraph* in those days, I could appreciate why Bob Marshall was said in some quarters not to have the strength of personality to insist on being given complete control. He was a thoroughly decent man, with considerable experience of footballing affairs, and a ready help to a young journalist still very wet behind the ears, but he lacked the forcefulness to stand up to the board members who were not on the same wavelength. Nor was he aided by a change of scouting policy whereby the North-East that had proved such a rich source of talent was neglected in favour of a focus on Scotland with no appreciable benefit.

The first big loss to Chesterfield's playing strength after Marshall's appointment came in the summer of 1949 when Tommy Capel followed the path Harold Roberts had taken in rejoining Bob Brocklebank at Birmingham. The next departure of note was that of Norman Kirkman, a full-back who had cost £4,500, the biggest fee received by Rochdale up that time, when signed for the Spireites by Brocklebank towards the end of 1947 after being given a free transfer by Burnley. Brocklebank had been Burnley's captain when the Bolton-born Kirkman had moved to Turf Moor shortly before the war after first being taken on as an amateur by Joe Smith, the Blackpool manager who had converted him from a forward into a defender.

It was at inside-left that Kirkman had been drafted into the Folds Road Central School team that also included Tommy Lawton and went unbeaten in the Bolton schools league for three seasons. The inside-right in that side was Jackie Knight, like Lawton and Kirkman an early Burnley recruit, who played for Chesterfield between helping Preston to the Second Division title in 1951 and going into the Third South with Exeter City. Knight was afterwards with Bath City and worked as a stonemason.

Kirkman's exit from Chesterfield was not one of those directly due to the club's urgent need for money. He refused to re-sign because he had been unable to settle in the town. The move took him to Leicester, but was ill-fated from the debut he ended in hospital with a broken nose. After only five games he was relegated to the Reserves, and after only a few months, in January 1950, rumours of discontent in the dressing room were confirmed when he was put on the transfer list with Alex Scott, another full-back, and goalkeeper Gordon Bradley, each at his own request. Scott and Bradley had been in the team beaten by Wolves in the FA Cup final the previous April. Bradley went to Notts County, Scott to Carlisle, Kirkman to Southampton.

Kirkman was needed by the Saints to fill the gap left by the transfer to Colchester of their former captain, Bill Rochford, an FA Cup winner with Portsmouth against Wolves in the last pre-war final at Wembley. But again Kirkman failed to gain a regular place, and the fates continued to conspire against him when rheumatic fever kept him out of action for the last few weeks of the 1951-52 season after Exeter City had appointed him player-manager following George Roughton's move in the opposite direction to manage Southampton. Kirkman had played for the RAF during the war, in which he had served as a navigator, but he had been in his mid-twenties before first playing in the League with Rochdale, and he made only 136 appearances at that level (41 of them for Chesterfield) before, in March 1953, he accepted a lucrative offer to manage Bradford after Vic Buckingham's move to West Bromwich.

Yet again, however, fortune did not smile on Kirkman. In January 1955 he left Park Avenue complaining of a 'thoroughly raw deal, disgusted with the treatment I have had'. Bradford's directors announced that they had been 'reluctantly compelled' to dispense with his services as one of the economies they were having to make because of the deterioration in the club's financial position. Kirkman, on the other hand, claimed he had been told that 'one of the reasons why I was being sacked was that there had not been the necessary discipline among the playing staff'. He added: 'The truth is that I have wanted to take strong disciplinary action with certain players, but have been far from having the necessary backing from the board.' He also stated that he was going out of the game for good, but in the 1960s had a spell as manager of Northwich Victoria.

The transfer of Hugh McJarrow to Sheffield Wednesday in March 1950 was another crucial depletion of Chesterfield's playing strength, soon followed by a further bid from Leicester that took away Reg Halton. This strong-tackling wing-half had first caught national attention as one of the guest players Arsenal fielded in their fogbound farce of a match with Moscow Dynamo in November 1945, but his entry into League football dated back almost nine years beyond that to his scoring debut for Manchester United against Middlesbrough. He was given only a few more chances by United, and not many more by Notts County, before also playing pre-war for Bury, with whom he completed a century of games before his transfer to Chesterfield in December 1948. In moving to Leicester in September 1950, he was signed for the third time by Norman Bullock, the manager who had also taken him to Gigg Lane and Saltergate. After more than 250 matches in all, 60 or so for both Chesterfield and Leicester, Halton was player-manager at Scarborough.

Late in the year of Halton's transfer to Leicester, a move in the opposite direction was made by Walter Harrison, a wing-half whose century of games for City had included the 1949 FA Cup final won by Wolves. Harrison, who had joined Leicester from Navy football, was Chesterfield's only ever-present in his first full season with the club, but he was just one game short of a career total of 200 in the League when he left for Corby Town in 1953.

Bob Marshall's enforced loss of key players quickened after relegation with the exits on successive days in June 1951 of Ray Middleton to Derby and Gordon Dale to Portsmouth, soon followed during that close season by the unloading of five others who had imposed less influence.

Dale, a clever, naturally gifted outside-left, was signed for £500 by Bob Brocklebank early in 1948 after being spotted with Worksop Town by Cyril Oxley, a former Chesterfield player. From the juniors and Reserves, Dale progressed to being given his first League chance by Marshall at Fulham in March 1949, and he quickly attracted scouts as he consolidated a regular place with his tricky displays. At his best he was one of the best wingers then in the game, but there were also days when he was so exasperatingly intricate, and consequently less effective, that he had to endure barracking. Throughout his career he had a habit of not being content to beat a man just the once, and that did not go down well with the frills-spurning frequenters of Saltergate.

Criticism at Chesterfield reached the point where Dale asked to be left out of home games, and he even considered asking for a transfer before he regained the form that silenced his Derbyshire detractors. Indeed, he was the player the fans carried off shoulder-high from the Saltergate pitch after his outstanding display, crowned with his first senior goal, in the Cup defeat of Middlesbrough. The publicity attracted the renewed interest of other clubs, however, and resistance to the offers made for him melted away with Chesterfield's return to the outposts of the Third Division North. The one accepted, of £20,000 at a time when the record was the £34,00 Sheffield Wednesday paid Notts County for Jackie Sewell, was the most Portsmouth had forked out for a player, and the most Chesterfield had received.

Yet Dale did not immediately win a regular place with Portsmouth, who began the 1950s as League champions, for a second successive season, but ended the decade down in the Second Division – then in the Fourth by the late 1970s. Dale's debut for Pompey was delayed for a month by an injury suffered in the club's practice match in August 1951. He had still to get into double figures for League appearances just over a year later because of further fitness setbacks, and he made only just over 100 in a little over six seasons, scoring almost twenty goals. He asked for a transfer after losing his place to Scottish international Jack Henderson, but did not get one until near the end of 1957, when he was one of two well-known players on whom Exeter City spent about £12,000. The other was Johnny Nicholls, a forward from Cardiff who had been capped twice by England while with West Bromwich. Dale was the costlier at £7,000, then an Exeter record.

The feeling lingered that Dale did not make the most of his talent after leaving Chesterfield. His descent into the Third South snuffed out any last hopes of the international career that had been predicted for him, and after another century of League games for Exeter he went into the Southern League with Chelmsford City. On retirement from playing, he became a newsagent back at Portsmouth, where he died in 1996.

The other players who left Chesterfield in the wake of their relegation in 1951 included four forwards – Bobby Foster, Dave Massart, Stan Machent and Jack Marsh – and goalkeeper Ken Oxford. Of those forwards, Foster, a Sheffield-born product of the club's junior side, was the least experienced when he left Chesterfield, having been given only four senior chances, but he went on to score 41 goals in 101 matches for Preston before making Rotherham his third League club. He had been taken to Saltergate not long after Machent, for whom, in December 1947, Chesterfield paid Sheffield United one of their biggest fees up to that time, yet he would have cost them only the signing-on £10 if he had not been released after having several trials with the Spireites, his home club, before joining the Blades during the autumn of 1948.

Machent moved to Hereford United in July 1951, having scored seven goals in 21 League games for Chesterfield. After then having a season with Buxton he rejoined Chesterfield as player-coach to the third team in September 1954. There was a soccer curio attached to his first signing for the Spireites. He had a brother, Arthur, who had been taken onto the Saltergate playing staff in November 1927. It must surely be unique for there to be a gap of twenty years between two brothers joining the same club.

The burly Massart, a real old-fashioned type of centre-forward, left Chesterfield in the same month as Machent. He had arrived from Bury only just over five months earlier, £6,000 having been expended in the hope that he could score the goals that would ward off relegation. On his past record there was good reason to think so, especially if he could rely on a good supply of centres from the tricky Dale. He had been regularly among the goals for Walsall and Bury after playing only intermittently in Birmingham's first team on turning professional with his home club shortly before the 1939-45 war (he had been born in the city's Yardley district). He scored regularly for Birmingham's reserve side between his few senior opportunities until wartime service took him to the Middle East with the RAOC, but after his demobilisation in April 1946 he turned out only three times for the club in the Second Division before his former Birmingham clubmate, the ex-England goalkeeper Harry Hibbs, snapped him up for Walsall in July 1947.

Massart got off to a spectacular start with the Saddlers. He did the hat-trick in each of his first three home games. By the March of that 1947-48 season his goals tally stood at 23 goals in 27 Third South appearances, encouraging Second Division Bury to boost their escape from relegation with a £2,000 investment. He repaid them with 45 goals in 85 League matches over three years, heading their scoring list for two consecutive seasons, before Chesterfield also turned to him in the hope of rescue.

Massart was signed on the first day of February in 1951. Two days later, Chesterfield dropped into one of the relegation hot seats for the first time that season by conceding three goals without reply at home to promotion-seeking Cardiff City (they finished third), but Massart opened his Chesterfield account next time out, if in another defeat, back at Birmingham. On Good Friday he also scored against another of his former clubs, twice equalising in a draw at Bury – and there would have been a hat-trick winner in the last minute but for a daring save by goalkeeper Goram.

Five Massart goals in eleven games for the Derbyshire club were too little too late, however, and off he went to continue his plundering with Weymouth in the Southern League. His 114 goals in 156 matches made him one of only three players to complete a scoring century for the Dorset club in that competition. Two more of his hat-tricks came in successive games. When he retired from playing in 1956, his benefit match against an FA team drew a crowd of about 7,000, well above Weymouth's usual home attendance. He remained in Weymouth to run a post office, then a hotel, and he died in the town in December 1993, aged 74.

Jack Marsh reached Chesterfield via Notts County, Coventry City and Leicester City. He started with Mansfield Boys Club (he was born in that Nottinghamshire town in 1922), and first played for Notts County during the Second World War. He was the centre-forward who had to give way when Tommy Lawton, then England's current attack leader, made his sensational move into the Third Division from Chelsea in November 1947, but he carried on in other forward positions except inside-right until his transfer to Coventry in October 1948. He made fewer than two dozen League appearances for both Coventry and Leicester, but his 26 games for Chesterfield took his career total just beyond the century before he left for Worksop Town in August 1951. His goals tally was modest – 33 in the League, just four for Chesterfield.

From Worksop, Marsh moved to Gainsborough Trinity, then back to Derbyshire with Ilkeston Town, where he did a Revie in playing as a deep-lying centre-forward under a plan to which he also gave his name. Like Revie, he was difficult to pick up, and he so successfully began attacks in which he arrived late to finish them off that he averaged a goal a game, his three hat-tricks including four against Grantham Reserves, until a thigh injury in the February of the 1955-56 season cost him a regular place. Even then, although still not fully fit, he scored four more times in a home match with Potton United. His 51 games in two seasons with Ilkeston produced 47 goals

Ken Oxford joined Chesterfield after an unsuccessful trial with Derby County during the summer of 1950. That was the year in which.he was called up into the RAF for National Service, but that was not the reason why he never made the Spireites' first team. He was kept out by the immovable presence in their goal of Ray Middleton, who, with Gordon Dale, was an ever-present in the relegation season of 1950-51. Immovable, that is, until Middleton departed to Derby – and then, ironically, came Oxford's own exit to Norwich City less than a fortnight later, early in the July of 1951 in which Bert Lomas was brought in from Rochdale as Middleton's replacement and Larry Platts taken from Nottingham Forest as the deputy. After thirteen seasons with Forest, Platts was with Chesterfield, Burton Albion and Stockport County within the next year, then player-manager of Deal Town. Lomas also did not stay long at Saltergate, leaving for Wigan Athletic in the summer of 1952. That was when Ron Powell came in to become a first-team fixture for much of the next dozen years.

At Norwich, Oxford found himself again the understudy, this time to Ken Nethercott, and it was not until Nethercott asked to be rested after 136 consecutive games that Oxford first played in the East Anglian club's Third South side in an away match with Crystal Palace, who won 1-0, on Christmas Day in 1953. It was only his second League match in more than five years, the first having been made for Manchester City in a goalless draw with Arsenal at Maine Road in April 1948. Oxford had joined City from Ardwick Lads Club the previous November, but he had been released later in that year of his debut and then fallen on more stony ground at Derby.

But things at last began to look up for this son of Oldham after his move to Norwich. He represented the Football Combination against a Dutch XI, and the Third South against the North while with the

Canaries, whose first-team goal he guarded in 135 more games before making the most of an unexpected second chance at Derby. The Rams' manager, Harry Storer, signed him for £4,000 in December 1957 to replace Terry Webster, who moved on to Skegness Town. For 2½ seasons Oxford was a regular choice, and he made 162 League and Cup appearances, earning a benefit cheque, before going to Doncaster, then Port Vale. Even the arrival of former England goalkeeper Reg Matthews from Chelsea did not end Oxford's first-team days with Derby. Tim Ward, the former Rams and England wing-half who had succeeded Storer as manager, recalled him when illness kept out Matthews on the opening day of the 1962-63 season, and, after saving a penalty in a 3-3 draw at Huddersfield, Oxford kept his regained place until the following March. He completed his career with Boston United, serving them, in turn, as reserve-team coach, caretaker manager, and manager until the 1970s. He also kept goal for the ex-Rams team into his late 50s. Quite a decent record to look back upon after such an unprepossessing start.

9

Dave Blakey takes appearances record from Ron Powell

It was early in Teddy Davison's second spell as Chesterfield's manager that goalkeeper Ron Powell and full-backs Freddie Capel and Tommy Flockett came together to form one of the best defensive units in the club's history.

Ferryhill-born Flockett took over as Capel's partner following Stan Milburn's transfer to Leicester. Signed for £800 in April 1949, he became a big favourite with the Saltergate crowd for his consistent reliability and uncomplicated style, making exactly 200 League appearances before leaving for Bradford City in 1957. He was spotted by Harry Dormand in the same Spennymoor United team as wing-half Jimmy Smallwood, a face worker at his local Bearpark colliery in County Durham who followed him to Chesterfield in October 1949.

Smallwood, too, was very popular with the fans, right from showing his full commitment to the cause by playing on with a head wound that needed five stitches when he made his first-team debut in a home game against Sheffield Wednesday on the last day of 1949. No wonder the young John Osborne looked up to him as 'the type that the ordinary bloke on the terraces could associate with, never giving less than 100 per cent every week and proud to be playing for the Spireites'.

Yet Smallwood, a £1,000 bargain first signed as a semi-professional, was so uncertain of making the grade when he accepted full terms two months later that he originally thought of planning ahead for only one year, to see how he went on. He stayed for quite a lot longer than that – as a player until the end of the 1960-61 season, surpassing 350 League and Cup games, and afterwards in other capacities right up to the mid-1980s. On joining the ground staff after hanging up his boots, he spent a season as the Reserves' trainer before stepping up to the same job with the first team in 1962. Then, from November 1967 to 1986, Smallwood was the club's groundsman, a role he combined with being a steward at Saltergate on match days besides playing a prominent part in the reformation of the Supporters' Club. A back injury eventually enforced his retirement, but he continued to show a keen interest in how Chesterfield were faring until his death during the first week of February in 2010 at the age of 84. There was a minute's applause in Smallwood's memory before Chesterfield's next match, won 2-1 against Lincoln City at Saltergate.

In contrast to Smallwood's long service, Freddie Capel and Tommy Flockett were both released by Chesterfield much earlier than they should have been. Capel, who had joined the club early in 1948 as an amateur half-back from the Manchester works team, the Goslings, that also launched his brother Tommy's career, kept remarkably fit during close seasons by working with the equally dedicated Smallwood in the scrap yard at Staveley Works. That he still had much to offer was shown when his farewell game in April 1957, a year after his well-earned benefit match against Leeds United marked the end of a sequence of 178, taking him to an overall total well beyond 250. He moved to Buxton, and later derived great satisfaction from putting something back into the game as manager of several local junior sides.

Flockett was challenged for his place by the emerging Gerry Clarke, but he did not finally surrender it until he was forced to leave at the same time as Capel, shortly before his 30th birthday. An error of judgment in his case was also emphatically demonstrated when he put in another seven seasons with Bradford City, earning a second benefit and more than doubling his total of League appearances to 427. And when he finally did give up playing he reappeared on the Saltergate scene, working with the young players there on settling down in Chesterfield. He was 70 when he died in 1997.

After Flockett's premature move to Valley Parade Gerry Clarke went on not only to amass some 400 games for Chesterfield up to 1968, but also to give the club further excellent service on the coaching staff and as assistant manager before becoming Brighton's trainer-coach in July 1974. His lengthy service as a Chesterfield player partly coincided with the longest of the lot – that of Dave Blakey, who took the club's appearances record from Ron Powell with 617 games in the League and 658 in all. And those figures could have been even bigger if Blakey had not had to wait five years for a regular place after being signed from East Chevington Juniors, a Northumberland side, in June 1947. That delay was largely due to National Service, during which he played for an Army team against an FA XI that included Ray Middleton and Stan Milburn, but there was also the decision to promote Bill Leivers over Blakey when Ken Booker left.

It was an injury to Booker that gave Blakey his first League chance in Chesterfield's second match of the 1948-49 season, drawn goalless at West Bromwich on the Wednesday evening of 25 August. Brought in from the 'A' team, he acquitted himself well, despite the extremely windy conditions, in this line-up: Middleton; Milburn, Bell; Machent, Blakey, Robinson; Hudson, Withington, Brown, Capel, Roberts. (this was the week during which Peter Robinson was joined by his younger brother Bill on the club's professional staff).

Chesterfield were denied both points by a brilliant save by Albion's goalkeeper, Jim Sanders, from Jimmy Brown, a former Motherwell centre-forward who was soon on his way out to Bradford City. A week later, following another scoreless game at home to West Ham, Middleton was the star performer in ensuring that there would again be no goals in the return match with the Throstles. His saves included one from a penalty taken by Davy Walsh, the Irish international on whom Blakey kept a close watch. That was the season in which Albion snatched the second promotion place behind Fulham after Southampton had surged eight points clear at the beginning of April. But the Saints had then lost leading scorer Charlie Wayman through injury, and their lead had been whittled down to one point by the time they travelled for their final match at the end of the month – and that was at Saltergate, where Chesterfield toppled them with a goal from Hugh McJarrow.

For incident in a match that season, however, the Spireites, and Blakey in particular, looked back with most pleasure on a 4-3 victory away to Cardiff City, who finished fourth. Booker was back by then, in early November, but a deputy was needed at inside-left for Tommy Capel, and Blakey was the surprise choice And what a success he made of it. He provided the pass from which Chris Marron quickly wiped out Cardiff's fourth-minute lead, then caused the mix-up from which Chesterfield went ahead with an own goal, and finally scored twice himself. His first League goal was the best of the bunch, a tremendous shot under challenge from two defenders.

Victory against such strong opposition was all the more remarkable for the fact that Chesterfield's attack was completely different from the one fielded in the opening weeks. It was composed of players who would not feature in it regularly except for Marron, who netted almost 50 goals in just over 100 games for the club before taking his respective career totals to 70 and just over 160 with Mansfield and Bradford Park Avenue. After that he was Heanor Town's player-manager. There were critics who felt Marron was not used as often as he should have been in the relegation season of 1950-51. For that game in Cardiff in 1948, Marron had Bert Johnson and Joe Holmes on his right flank, with Blakey partnered by Danny Smith on his left. Johnson had played a few times for Everton in the First Division, but soon left for Witton Albion; Holmes, signed from the Parkhouse Colliery side, stayed longer, but with restricted chances, before joining Matlock Town; Smith, a Scot from Coltness United, played only a few more League games for Chesterfield than he had done for WBA, but afterwards got into three figures with Crewe before moving to Corby Town.

A number of Blakey's other early, irregular first-team opportunities were made in the forward line, explaining why this redoubtable defender scored as many as twenty League goals, plus another in the Cup. Not until his 43rd game, won 3-0 at home to Accrington Stanley on 6 September 1952, did he get into the side at centre-half to stay. That was the start of a sequence of 244 League appearances, broken on the last day of November in 1957 when injury kept him out of a drawn game at Mansfield. He also missed a home draw with Crewe, but then reclaimed his place from John Allison, a former Blyth Spartans pivot who became a Durham policeman, until late the following March, when he was sent off for dissent only thirteen minutes into the roughhouse of a home match that Bradford City won with a penalty.

During those early years of the 1950s Blakey was at the heart of a defence that remained unchanged for 62 League and Cup games until George Brown, a Liverpudlian wing-half later with Peterborough, ended a run of 72 senior games in missing a Northern Section visit to Carlisle on 5 February 1955. That gave Maurice Galley, a 20-year-old from Clowne, the first of just over 50 League chances before his move to Boston United.

Blakey was dropped for the first time at the start of the 1963-64 season, but for just one match. It was the only League game his replacement, Ronnie Hinton, played for Chesterfield after arriving from Doncaster Rovers; he left for Denaby United not long afterwards. Back came Blakey until he had to contend with a much stiffer challenge from Albert Phelan the following season. The years were catching up with Blakey by then, and Chesterfield were thankful to have someone as reliable as Phelan to call upon. Phelan was signed as an amateur in 1962 and turned professional two years later after graduating through the junior and reserve sides. He became a regular member of the side in the 1966-67 season, at the end of which Blakey retired from playing after spending most of it in the Reserves.

Phelan was the quiet man of the team for some 400 games in filling the role of what became known as a sweeper, in reading the play so well, that he covered his colleagues besides blocking the way down the middle. Indeed, he made it all look so easy that it was said he probably did not get the recognition he deserved. He was another who still had a great deal of footballing life left in him when he moved to Halifax Town in 1975 with midfielder Ray McHale in exchange for Terry Shanahan, who was later with Millwall, and £3,000. Phelan also became a very popular figure at The Shay, then spent five years at Boston, the last two as manager, before scouting and coaching for Sheffield Wednesday.

Dave Blakey was brought back for an emotional first-team farewell in Chesterfield's final home Fourth Division match of the 1966-67 season, won 2-1 against Port Vale on 8 May. The pity was there were not many there to see it, just 2,605. Blakey's senior career had lasted almost 21 years, earning him a Football League long-service medal, in those days, long before the Bosman ruling, when the retain and transfer system tied players to their clubs for as long as they were wanted. Blakey did, in fact, ask for a move. That happened during a dispute over a benefit that dragged on for six years before he was finally granted one, jointly with Ron Powell, in April 1964 for a match between a Manchester City XI and an International Stars team.

Blakey first became eligible for a £1,000 benefit in April 1958, but chairman Harold Shentall refused to grant him one because the club was heavily in debt and such payments were not compulsory. Two years earlier, the financial situation had been so desperate that Teddy Davison had said Chesterfield could not afford the expense of another possibly fruitless journey when Rochdale requested a return visit four days after the match there between the clubs had been postponed because of the icy weather. Rochdale, themselves badly in need of money, had suggested a Wednesday evening under floodlights, and it would have been the first such League fixture if Chesterfield had agreed and permission had been granted. The League had only recently decided to consider whether or not to allow games to be played under lights, and just over a month later, on 22 February 1956, the distinction Chesterfield could have shared went to the match in which Newcastle defeated Portsmouth 2-0 at Fratton Park. Even then, however, there was almost a complete black-out. The main fuse in the grandstand blew out half-an-hour before the scheduled kick-off, and electricians located the trouble with only ten minutes to spare, delaying the start by ten minutes. For Chesterfield there was still a floodlight distinction to come. In 1963 their purchase of a second-hand set of lights from Sheffield United made them the last League club to install them. The cost of a new set four years later was offset by the sale of John Osborne to West Bromwich.

A year after the first rejection of a benefit for Blakey, a surplus of £2,308 was declared by Chesterfield on the past season, and it was then that he went on the transfer list at his own request because a benefit continued to be withheld. With no acceptable offer received, Blakey soldiered on, as popular as ever, as both player and skipper, with his team-mates and fans – so much so that by 1962 he was talked about as the club's first player-manager when a vacancy occurred with the exit of Teddy Davison's successor, Dugald Livingstone, an ever-optimistic Scot who had taken Newcastle United to an FA Cup final victory in 1955 but had found the task of keeping Chesterfield out of the new Fourth Division beyond him in 1961. Livingstone left after an application for re-election to the League had been avoided only by victories in the last two games of the following season.

Instead of looking to Blakey, however, the directors at Saltergate gave the manager's job to Tony McShane, an Irishman who had been an attacking, if inconsistent, half-back with Plymouth Argyle and Swindon Town, then manager of Goole Town and Scunthorpe United. McShane had been with Plymouth in their Third South title-winning season of 1951-52, and had taken over a Scunthorpe side newly promoted to the Second Division as the last Third North champions of 1958 before the formation of the Fourth Division. Although unable to guide Chesterfield out of that new lowest section of the League during his five seasons at Saltergate, McShane at least helped to find a solution to Blakey's benefit problem. Another unusual item on his CV was as the scorer of a hat-trick of penalties for Plymouth Reserves.

The improvement in Chesterfield's financial position in 1959 was short-lived. A loss of £25,661 was reported after the next season, prompting the chairman to observe: 'This is not running on a shoestring. It is below the breadline.' When a roof was needed for the Kop terrace it was the Supporters' Club that paid for it. In such alarming cash-strapped circumstances the failure to avoid another relegation was scarcely surprising. There was an early alarm signal with the concession of seven goals away to Port Vale, soon followed by seven games from which only one point was taken, and then by a club record of nine consecutive League defeats that included a 1-5 trouncing at Newport. What was surprising was that amid all this trauma in the Third Division the club embarked upon an FA Cup run of six games, three of them replays. In the League they won away from home only once that season, at QPR, yet in the Cup's first and second rounds they triumphed at Doncaster and Oldham after 3-3 and 4-4 draws at Saltergate. Then they held First Division visitors from Blackburn to a scoreless draw before losing by three goals at Ewood Park.

A sixteenth away defeat in Division Three, by the odd goal of seven at relegation companions Colchester, brought the sad 1960-61 season to a close with these final positions at the bottom of the table:

Season 1960-61	P	W	D	L	F	A	Pts
21. Tranmere	46	15	8	23	79	115	38
22. Bradford C	46	11	14	21	65	87	36
23. Colchester	46	11	11	24	68	101	33
24. Chesterfield	46	10	12	24	67	87	32

In the face of so much adversity Keith Havenhand did remarkably well to top Chesterfield's League scoring list with 21 goals – ten clear of the only other player to reach double figures, Terry Foley, a centre-forward from Portsmouth who soon afterwards left for Yeovil Town. The powerfully-built Dronfield-born Havenhand, an England youth international, spurned approaches from Sheffield Wednesday and Wolves before leaving his employment as an apprentice centre lathe turner to sign professional forms for Chesterfield. He was only sixteen years and 227 days old when he made his first-team debut at the end of the 1953-54 season, and, despite a call-up for National Service, he settled into the side two years later while also a member of the club's successful FA Youth Cup XI.

Havenhand was one of four players who took part in all of Chesterfield's 46 League matches on the way down to Division Four. The others were Gerry Clarke, Jimmy Maddison and Gerry Sears. Maddison, a slightly-built but tricky left-winger, added 100 games for Chesterfield to the near-300 he had played for Grimsby before leaving for Cambridge City. Sears was a one-club man, rewarded for patiently waiting, like Blakey, for some five years for a regular first-team place – despite making a scoring League debut in April 1953. An ever-present for three seasons after at last being given a good run in the side from the second match of the 1958-59 season, at a time when the team was constantly changed, he moved up to seventh in the list for the club's individual appearances by becoming another to exceed 400. And, again like Blakey, there could have been more. He never fully recovered from a back injury suffered against Exeter City in February 1968. Forced into premature playing retirement, he ran his own milk round for six years before finding employment at the Tube Works in Chesterfield.

Brian Frear, an inside-forward from Huddersfield Town who scored more than 80 goals in nearly 300 games before going to Halifax, was the next most regular member of the side that slipped into the League's basement, missing only two matches. After him came Ron Powell (43 games) and Dave Blakey (39). After retiring from playing six years later, Blakey stayed on at Saltergate for a short time to run Chesterfield's auxiliary fund, a job that chiefly entailed selling tickets. He left in November 1967, finding the more active involvement in the game for which he craved as a prolific discoverer of new talent. He was led to scouting first for West Bromwich Albion by a link with Alan Ashman, a former Carlisle centre-forward who was just venturing into management at the Hawthorns. A year later, another link, this time with Jimmy Adamson, who was then coach at Burnley, and soon to be manager, after winning England caps as a wing-half with the Lancashire club, took him to Turf Moor.

Blakey recalled: 'I was assessing teams Albon were due to play. I watched Burnley, and told Jimmy that West Brom would beat them 5-0. It was 7-1. Burnley offered me a place. Bob Lord, their chairman, interviewed me and wanted to know names of people I knew in football – my connections, my contacts, scouts who operated for me. I told him straight he wasn't getting any of that. I got the job.' Burnley certainly reaped big dividends. As their chief scout, Blakey produced talent worth more than £2 million. Players he brought to the club included Martin Dobson, Brian Flynn, Ray Hankin, Steve Kindon, Leighton James, Geoff Nulty and Bill Rodaway. Quite a list! He had to be at his most persistent and persuasive to land Flynn, a coming Welsh international who, at 5ft 4in, was one of the smallest players in League football. 'The boy's family wanted to think about it overnight. I stayed on. Somebody moved out of a bed and I slept at the same house. Brian signed the following day.' Shades of the tactics employed by Brian Clough when he persuaded Archie Gemmill to join Derby County. Clough even helped with the washing-up next morning.

Blakey was constantly on guard against an error that traps many scouts – of looking at a player, or pretending to look, far too much. 'All the time,' he said, 'I hears scouts saying this lad's not bad, but he can't head a ball. Or some other boy is all right-footed. Imagine if somebody sometime might have thought that way and decided they didn't want Puskas.'

In July 1976, Blakey turned down a £50,000 five-year contract with a London club, among other offers, to accept the appointment as Sheffield Wednesday's chief scout. 'He came here for maybe a third of the pay he could have had elsewhere,' said Len Ashurst, then Wednesday's manager. 'I can explain that,' countered Blakey. 'As a Chesterfield player I used to come to Hillsborough in awe, and I think things can happen there again. I'm not sure about Burnley. Jimmy Adamson was right. They could have been the team of the Seventies, but too many players were let go' (Flynn among them; he went to Leeds, but had a second spell at Burnley). 'With Wednesday I am sure I can help make things happen.'

But it was not to be. Wednesday were then humble members of the Third Division, and they still were when Blakey left in just under a year.

The Owls would eventually rise to the FA Premier League, but not until 1992, and to an FA Cup final, but not until, as losers, in 1993 (the year in which they were also runners-up for the League Cup, a trophy they won in 1991). On the last day of May in 1977, Blakey replaced Peter Doherty, the former Northern Ireland manager, as Sunderland's assistant manager in charge of scouting. After that he had two spells as Leeds United's chief scout, ending in 1988. Although living in the Doncaster area, he was back at Saltergate as a spectator into the 21st century, usually on behalf of Doncaster Rovers.

As had happened before, relegation for Chesterfield in 1961 made it inevitable that they would be unable to hold on to all their best players. In October that year, Keith Havenhand's need for a higher grade of football was answered by the £10,000 transfer to Derby County that raised him to the Second Division status the Rams had regained with the considerable aid of another signing from Saltergate. Teddy Davison had gone back to Sheffield Wednesday for Dennis Woodhead, paying £2,000 in September 1955 for a strong-running winger and emergency centre-forward. Woodhead had recovered from a broken leg to help the Owls to two promotions from Division Two and been their top scorer with 21 goals during the 1953-54 season in which they reached the FA Cup semi-finals.

Woodhead, whose grandfather Billy Betts had also played for the Sheffield club, did the hat-trick on his Chesterfield debut in a 7-2 home win over Rochdale, but he made only fourteen other appearances for the Spireites before Derby's manager, Harry Storer, saw him as just the man, for an outlay of £1,500, to add experience, good distribution and powerful shooting to the team that rose from the Third Division North in 1956-57. On Easter Monday that season Woodhead was among the scorers in the 7-1 defeat of Chesterfield at the Baseball Ground.

Short as Woodhead's stay at Saltergate was, there was still time for him to form an all-Chesterfield left wing with George Smith for the North against the South in the Third Division's televised representative match that attracted a crowd of 14,000 to Peel Park, Accrington in October 1955. Although neither scored, they played a prominent part in the 3-3 draw, in this team: Minshull (Southport); Fleming (Workington), Kenny (Carlisle); Stokoe (Workington), Ryden (Accrington), Ryan (Derby); Webb (Bradford City), Broadis (Carlisle), Connor (Stockport), Smith, Woodhead (Chesterfield).

Woodhead, whose days with Wednesday – dating back to his signing as an amateur in June 1942 – were interrupted by wartime RAF service in which he flew over 30 bombing missions as a flight engineer, left

Derby for Southport early in 1959, but, on League orders, he was transferred back a month later because of knee trouble. His senior career of 343 games and 108 goals ended soon afterwards, but he was subsequently with Frickley Colliery, Retford Town (both as player-manager) and Worksop Town before returning first to Chesterfield, as lottery manager, and then Hillsborough, where he succeeded Derek Dooley, who had been promoted to manager, as commercial development officer. He took early retirement aged of 62 in 1987, eight years before his death.

At Derby, Keith Havenhand rejoined Barry Hutchinson, another Derby recruit from Chesterfield who had played for the North against the South (at left-half at Stockport in April 1957). Hutchinson had made the move during July 1960 in exchange for wing-half Albert Mays, full-back Roy Martin and a fee of £2,025. Hutchinson, whose father, Jimmy, had played for Bournemouth, Lincoln an Oldham, was converted into an inside-forward by the Rams and averaged a goal every two games in scoring 57 in 116 appearances before moving to Weymouth in July 1964 and helping them to the Southern League title.

Havenhand, whose 176 games for Chesterfield had produced 58 goals, looked likely to enjoy similar success when he scored fourteen times in 29 games in his first season with Derby, but a cartilage operation then halted his progress and near the end of 1963 he dropped back into the Fourth Division with Oxford United, his price reduced to £4,000. Even down there he could not command a first-team place, and after eighteen months with King's Lynn he retired from football to turn his hand, soon afterwards, to running a driving school.

Hutchinson, who had been an amateur with Bolton Wanderers before beginning his seven years with Chesterfield in 1953, earned a return to the Football League with his 46 goals for Weymouth in the 1964-65 season. Six months with Lincoln were sufficient to make him their leading scorer of 1965-66 with twenty goals. In February that season he departed to Darlington and repaid their £5,000 investment by boosting their push to their first promotion for more than 40 years as runners-up in the Fourth Division. Further service at that level with Halifax and Rochdale increased his League tally to 116 goals in 367 matches, after which he completed his playing career with Bangor City in the Northern Premier League.

10

Promotion with 'Gentleman Jim'; Ernie Moss top scorer

Chesterfield spent nine seasons in the Fourth Division, finishing in the bottom half of the table in all but two of them, and at the bottom of the top half in one of the others, before climbing out as champions in 1969-70. The manager who guided them to their first silverware for 35 years was Jimmy McGuigan, a Glaswegian who had already gained promotion from the same division with Crewe Alexandra, and would do so again with Rotherham United.

McGuigan was a winger in junior football with Bonnyrigg Rose Athletic before signing professional forms for Hamilton Academical in 1946. One season later he moved into England, playing in turn for Sunderland, Stockport, Crewe and Rochdale. Just over 200 of his 334 Football League appearances were made for Crewe, with whom he became coach in 1959, then manager in March the following year. Their promotion from third place in 1963 was the first they had ever achieved, but they dropped straight back, third from the foot of Division Three, and in November 1964 McGuigan moved to Grimsby Town.

At Blundell Park 'Gentleman Jim' took over a team second in the Third Division, but they fell away in the second half of the season to finish tenth. He did well to maintain a mid-table position a year after the scrapping of the reserve squad for economy reasons, especially as he had to rely on members of the youth side in emergencies, but his task was made even more difficult when he was not consulted about the sale of key players. The directors took it upon themselves to part with goalkeeper Charlie Wright, and soon afterwards they broke up a potent strike partnership with the transfer of Matt Tees and Rod Green. All three went to Charlton. That made a decline on the field inevitable, and in July 1967 the board announced that results 'do not prompt us to desire to renew his contract'. It was due to expire in four months' time, but, his position having been made untenable, McGuigan resigned immediately.

So it was that a man with promotion credentials was on hand when Chesterfield were looking for a successor to Tony McShane, who had left Saltergate the previous May. It took McGuigan a little time to sort out a side that had slumped into one of the blackest periods of the Spireites' history, and after an escape from the League's lowest sphere had slipped from his grasp in his first season (a final position of seventh, five points adrift of Crewe, who went up again in the fourth and last qualifying place), the tumble to twentieth of 1965-66, immediately above the four clubs that had to seek re-election, was repeated in 1968-69. But what a transformation there was in the team's fortunes the next season. Points were increased from 41 to 64, wins from thirteen to 27, and defeats decreased from eighteen to nine. McGuigan was the Bell's Manager of the Season for Division Four. This was how the promoted clubs finished:

Season 1969-70	P	W	D	L	F	A	Pts
1. Chesterfield	46	27	10	9	77	32	64
2. Wrexham	46	26	9	11	84	49	61
3. Swansea	46	21	18	7	66	45	60
4. Port Vale	46	20	19	7	61	33	59

Wrexham were unbeaten at home; Swansea and Port Vale both lost only once on their own ground; Chesterfield suffered three defeats at Saltergate – by an only goal to both Port Vale and Chester, the odd goal of three to Grimsby. The FA Cup and League Cup were no distraction for the Spireites. They were swept out in the first round of both – respectively by three Tranmere goals at Prenton Park, and by one from Bradford City in a replay at Saltergate.

Only one player appeared in all of Chesterfield's matches that season, even though just nineteen, including substitutes, were called upon altogether, and he was also the only player to represent the club throughout those years of their first spell in the Fourth Division – a constant choice after appearing just half-a-dozen times at the start. He was Albert Holmes, another of the big names in the Spireites' story. Apprenticed as a fitter with the East Midlands Gas Board, Holmes turned down an offer from Rotherham United in order to complete his studies, playing for his local Gas Board team in the meantime. He then joined Chesterfield as a part-time professional in 1960, and signed full terms the following year. His long and distinguished career with the club stretched across 510 games, 471 of them in the League, until 1976, when he saw out his playing days with Boston United and afterwards reverted to being a gas engineer, self-employed. His son followed him as a professional footballer, but Chesterfield were not among the six clubs with which Paul Holmes totalled just over 400 League games, topping the century with both Torquay United and West Bromwich Albion.

Albert Holmes almost left Saltergate three years before he did, for in 1973 he was freed by McGuigan and verbally agreed to join Scunthorpe

United. Only a few days later, however, McGuigan himself departed, resigning after a dispute about bonuses for senior players, and Chesterfield left Holmes in a quandary by then offering him a new deal for the next season and also inviting Ron Ashman, the man who had tempted him to Scunthorpe, to become their new manager. Off Holmes went on holiday, uncertain of which club he would be playing for, and when he returned he found he was clear to re-sign for Chesterfield because Ashman, a former Norwich City captain, had moved the short distance from Scunthorpe to become the new manager of Grimsby Town instead of accepting the post in Derbyshire.

McGuigan promptly found a new opening at Rotherham, and remained there until November 1979, when he was Stockport's choice to succeed Mike Summerbee, the former Manchester City and England forward, after they had been rejected by Harry Gregg, then Manchester United's goalkeeper coach, and Oldham's Jimmy Frizzell. A 0-5 defeat by Newport, Stockport's heaviest at home that season, was a far from ideal start for McGuigan, but, although he was unable to get County out of Division Four, stomach trouble, which kept him away from his post for several months, was the reason why he was forced out of the game in April 1982 with three weeks of his contract to run. Eric Webster, who had already doubled as Stockport's head groundsman and reserve team trainer, deputised in his absence, and chairman Alan Kirk was so pleased with results during that period that Webster became McGuigan's successor. Three years later, however, the new manager was back to being the groundsman. Stockport were knocked out of the FA Cup by Telford United in 1983-84, and had to seek re-election the following season.

Albert Holmes, consistent and hard-working, made his name as a defender, renowned for the trademark sliding tackle out of which he usually came with the ball, but he was sometimes called on to pep up a misfiring forward line. That enabled him to get into double figures for goals, just, and the one for which he was best remembered bamboozled the Cambridge United goalkeeper from some twenty yards in his final season. A testimonial would have been a most deserved reward for such loyal service, but Holmes, in a reversal of the Blakey situation, refused one in 1976, feeling that there was no point in having it arranged with the club again going through a lean time that was reflected in declining gates. In any case, typical of the man, he considered that the fans had already paid enough to watch him over the years.

But for niggling injuries, Holmes would have been an ever-present in more than three of his seasons with Chesterfield, and thus even more closely challenged Blakey's appearances record. The circumstances in which he missed an FA Cup-tie with Bradford City were worthy of a place among soccer's oddities. Perfect balance was one of his playing attributes, yet he missed his footing in injuring an ankle while parking his car.

The other most regular members of Chesterfield's 1969-70 promotion team were Albert Phelan, who missed only one match, Kevin Randall and Ernie Moss, who were both absent from just two, Tom Fenoughty (43 games), John Archer and David Pugh (both 42), Charlie Bell (37), Alan Stevenson (35), Tony Moore (30) and John Lumsden (23). The club began the season with a line-up of: Humphreys; Holmes, Lumsden; Pugh, Bell, Phelan; Foley, Randall, Fenoughty, Archer, Martin. They ended it with: Stevenson; Holmes, Hickton; Fenoughty, Bell, Phelan; Pugh. Moss, Randall, Archer, Moore.

Randall and Moss were two more of the Chesterfield greats. Moss, who, with Stevenson, had been among the club's junior winners of the Northern Intermediate League Cup the previous season, was top scorer with twenty goals towards promotion, two ahead of Randall. Between them this pair scored almost 300 goals in their careers with Chesterfield, Moss becoming the club's all-time leading League and Cup marksman with 192, all but 30 of them in the League, in his three spells at Saltergate that spanned nearly twenty years and included another promotion as Fourth Division champions in 1985. Randall netted 96 for the club in the League, 105 in all.

This potent partnership would almost certainly never have materialised, however, but for McGuigan's intervention. Soon after Moss left his job as a clerk in the Derbyshire County Council education offices at Matlock to join his home club from the local Tube Works side in April 1967, the manager described him as 'a big, willing bloke, a charming fellow who had raw potential. His balance was nil, therefore his ball control was nil. He knew where the goal lay, but couldn't often hit it'.

That was indeed the case in the season before promotion was won. Moss made his League debut against Bradford at Park Avenue on 26 October 1968 (a few days before signing professional forms), but he failed to score either in that match or the sixteen others in which he played as Chesterfield went so close to relegation. McGuigan worked hard to rectify that weakness in training, with the gratifying outcome that made Moss the spearhead for promotion and beyond. Even so, a good many of his goals (four of them in one match with Newport on the way out of Division Four) still came from the heading skills he had already possessed. He took full advantage of the height that enabled him to tower over defenders, but was more of a 'gentle giant' than an over-robust player. Wholehearted was the word for his style. 'For me,' said Moss, 'competing was all about the pride and dignity of honest endeavour. Winning wasn't all about riches and rewards. It was about preserving one's sporting integrity; it was about honour.'

Appearances for eight other clubs besides Chesterfield took Moss to a Football League total of 749, putting him fourteenth in an all-time list headed by Peter Shilton with just over 1,000. Goalkeeper John Burridge surpassed Moss's total with 771 in 28 seasons, but 80 of them were with Scottish clubs.

In his first spell with the Spireites before leaving in January 1975 for Peterborough, who paid their then record fee of £25,000, Moss scored 95 goals in 271 League matches, taking his season's tally into the customary double figures despite missing a few months of 1970-71 with ruptured ligaments suffered at Swansea. In his second, brought back after helping Mansfield to the 1976-77 Third Division title in a further profitable link-up with Randall (30 goals between them), he scored 33 in 107 games. In the third, after being with two clubs, Port Vale and Doncaster Rovers, that were promoted to the Third Division, he scored 34 in 91 and was again a prominent figure as Saltergate was once more the home of the Division Four champions in 1984-85, two seasons after relegation. Moss was named Port Vale's Player of the Year in 1982, and Chesterfield supporters voted him their cult hero No 1. He was also elected one of the Fans' Favourites by the Professional Footballers' Association.

Kevin Randall, who was born at Ashton-under-Lyne, played in the same Manchester United youth team as George Best before leaving his job with a law stationery firm in 1965 to become a professional footballer with a £750 move to Bury from Droylesden, the club from which his uncle Maurice had previously joined Crewe Alexandra. Kevin was released, however, after only four League games alongside another future international, Colin Bell, and Tony McShane did his best piece of business for Chesterfield by snapping him up in July 1966, the month in which English football scaled new heights with the winning of the World Cup.

Randall made his debut for the Spireites on his 21st birthday, 20 August 1966, and the following week scored in a 3-0 defeat of Barnsley, the first of the goals that have made him the club's third highest League and Cup goal-getter, behind Moss and Herbert Munday (who had the biggest total overall, but is second to Moss with the exclusion of his games outside the main competitions). 'Kevin was almost telepathic,' said Moss. 'He was the best crosser of a ball I've ever known, and I had the best understanding with him than anyone I've ever played with.' One

Randall goal of special memory was scored in a third-round FA Cup-tie at Stoke in January 1972, a match in which he gave arguably his finest display. It was hailed as the goal of the game, a clever chip over the goalkeeper – none other than Gordon Banks. Chesterfield did not deserve to lose, by the odd goal of three, and Stoke's manager, Tony Waddington, acknowledged that the standard of football was 'the best we've seen here all season'.

Randall recalled that he earned £20 a week in his first season with Chesterfield, plus £1 for every 1,000 supporters above a gate of £8,000. It was not at all to the liking of most Saltergate supporters when their favourite of 282 games was sold to Notts County for £20,000 a few months after giving Stoke that Cup scare. And their displeasure over his loss considerably deepened when he not only helped the Magpies into the Second Division as runners-up in 1972-73 but also earned a Third Division championship medal with Mansfield four years later. On both those occasions he was his team's top scorer, with nineteen goals for Notts, seventeen for Mansfield. York City paid £8,000 for him in October 1977 after he had lost his place at Field Mill mainly due to a pelvic injury, and in exceeding a century of appearances for them he took his total of League and Cup games to nearly 600. His final goals tally was in the region of 200.

On retiring as a player, Randall coached York's youth team before being their caretaker manager between the departure of Barry Lyons in December 1981 and the appointment of Denis Smith in May 1982. Then, in 1984, Randall was back at Chesterfield as coach, physiotherapist and assistant manager to John Duncan, from whom he took over as manager when the former Tottenham striker left for Ipswich. It was a sentimental return for the man who was said to have achieved 'almost God-like status among the Saltergate faithful', but not, ultimately, a happy one. The team struggled, and Randall was dismissed in October 1988 after eight defeats in ten games.

After that, it was also back to Mansfield as youth development officer, then to Goole Town as manager, and, in February 1993 to Chesterfield again as assistant to the reappointed Duncan. He later became QPR's chief scout. Until 1990 Randall played Lancashire League cricket for Chesterfield Taveners, and such was his continued enthusiasm for football that he turned out for Pilsley Star in the Chesterfield Sunday League when he was more than 50 years old. He was 49 when he last played for Chesterfield, against his first club, Droylesden – and converted a penalty in a 3-2 win.

It was on a day when Randall missed a penalty, in a home match with

Southport in February 1967, that Chesterfield won narrowly despite also conceding a freak goal. Shortly before half-time their goalkeeper, Brian Arblaster, placed the ball in the goal area, mistakenly thinking a free-kick had been awarded. Tommy Spencer, the visitors' inside-right, dashed forward and hit it into the net. Other goalkeepers have been made red-faced in similar circumstances — among them another of Chesterfield's, none other than Ray Middleton.

At Newcastle in September 1947, the Spireites had already conceded a second-minute goal to Roy Bentley when, six minutes later, there was a confident appeal for offside as Jackie Milburn ran through to take a pass from Charlie Wayman. A linesman flagged, and on gaining possession Middleton placed the ball for the free-kick he thought had been awarded. But the referee had not blown his whistle, and as Middleton went back to take the kick Milburn nipped in to extend the lead. Even then, however, there was a happy ending for Chesterfield. They recovered to win deservedly by 3-2 with goals from Dennis Howsham, a free-transfer forward from Sheffield Wednesday, and Harold Roberts either side of a fine example of Billy Linacre's opportunism. With goalkeeper Fairbrother and full-back Craig undecided about which of them should take the ball in the goalmouth, the winger, man of the match, dashed in between them to equalise.

On the subject of penalties, it is interesting to note that Ernie Moss was proud of the fact that he scored all his League and Cup goals without the aid of a spot kick. Ironically, he missed the only one he ever took, in his 1986 testimonial match against Sheffield United, the club that also provided the opposition when Randall had his testimonial in 2007. For Randall, the occasion was given an extra fillip by the commissioning of an action painting of himself by his friend the local artist David Charlesworth. Proceeds from the sale of the prints, signed by both subject and artist, went towards the testimonial fund. Randall's friendship with Charlesworth dated back to 1984, when his great interest in steam engines led him to visit the artist's first public exhibition at the Peacock Centre in Chesterfield. 'I was a train-spotter as a boy,' said Randall, 'and have always had a fondness for steam engines. I loved David's work so much that I bought a couple of pencil sketches, and we have been friends ever since.'

Ernie Moss's third spell as a Chesterfield player ended on Christmas Eve in 1986, when he joined Stockport County with Phil Brown for a combined fee of £10,000. Brown, a winger, had played in not far off 100 first-team games after being signed under the club's apprentice scheme, which had first produced John Beresford and Ian Sharpe in 1962. Three

years after that, a team fielded against Notts County included nine players who had been born within fifteen miles of Chesterfield.

Brown and Moss parted company for the 1987-88 season. Brown was
then leading scorer for Lincoln City's GM Vauxhall Conference champions in their return to the Football League straight after being the first
club to be automatically relegated from it; Moss joined Scarborough,
Lincoln's predecessors in promotion from the Conference, for their first
Football League season under the management of another former
Chesterfield clubmate Neil Warnock. Brown and Moss were later together again with Kettering Town, Gainsborough Trinity and Matlock Town.
Moss was first at Kettering as a player, heading their scoring list with seventeen goals at the age of 40 in the 1988-89 season they finished as
Conference runners-up to Maidstone. He returned in 1990 to Kettering
(for whom Brown was top scorer in 1992-93), then had a final year there
as assistant manager around the turn of the century before becoming
manager of Matlock Town, for whom he had played after first leaving
Kettering. When Moss finally moved from Matlock to manage Hucknall
Town in 2004, Brown moved up from playing to be the club's joint manager with Gareth Williams, a partnership that lasted for more than four
years before both were dismissed.

Moss ended his days in the Football League after a brief stay on loan
from Scarborough at Rochdale (Lincoln were his other League club). It
was from Rochdale that he went to the first of his three stints at
Kettering. He also played for Shepshed Charterhouse before embarking
upon his 15-year career in management outside the Football League as
assistant manager of Boston United in 1992.

In 1997 Moss led Gainsborough Trinity to a trophy double with victories in the finals of the Northern Premier League Challenge Cup,
against Boston, and the Peter Swales Shield, against Leek Town, the
league champions. Trinity again reached the Challenge Cup final the next
year, but lost to Altrincham. Another setback for Moss as Leek's manager, sacked after prompt relegation, followed, but in 2004 he saw Matlock
to promotion to the Unibond League's Premier Division. His subsequent
spells with the Towns of Hucknall and Belper were unsuccessful, but
Chesterfield benefited again from Moss when he coached youngsters in
the club's community scheme and undertook scouting missions. Away
from football, he established a sports shop with Geoff Miller, the former
Derbyshire and England cricketer.

Another of Chesterfield's 1970 promotion winners was also a Matlock
Town manager. Tom Fenoughty held that job for 4½ years after being
associated as player, then approaching his mid-30s, with something

unique in soccer history. He and the younger Mick and Nick Fenoughty made Matlock the first club to field three brothers at Wembley when they met Scarborough in the FA Challenge Trophy final on 26 April 1975. What was more, Tom and Nick scored in Matlock's 4-0 victory.

In addition to the Milburns already mentioned, Alan Keen, who played more than 60 times for Chesterfield in the mid-1950s before leaving for Cheltenham Town, was also one of three brothers who have a special place in the soccer annals. He appeared with Jack and Herbert in the same Barrow team before his transfer to Saltergate in 1954. The first case of this kind was provided by John, George and William Carr, who first turned out together for Middlesbrough on New Year's Day in 1920. Others have included Albert, Bob and Ron Stitfall at Cardiff, Cyril, Gilbert and Ken Beech at Swansea, Arthur, Fred and Harry Tomlinson at Doncaster, and Danny, Ray and Rodney Wallace at Southampton.

There was almost a father and son, besides three brothers, in Matlock's team at Wembley. Peter Swan, the former Sheffield Wednesday and England centre-half, was then the Town's player-manager, but he decided not to include his son Carl, who had played in the quarter-final against Goole and the two-leg semi-final against Burton Albion. 'I would have loved to have played Carl,' he said, 'but we are at full strength and he had been mainly a stand-in.'

Swan had been reinstated in June 1972 after being jailed for four months, and banned from football for life, for his involvement in a betting scandal along with several other players. Two of them were his Wednesday clubmates David ('Bronco') Layne, who had been in the same Sheffield Boys team as Gordon Banks, and Tony Kay. They placed £50 bets that their team would lose at Ipswich, and when the Suffolk club, then champions, won, they each collected £100. 'There was never any question of our throwing the match,' said Layne, who was seriously injured, and his wife Carol killed, in a car crash six months after his release from prison. 'Our side was never in a position to win that day. All we had done was send off our £50. Only later did we realise what a big thing it was.'

Swan played again in the League for the Wednesday and Bury before joining Matlock in July 1974. He left there at the end of the 1975-76 season, and it was then that Tom Fenoughty took over – to be followed in December 1980 by none other than Swan, who was reappointed after managing Worksop and Buxton, but dismissed a year afterwards when Matlock were bottom of the Northern Premier League. The job then returned to the Fenoughty family, Mick taking over and going on to complete fourteen years with the club before resigning in 1985 to concentrate on his other work as the Northern Area sales representative for an international medical drugs firm.

Tom Fenoughty was one of the many Sheffield United or Sheffield-born players who have made the move to Chesterfield over the years, putting those frequent dealings with Manchester City that have already been referred to well and truly in the shade. Fenoughty, whose birthplace was Rotherham, joined the Blades from Sheffield FC in 1964 and made one short of a half-century of League appearances for them before going to Saltergate. His arrival in the close season of 1969, combined with that of John Archer from Huddersfield Town, completed manager McGuigan's transformation of a team of no-hopers into promotion winners. Fenoughty, chiefly a midfielder, played in 110 League and Cup games for the Blues (as the Spireites have also been known).

Archer, who was born at Biddulph in Staffordshire, entered League football with Port Vale after graduating through their youth team, and he also played for Bournemouth and Crewe before McGuigan saw him as the inside-forward he had been looking for. His 116 games and 22 goals for Chesterfield increased his League totals to 333 and 76, after which he became manager of Sandbach Ramblers.

Charlie Bell was another player imported from Sheffield United, one of McGuigan's earliest and most inspired signings for Chesterfield, who imposed a great influence on the escape from Division Four. The Bramall Lane club made him a professional in the same year as Tom Fenoughty, but he played only three times in their first team, as a forward. He began with Chesterfield in midfield, and also turned out for them up front, before injuries to others led to his taking over as the regular centre-half. It was then decided that, although he was the right height for that position, his physique needed building up, so he was put on a weight-training course. As a result, he developed into one of the best central defenders in the League, described in one *Derbyshire Times* report as 'the bastion of the sea-blue fortress'.

For more than 150 matches Bell stood steadfast in Chesterfield's cause, but he was then replaced by Eric Winstanley and followed McGuigan to Rotherham after being rejected by Barnsley on medical grounds. He ended his footballing career as coach at Stockport, then became a sales representative, based in Sheffield. Winstanley stayed with Chesterfield long enough also to get into three figures for appearances, but he was a Barnsley man first and foremost, by both birth and dedication, and hailed among supporters at Oakwell as a legendary figure. After playing more than 400 times for Barnsley, a good many of them as captain, he spent over twenty years on their coaching staff and was twice caretaker manager. His service with the club began with his signing as a professional in May 1962, and ended in June 2011 when he left to join the Saint Kitts and Nevis team in the Caribbean as technical director. He was subsequently a coach with Doncaster, Scarborough and York, then went abroad again, to South Africa in 2009, to join Supersport United's development project.

Joe Devine welcomes his fellow countryman Tom Lyon to Chesterfield after his transfer from Blackpool in 1938

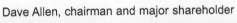

Dave Allen, chairman and major shareholder

Dema Glassworks before the building of the new stadium

George Smith celebrates his 90th birthday

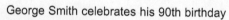

George (left) and Stan Milburn, partners at full-back

Joe Devine and Ollie Thompson, on the
coaching staff either side of World War II

Fred Capel

Harry Clifton

David Blakey, holder of the
club's appearance record

Billy Kidd

Jimmy Smallwood

DIVISION FOUR CHAMPIONS—CHESTERFIELD

Back row (left to right): S. Walker, P. Carline, J. Moyes, M. Wright, J. Lumsden, G. Martin. Centre: K. Randall, E. Moss, C. Bell, A. Stevenson, A. Humphreys, A. Phelan, T. Fenoughty. Front: J. McGuigan (manager), D. Pugh, R. Hickton, J. Archer, A. Holmes, A. Moore, G. Clarke (trainer).

Albert Phelan

Dennis Westcott in action for Blackburn Rovers, beating Jack Chisholm of Sheffield United

Horace Wass

Gordon Dale

Billy 'Legs' Linacre

Tommy Flockett

Willis Edwards

Ken Booker

Charlie Bell

Hugh McJarrow

Sean O'Neill

Chesterfield's 1937-38 squad

Team photo from 1951-52. Back: McLeod, Southall, Milburn S, Leivers, Lomas, Smith. Front: Knight, Capel F, Marron, Harrison, Wilson

11

Blades connection;
Arthur Cox the big spender

Chesterfield made the strongest of all their Sheffield United connections with the appointment, on the first day of September in 1973, of the man who took over the manager's job Jimmy McGuigan had so abruptly left the previous May. He was Joe Shaw, clear holder of the Blades' appearances record with 632 Football League games and an overall total of more than 700 with the addition of cup-ties and friendlies. His statue stands outside the club's ground at Bramall Lane.

There was also a link with the North-East of England that has been such a happy hunting ground for Chesterfield over the years, for Shaw was born, on 23 June 1928, at Murton in County Durham. Although he played for Durham Boys at county level, and first turned out for Sheffield United at the age of sixteen, he did not graduate straight to Bramall Lane from schools soccer. He worked at Upton Colliery, near Doncaster, and was in the team there as an inside-forward before beginning in July 1945 a professional career with United, his only League club as a player, that lasted as a member of the first team until February 1966.

For much of that time Shaw, despite his lack of height (5ft 8in in his socks), was a resolute centre-half, regarded at his peak as the best of that time in England not to win an international cap. In the obituary published in *The Independent* after Shaw's death in November 2007, Ivan Ponting described him as 'the trusty bulwark at the core of the United rearguard'. The closest Shaw got to representing his country in a full international was to be selected as the only reserve for the match in which Scotland were beaten 2-7 at Wembley in 1955. A vacancy did occur at wing-half, a position in which Shaw also played, when Huddersfield's Bill McGarry dropped out through injury, but Ken Armstrong, of Chelsea, was brought in to fill it. So the spurned Shaw had to be content with playing twice against Australia on an FA tour in the early 1950s and making a couple of appearances in the Football League XI.

Shaw wore Sheffield United's red and white stripes in two League North matches of the transitional 1944-45 season, the first of them in a 3-1 victory over Huddersfield Town on 2 April, when he was only sixteen years an 285 days old. He made his Football League debut in a 1-2 home defeat by Liverpool on 30 August 1948, but missed most of the match with a bleeding nose. He was off the field when the visitors went ahead midway through the first half, and absent for much of the second. United were relegated that season, and for the next few years, during which, in 1953, they were Second Division champions, Shaw played at wing-half until manager Reg Freeman switched him to central defence, and made him captain, after two heavy defeats at the start of the 1954-55 season.

That was the turning point of Shaw's playing career. It quickly became clear that this was his natural place on the field. Superb anticipation, the ability to read a game, speed over short distances, and remarkable agility in recovery were his strong points. He made it all look so easy. Joe Mercer, the former Everton, Arsenal and England wing-half, preferred a more physical presence at the heart of defence when he took over as manager, but, after several unsuccessful attempts to provide it with new signings, he came to realise his mistake and apologised to Shaw for ever doubting him. With John Harris, who had been a sterling centre-half himself with Chelsea, then at the helm, Shaw's experience and expertise were vital as United won promotion again in 1961 and also reached an FA Cup semi-final in which they lost to Leicester only after a second replay.

Shaw was still going strong in his 30s, enjoying a third spell as skipper, and he celebrated his 600th League appearance in a 2-1 victory against West Ham on 6 February 1965. The Hammers were also the opposition when he finally stepped down from the first team just over a year later, after which he helped youngsters along in the Reserves, then briefly coached at Bramall Lane before going into management with York City in November 1967. That, though, was not a happy venture. Re-election to the Fourth Division had to be sought at the end of that season, and he resigned shortly before the start of the next one. He was next Fulham's chief scout before accepting the offer from Chesterfield, who had recently had a change of chairman with Dan Newton taking over following the death of Harold Shentall.

Chesterfield went close to getting back into the Second Division in Shaw's first season of 1973-74, occupying the third promotion place as late as the middle of March, but they lost three of their last four matches and finished fifth. The sale on transfer deadline day, 15 March, of goalkeeper Jim Brown had a big bearing on the failed challenge. He went to Sheffield United for £60,000 two days after going on as a substitute for Scotland in an Under-23 match at Newcastle against an England side that included his Saltergate predecessor Alan Stevenson. It was a sudden deal that came as much of a surprise to the player himself as to the fans with whom he had become a real favourite, a notable addition to the club's list of outstanding goalkeepers.

There had also been an unwelcome aspect of Brown's £6,000 signing by Chesterfield in December 1972 after he had impressed against them for Albion Rovers in a pre-season friendly arranged following the transfer of midfielder Sam Ferris to Saltergate from the Coatbridge club. Chesterfield blamed the Christmas postal rush for being pushed into the bottom half of the Third Division by order of the Football League after having revived hopes of a promotion bid with eleven points from their last seven games. They had to replay their Boxing Day match at Blackburn, which they won 2-1, because, on beating Brighton to Brown's signature, they fielded him before the proper registration of the transfer forms that had been posted to the League's headquarters at Lytham St Anne's on 22 December.

'We acted in good faith,' said Arthur Sutherland, the club's general manager and secretary, 'but the postal delay was so great, even for first-class mail, that the forms did not reach the authorities in time.' The League's Management Committee took the view, however, that the regulations were clearly laid out, and that Chesterfield should have realised the forms would be delayed in the post. The ruling may have seemed harsh because there was no deliberate attempt to contravene the regulations, but it was not as harsh as in the two previous cases of fielding an ineligible player. Sunderland had been fined £50 and had two points deducted for giving goalkeeper Ned Doig his debut in 1890 before his registration had gone through, and Stockport had also been docked a couple for putting James Smith into their team in 1927 without permission. Chesterfield at least had the chance to keep the points, which they duly did the following March by completing a double over Blackburn in the rearranged game with a penalty converted by Jackie Sinclair, a winger on loan from Sheffield Wednesday.

In Chesterfield's first League match of 1973, Frank Large, a much-travelled forward newly arrived from Northampton, scored against Swansea what would have been his 200th League goal but for the expunging of the one he had netted against Blackburn on Boxing Day. He had to wait only a few more weeks, however, to top the double century in a 2-2 draw at Plymouth. The season ended with Blackburn in third place, just those two points behind Notts County, who went up with Bolton Wanderers. Chesterfield finished sixteenth, only a couple of points above the drop.

Large, a former railway worker, had quite an on-going association with Northampton Town. His move to Chesterfield at the age of 32 was his third from that club, prompting him to remark: 'The funny thing is I've never asked for a transfer. This time I thought I was at my last port of call, but Northampton are in a bit of money trouble, so selling me was a way of helping their financial affairs. In fact, the club have made almost £90,000 out of selling me in the past [to Swindon and Leicester], but this time the transfer was different. For once I didn't want to move because I was at last putting some roots down. With four children I thought it was time to get settled.' But Large, a Yorkshireman who had also been with Halifax, QPR (who converted him from centre-half to striker), Carlisle, Oldham and Fulham before Chesterfield, went even further afield after scoring fifteen goals in 46 League games for the Spireites – to Baltimore in the United States, where he joined the Comets. After retiring from playing football he helped his son Paul to manage Westport United and Ballina Town in Ireland, and also played cricket for the County Mayo club.

Jim Brown, who won his one full cap while with Sheffield United when Scotland failed to qualify against Romania for the European Championship, also played in America, for Detroit Express, Washington Diplomats and Chicago Sting, before returning to Britain and playing three times in Cardiff City's League side. He was next with Kettering, from where he rejoined Chesterfield in 1983 and increased his total of League appearances for them to 182. It was during his second spell at Saltergate that he was in the team that suffered the record 0-10 defeat at Gillingham in September 1987 (after not conceding a goal in their previous four games that season). But no blame was attached to Brown. He was badly injured in trying to save at the start of the deluge. He should have been substituted, but resolutely carried on – and did not reappear in the side until Boxing Day

Brown had not long been back with Chesterfield when, in October 1983, he had an experience of a very different kind. The first of the two goals in a home win against Stockport made him one of the goalkeepers who have strayed from the job they were paid for by scoring in a League match, his long clearance freakishly beating the desperate leap of his opposite number, Mick Salmon. Two years before, Brown had been the first goalkeeper to score in the North America League, while playing for the Diplomats against Atlanta.

As Brown's playing career drew towards its close, another post opened up for him at Chesterfield. While still keeping goal, he was an ideal choice to take over as the club's commercial manager in 1986, and he was instrumental in the setting-up of the 'Blues on the Move' lottery that did so much to secure the Spireites' future after they had been in great danger of extinction three years before. They had then been nearly £360,000 in debt, also facing a bill of about £1,000 for the repair of seating in the

Cross Street stand that had been ripped out by Millwall fans during a 1-0 win that had kept the London club in Division Three.

The financial hole into which Chesterfield had fallen remained frighteningly deep despite their announcement in January 1984 of a profit of £4,171 on the past financial year, following several seasons of heavy losses. They were more than £400,000 in the red when, on 14 November 1985, a life membership 200 Club was launched with a £100,000 target. For a once-only payment of £500 supporters were to get one Centre Stand ticket, or two terrace tickets, for life.

Jim Brown still had his most important role to play at Saltergate (more of that in its turn), but first his playing career took a most unexpected twist when, in his 41st year, he was named as the team's substitute, but unused, goalkeeper on a dozen occasions during the 1993-94 season. He also filled that role at the 1995 play-off final in which Chesterfield defeated Bury at Wembley, and, at the age of 45 years and 188 days, for a first-round FA Cup-tie against Northwich Victoria, won with an early goal, in 1997.

In marked contrast to Brown's long service to Chesterfield, Joe Shaw's was disappointingly short. He was unable to keep the club among the front runners after starting with that promotion near-miss. Player unrest led to a number of departures – among them (shock, horror!), that of Ernie Moss, a move that could not have been bettered for getting the manager on the wrong side of supporters. After two seasons of mid-table mediocrity, Shaw was also irrevocably on the wrong side of the board, on which P C J T Kirkman OBE had followed Dan Newton as chairman. The directors' patience ran out when a poor start was made to the 1976-77 season, and Shaw pre-empted a sacking by resigning after two heavy defeats – by 0-6 at home to Bury and 1-4 away to Sheffield Wednesday – had dumped his team into the relegation zone. A sad and most unfitting end to the career of one of soccer's true stalwarts.

The choice of Arthur Cox to succeed Shaw made him Chesterfield's first manager without a senior playing pedigree since the appointment of Jim Caffrey in 1920. Cox, who was born at Southam, a small town near Leamington in Warwickshire, on 14 December 1939, joined Coventry City from school in 1955, and he appeared to have a bright future as a player, although still to get into the first team, when his right leg was broken so badly that it brought his playing career to an abrupt and untimely halt. He was only eighteen. The club kept him on as a member of their coaching staff, and during his nine years in that role he suffered another cruel blow through the death of his first wife in a road accident. From Coventry, where he latterly ran the youth team, he went to Walsall as chief coach, then also coached at Aston Villa, Preston, Halifax, Blackpool and Sunderland.

The crew-cut Cox, a tough and honest down-to-earth character with the look of a sergeant-major, gained his first experience of management as briefly caretaker at Villa Park in December 1968 between the departure of Tommy Cummings, the former Burnley centre-half, and appointment of that man of many clubs, the colourful Tommy Docherty. At Preston, Cox's coaching efforts were first rewarded with a trophy. North End had just been relegated when he joined them in 1970, but they went straight back up as Third Division champions in his first season with the Deepdale club.

After being with Alan Ball Senior, father of one of England's World Cup winners, at Halifax, Cox rose to assistant manager with Blackpool, but it was at Sunderland that he first became well known when he combined his coaching with being assistant to manager Bob Stokoe, the former Newcastle defender. Stokoe declared that 'Arthur Cox, our coach, prepared the lads magnificently for Wembley' after the then Roker Park club had hit the headlines with their shock defeat of hot favourites Leeds United in the 1973 FA Cup final, but Cox resigned 'for personal reasons' in March 1976. He was replaced by Ian McFarlane, who was lured from League Cup winners Manchester City in time to see Sunderland gain promotion that season as Second Division champions.

Off Cox went to Turkey to manage Galatasaray, but his wife could not settle there and on returning to England he was beaten to the Mansfield post by Peter Morris before successfully applying to Chesterfield. Morris, a Derbyshire man, had played for Mansfield before helping Ipswich and Norwich to the Division Two title and being a League Cup finalist with Norwich. Cox moved into the manager's chair at Saltergate on 8 October 1976. Characteristically forthright, he came with no promises, but made it clear he would not hesitate to take what others might well regard as unpleasant decisions if he considered them to be in the club's interests.

One of those unpleasant decisions (for the opposition) was made within a few weeks of his arrival when Chesterfield rose from twentieth to eighth in the Third Division table with an unbeaten run of seven games culminating in a 7-0 home win against Bury. Half the pitch for that match was icebound, so Cox gave his players an advantage by sending them out in pimple-soled boots. The visitors had brought only their usual studded boots, and when their officials said they wished to go into town to buy appropriate footwear Cox resorted to a double deception. He did not order the taxi he said he would get for them, then came up with an imaginative excuses for its absence.

The Bury men eventually made their own arrangements, but Chesterfield were four goals ahead by the time they got back with the boots. Four of the eventual seven were scored by Rodney Fern, a nippy forward formerly with Leicester and Luton who totalled 125 in 448 games in a League career he ended with Rotherham. At Leicester, Fern was likened to the comedian Marty Feldman by commentator Hugh Johns because of his curls. But well before he reached Chesterfield, for whom he completed a half-century of goals in just over 150 appearances, he shed them in favour of sporting a Mexican-style moustache.

From that big beating of Bury, Chesterfield went into another decline with just one point from ten games, and their final position eighteenth, three points above the relegation trapdoor, spurred Cox into another decision that was not entirely popular. He ordered his players in for training throughout the close season. It paid off with a flying start that shot the Spireites to the top of the table, and, although injuries to half-a-dozen key men subsequently influenced a slide to halfway, Blackpool were sufficiently impressed with what Cox was doing to want him as their manager. Chesterfield warded them off with the offer he accepted of a five-year contract.

Cox was soon busy in the transfer market. With the £80,000 sale of goalkeeper Steve Hardwick to Newcastle, he still had some money to spare after the purchase of two forwards, Rick Green from Scunthorpe for £20,000,and Stuart Parker from Southend United for £15,000, plus midfielder Ricky Heppolette from Crystal Palace for £16,000, and full-back Colin Tartt from Port Vale for £15,000. Green and Tartt both went back to where they had come from, Green after being sold to Notts County while Cox was still manager, Tartt taking the direct route back to Vale Park after Cox had left.

Tartt proved the wisest investment. He made more than 180 League appearances for Chesterfield, each of the three others fewer than 50. Heppolette, who was born in India, moved to Peterborough United, Parker to Sparta of Rotterdam. Parker had no fewer than eighteen clubs as a player, beginning at Blackpool in 1972 and ending with Hyde United in 1989. He scored twice in Blackpool's defeat of Napoli in an under-21 tournament in Italy in 1974, and ten years later helped Drogheda United to win the League of Ireland Cup.

Cox also showed a profit on the transfer out of two other goalkeepers besides Hardwick. Steve Ogrizovic's sale to Liverpool for £75,000 (as deputy for England's Ray Clemence before making good at Coventry) was followed by that of Glan Letheran, whom he bought for £10,000 from Leeds United to follow 'Oggy', and then sold to Swansea City for

£50,000 nearly two years later. Letheran was a Welsh international at Under-21 and Under-23 level, but only an unrequired substitute, a dozen times, for a full cap. He joined Chesterfield after being loaned to Scunthorpe by Leeds, for whom he played in just one League game but was on the subs' bench, also unused, for their 1975 European Cup final defeat by Bayern Munich.

Shortly before the 1978-79 season, Cox observed that 'it is reasonably easy to buy players if you are prepared to pay exorbitant fees'. A few days later he broke Chesterfield's transfer record by paying Leicester City £35,000 for midfielder Geoff Salmons. Here was another of the players with the Sheffield United connection. Salmons, who was born at Mexborough in 1948, joined the Blades straight from school and was an important member of their team that returned to the First Division in 1971. Both he and his manager, Ken Furphy, regretted that he had to leave when, just one short of 200 League and Cup games, he moved to Stoke City for £160,000 in July 1974. 'There is no cash available for sign-ings,' said Furphy. 'The only way I can buy is to sell players to raise the cash. We didn't want to let Geoff go.' Salmons expressed his feelings about it three years later when he briefly rejoined United on loan before his transfer to Leicester. 'I spent more than ten happy years at Bramall Lane before they sold me to Stoke,' he said. 'I didn't want to leave then. My heart has always been with this club. It's like coming home.'

Stoke were themselves in an uncomfortable financial position similar to the one that had compelled Sheffield United to part with Salmons to the Potteries when they had to release the player to Leicester – first on loan, then for a fee of £42,500. 'We spent a considerable sum on buying Peter Shilton, Alan Hudson and Geoff Salmons,' stated their manager, Tony Waddington, 'but we knew we had sufficient money for the deposits and could pay the rest back over a period. At that time, howev-er, we did not realise just how bad inflation would be, and how high inter-est charges would go. Then we were confronted with £750,000 needed for the repair of the Butler Street stand that was damaged by a gale.'

Stoke had hoped to patch up the wooden stand, but a week after the gale 30 tons of timber crashed through the roof, wrecking 1,500 seats. The club did not receive full insurance because only part of the stand was damaged, and they then found that the new one, built of steel, would need deeper foundations, increasing the cost. Shilton, Hudson, Jimmy Greenhoff, Mike Pejic, Ian Moores and Sean Haslegrave were other play-ers Stoke had to let go in a break-up of the team heading back to Division Two. 'It's the only way a club like ours can exist in an economic jungle,' commented Waddington, whose resignation soon afterwards ended a seventeen-year reign that made him the longest-serving among the managers of that time.

Salmons had not been long at Leicester when Cox came for him, but he played in 120 League games for Chesterfield, scoring fifteen goals, before leaving in May 1982. That gave him respective career totals of 449 and 41. A recurring hamstring injury restricted him to four first-team appearances, one of them as a substitute, in his last season with the Spireites, but, at 34, he carried on for while with Gainsborough Trinity.

Neither did Salmons remain long as Chesterfield's most expensive player. In the 1979 close season Bill Green, a central defender from Peterborough, and Alan Birch, a right-winger from Walsall, cost £40,000 each as Cox sought to improve a side that had just gone close to relegation, in twentieth place, despite playing football he considered 'far above the standard of the Third Division'. It included four regulars, Les Hunter and Ken Burton in defence, Andy Kowalski and Phil Walker in attack, who between them totalled more than 1,000 League appearances for the club.

Hunter went on to equal Ernie Moss, who made the first of his returns to Saltergate that season, in having three spells with Chesterfield; Kowalski and Walker both had two. Hunter, originally signed as an apprentice, was twice transferred to Scunthorpe, rejoined a second time from Lincoln, and finally left for Matlock Town. Kowalski was signed from Alfreton Town, went to Doncaster, returned from Peterborough, then moved to Boston. Walker joined from Mansfield YC, was transferred to and from Rotherham, and left again for Scarborough.

Walker was plagued by injury while with Rotherham, to whom he was first transferred in an exchange deal involving midfielder Mick Gooding, who had the misfortune to break a leg in only his fifth League game for Chesterfield, won at home to Newport on the first day of February in 1983. On recovering, Gooding played in only seven more before going back to Rotherham. Walker, on the other hand, made just over 200 League appearances for Chesterfield, but only 38 of them in his second spell with the club. Len Badger, a veteran full-back of more than 450 League games for Sheffield United, also broke a leg while with Chesterfield, a year after joining them in January 1976 – the month in which striker Steve Cammack was also signed from the Blades.

Arthur Cox completed his preparations for the 1979-80 season by bringing in left-winger Alan Crawford from Rotherham for the £30,000 he had just received from that club for Rodney Fern, and paying Leicester City £35,000 for midfielder John Ridley. Crawford took over from Walker, who switched from outside-left to follow Fern at the head of the attack. James ('Sean') O'Neill, an astute Shaw signing after being freed by Leeds, re-established himself as Tartt's full-back partner in place of Burton, who had gone to Halifax. The rejigged line-up played some sparkling football that was most freely expressed in a 7-1 home win against Reading.

Still, however, Cox was not satisfied. Chesterfield had a real chance of going up when they went into third place in March by beating visitors from Southend with a Kowalski goal, and the manager aimed to bolster it by splashing out nearly £300,000 the club could ill afford. Goalkeeper John Turner came from Torquay for £50,000, full-back John Stirk from Watford for £40,000 (Tartt moved to centre-forward with Walker's return to the wing), and midfielder Phil Bonnyman from Carlisle United for a club record £150,000.

But the hoped-for extra impetus was not provided. There were those who thought that Bonnyman's replacement of the popular Kowalski, who had dropped back to wing-half, adversely affected the team's morale, but the loss of Bill Green's leadership through injury was a bigger reason for the missed opportunity. Chesterfield lost only two of their last ten games, in succession, but that was enough to enable Sheffield Wednesday to pip them for the third promotion place behind Grimsby and Blackburn by one point.

The renewed debt into which those deals had plunged Chesterfield was further increased in July 1980 with the £100,000 signing of Danny Wilson from Bury. There was no doubting the ability of this Wigan-born midfielder, who would be capped two dozen times by Northern Ireland, but the serious financial consequences of his arrival quickly became all too evident when the club began to default on their payment of the fee's instalments. It was in these daunting circumstances, which so nearly led to the club's extinction, that Chesterfield lost their manager. Newcastle United, who had their own money troubles, made an approach, and on 4 September, Cox was announced as their successor to Bill McGarry. A minute's silence was observed at a Chesterfield pub.

On Tyneside, Cox built a team around Kevin Keegan, the former Liverpool and England human dynamo, that played some of the best football seen there for many years in winning promotion to the First Division in 1984. Yet the celebrations had still to die down when he caused a sensation by dropping back into the Third Division in Derbyshire. Derby County went into their centenary season with Cox as their ninth manager in eleven years – at an annual salary of £28,000 that was £7,000 below what he would have earned at Newcastle, also on a three-year contract.

Cox, who had rejected substantial offers from QPR, Hull, Portsmouth and Wolves, explained his choice of Derby by saying: 'The answer is that for a few clubs anything is possible, and Derby's marvellous support makes them one. In potential, this is still one of the biggest clubs in the land.' In 1986 he pulled off another promotion, and a year later the Rams were Second Division champions. Five years after that, Derby missed being founder members of the FA Premier League only through a narrow semi-final defeat in the play-offs.

A back problem forced Cox's resignation in October 1993, but, although never a manager again, he held a variety of posts as assistant, coach and chief scout before finally retiring in 2008. These included linking up again with Keegan at Fulham, the England team, Manchester City and back at Newcastle.

Cox's successor at Chesterfield in September 1980 was Frank Barlow, who, as a defensive midfielder, had been another player signed by the club from Sheffield United, for £15,000 in August 1972. His career in senior football began at 19, when, after being capped by England at schoolboy level, and turning down the chance to go to university, he signed professional forms for United, his home club, in 1965. He made 121 League appearances for the Blades, then 140 for Chesterfield, before he was forced to give up playing after being badly injured in a match with Southend United at Saltergate in December 1975. He was kept on as caretaker manager following the sacking of Joe Shaw, and then appointed first-team coach at the age of 31. So he was seen as the man on the spot with the right credentials to move up to the manager's hot seat.

12

Rangers beaten on path to Anglo-Scottish Cup

Frank Barlow was a reluctant manager. He protested several times while he held that job with Chesterfield that he did not really want it. He said he always felt more comfortable as a coach, which he was before being pressed into succeeding Arthur Cox. Yet he brought success in his first season in charge. The Spireites carried off the Anglo-Scottish Cup in March 1981. In fact, they are still the holders.

The reason why this trophy is still on display in the Chesterfield boardroom is that it has not since been at stake. The competition, created in 1975 as a reincarnation of the Texaco Cup with a similar format, was suspended indefinitely because the Scottish League no longer wished to take part. Jim Farry, their secretary, complained that it had become devalued by the absence of English teams 'from the upper echelon', with no guarantee that there would be stronger opposition from that quarter in the future. Which was rather rich considering that little Chesterfield had defeated mighty Glasgow Rangers (well, they were mighty in those days) on their way to the final.

The competition continued, with English clubs only, as the Football League Group Cup. An attempt was made in 1987-88 to revive the original knock-out tournament as the Anglo-Scottish Challenge Cup, but it was shelved after a poor attendance for the first leg between Coventry City and St Mirren. The second leg was never played. St Mirren had been the only Scottish winners of the Anglo-Scottish Cup the year before Chesterfield claimed it. Indeed, they had been the only Scottish club to reach any of its six finals, which were all played over home and away legs.

In the 1977-78 season St Mirren, members of the Scottish Premier Division, were beaten by Bristol City, who were then in the English First Division, but they had their revenge against the Ashton Gate club in the final of 1980, when City were also relegated. The other holders of the trophy were the first two winners, Middlesbrough and Nottingham Forest, both of the First Division, and Burnley, of the Second. Newcastle United were expelled from the 1976-77 competition for fielding a weakened team in the first leg of their quarter-final against Ayr United, and over the years English entrants were increasingly drawn from the lower divisions of the Football League.

With the addition to their 46 League games of four in the League Cup, six in the FA Cup and nine in the Anglo-Scottish Cup, Chesterfield played in 65 matches during the 1980-81 season, a record number outside the Football League's top two divisions. They finished ahead of Grimsby, Hull and Sheffield United in their qualifying group. All the knock-out stages were decided over two legs. Chesterfield drew 1-1 with Rangers in Scotland, Phil Walker scoring, and won 3-0 at home with two goals from Bonnyman, who had been given a free transfer by Rangers, and the other one from Moss. The gate at Ibrox was 12,000, in a stadium that had housed nearly 120,000 (against Celtic). The crowd of 13,914 for the return game was surpassed at Saltergate that season only for the visits of Sheffield United and Barnsley. The usual attendance there was then rarely above 6,000, and sank as low as just over 3,000.

The memorable defeat of the Scottish giants took Chesterfield to a semi-final in which they made harder work of beating Bury, who were then a Fourth Division club – and only a mid-table one at that. After edging to a 2-1 win at Gigg Lane, where Wilson and Crawford were their scorers, Barlow's men increased their advantage in the home leg with John Stirk's first goal for the club in the twentieth minute, but they survived precariously from the 65th minute in which the visitors closed the gap to 3-2 on aggregate.

In the final, their first in a senior competition for 114 years, Chesterfield were pitted against Notts County, who that season won promotion back to the First Division they had left as long ago as 1926. And what a mighty close-run thing it was. A first-half goal from Moss gained a slender lead to take to the second leg at Meadow Lane, where it was wiped out before the interval by Scottish international Don Masson. That was how the overall score still stood after 90 minutes, but Alan Crawford, who had been sent on as substitute for Bonnyman, scored the decider in extra time.

Chesterfield's team for the two matches of the final, with changes for the second leg shown in brackets, was: Turner (Gregory); Stirk, O'Neill; Wilson (Ridley), Green, Ridley (Kowalski); Birch, Moss, Kowalski (Bonnyman), Salmons, Walker. There were two substitutions in addition to the crucial one concerning Crawford. Tartt was called upon for both. He replaced Wilson at Saltergate, Stirk in Nottingham. The team fielded in the two games with Rangers was: Turner; Tartt, Pollard; Wilson, Green, Ridley; Birch, Moss, Bonnyman, Salmons, Walker. The Sheffield-born Paul Gregory who deputised for Turner at Meadow Lane had joined the club as an apprentice, and was later with Doncaster Rovers. Gary Pollard, who came through the Juniors, went to Port Vale the year after skipper Ridley was given a free transfer back to that club during the 1982 close season as part of the economy drive forced on Chesterfield in their desperately close brush with extinction. It was cold comfort for the Derbyshire club's officials to know that other clubs were having similar financial difficulties.

Another regretful decision had by then already been taken to part with Alan Birch, who had become a firm favourite of the fans, distinguishable not only for his tightly-curled perm. Given a free rein by Arthur Cox, Birch featured prominently in the successive fourth and fifth Third Division finishes of 1979-81 before, under the weight of the growing debt, the club took a downturn along the road that was so soon to lead to another relegation.

Birch left in circumstances even less straightforward than those in which he had arrived. Chesterfield had been interested in him since his fine display against them for Walsall in a scoreless draw at Saltergate in March 1979, but at the end of that season he had agreed terms with Mansfield Town after going to Field Mill for talks with manager Billy Bingham, the former Northern Ireland winger. However, on returning to the ground from an hour's lunch break in which the contract was being drawn up, Birch had found to his great astonishment that Bingham had been sacked, and, although Mansfield had still been keen to sign him, he had decided the move was no longer in his best interests. That was when Chesterfield had stepped in.

The bid Chesterfield received for Birch in August 1981 was of £200,000, their biggest for an outgoing transfer, from Wolverhampton Wanderers. It was money the Derbyshire club urgently needed to pay off a £25,000 debt to Leicester City incurred from the transfer of Martin Henderson, so that a ban imposed by the League on their signing new players might be lifted. That, however, did not happen until October 1982. Wolves were themselves in deeply in the red, and soon after signing Birch they went into voluntary liquidation, rescheduling their debts. The amount they eventually handed over to Chesterfield was £177,500.

Birch had to be sold at a big loss within a few months of moving to Molineux. He went to Barnsley, and from there he became another of the players who have had more than one spell at Saltergate. He rejoined Chesterfield in August 1983, two months into what would be the first of John Duncan's two stints as the club's manager after relegation had cost Barlow his job. But Birch was unable to repeat the success he had previously enjoyed with Chesterfield. He was a signing of the new chairman, Barrie Hubbard, and was not always in agreement with the manager. Rotherham paid £25,000 for him in March 1984, and he was also with

Scunthorpe and Stockport before ending his playing career outside the Football League at Frickley Athletic, Shepshed Charterhouse and Matlock Town. He then became a publican – first at the Nag's Head in Chesterfield's Derby Road, then at the Globe Inn at Tamworth in Staffordshire.

Frank Barlow was offered a place in the new Saltergate set-up that changes on the board heralded, but he declined out of loyalty to his back-room staff, the whole of which was sacked. Out went coach Bill Dearden, chief scout Harold Roberts and physio John Short. Dearden, another of Chesterfield's former Sheffield United players, had arrived from a second spell with Chester in 1977 and joined the coaching staff shortly before ending his playing career two years later. He soon found a new coaching post at Mansfield, where he spent eleven years before taking up a similar position with Port Vale. He was subsequently caretaker manager of both Vale and Mansfield before taking over as manager of Notts County, then coach at Blackpool and Milton Keynes. In 2008 he returned to Blackpool as chief scout, a role in which he also went back to Sheffield United three years later.

Barlow's exit from Chesterfield gave Scunthorpe United the opportunity they quickly grasped to appoint him assistant manager, and a year later, in August 1984, he became their manager in succession to Allan Clarke, the former Leeds and England forward, who resigned, along with chairman David Wraith, after promotion to the Third Division had been immediately followed by relegation.

Again, Barlow accepted the post reluctantly, yet he coped with it capably enough, although unable to inspire another promotion, before leaving in the spring of 1987. He would not return to management for almost twenty years, coaching in the meantime at Barnsley (where he briefly linked up again with Clarke), Sheffield Wednesday, Birmingham City, Bristol City and Walsall.

Then, at the beginning of 2005, Barlow became assistant to Nottingham Forest's new manager, Gary Megson, and when Megson left 'by mutual consent' after relegation and a struggle to maintain a push for promotion, Barlow was made joint caretaker manager with Ian McParland, the reserve team's coach. Under their direction Forest went ten games unbeaten, just failing to equal a club record of seven successive wins, but Barlow was only too ready to revert to coaching, along with McParland, when Colin Calderwood was appointed manager. Soon afterwards, Barlow joined Hull City, and once more he was pushed into the role of caretaker manager – for just two days while negotiations were completed for Phil Parkinson's release from Colchester United. Barlow reverted to being assistant manager, but he left Humberside in October 2006 when a disappointing start to the season provoked changes in the coaching staff.

Later that season, Barlow joined Bradford City as assistant manager, and during the following close season he took the same job with Wigan Athletic. By then he had turned 60, but manager Chris Hutchings saw him as someone he could 'trust implicitly when it comes to football knowledge'. But their association did not last long. Hutchings was sacked in November 2007, and Barlow yet again served as caretaker manager until Steve Bruce, the former Norwich and Manchester United defender, was appointed. Unfortunately for Barlow, however, that also pointed him to the exit, for Eric Black, who had worked with Bruce in the past, was brought in from Birmingham City as assistant manager and first-team coach. Once more, Barlow was soon back in business, on 9 June 2011. And, most fittingly, he completed the full circle by returning to Sheffield United – as assistant to none other than Danny Wilson, the player who had been transferred to Nottingham Forest in 1983 during Barlow's time as Chesterfield's manager.

From the sale of Wilson, who played for the Spireites in exactly 100 of his career total of League games in excess of 600, Chesterfield recouped £30,000 plus two players they already had on loan, Calvin Plummer and Steve Kendal. Derby were first in for Wilson, and Brian Clough, Forest's manager, revealed that the player would have gone to the Baseball Ground, where Peter Taylor, Clough's former partner, was then manager, if Barlow had not wanted the Forest pair.

From Wilson's viewpoint, however, there was the vital fact that Forest were in the First Division. It was because he wanted to play there that he had originally spurned Chesterfield (and Birmingham City). But he turned out only ten times in Forest's first team, and one of those was as a substitute. The man Barlow had been 'very sad to let go', describing him as 'the sort of player every manager wants, with pace and aggression and always giving 100 ;per cent', achieved his top-flight ambition with Luton Town and Sheffield Wednesday, who both paid £200,000 for him, after being in a Brighton side relegated to Division Three.

Wilson followed 110 Division One games for Luton, who have since dropped out of the League, with 62 for Wednesday (six as sub) in the FA Premier League after helping the Owls to promotion. He was a League Cup winner with both Luton and Wednesday, scoring a late equaliser in the Hatters' 3-2 defeat of Arsenal in 1988, but was on the losing side in three other Wembley finals – two of them with Wednesday in the League Cup and FA Cup, both against Arsenal, in the same 1992-93 season.

Then, in 1997, as manager, Wilson piloted Barnsley into what, under sponsorship, was then known as the FA Carling Premiership. It was the Yorkshire club's first rise to a place among the elite in their 110-year history. They immediately dropped straight out of it, but Wilson oversaw a fifth-round FA Cup defeat of favourites Manchester United before continuing a managerial career in which he has been with both Sheffield clubs either side of taking Bristol City to victory over Carlisle in the League Trophy final at the Millennium Stadium in Cardff in 2003, and Hartlepool United to promotion as Division Two runners-up to Walsall in 2007. Milton Keynes Dons and Swindon Town are the other clubs he has managed.

The debt Chesterfield incurred to Leicester City when Alan Birch had to be sold arose from their £70,000 signing in September 1981 of Martin Henderson, a forward who had been in Glasgow Rangers' Scottish Cup-winning team of 1976.

From Ibrox, Henderson went first to Hibernian, on loan, then to the United States, with Philadephia Fury, before entering English football with Leicester. He had scored two dozen goals in about 90 games for Chesterfield when, in October 1983, he followed the path from Saltergate to Port Vale taken over the previous few years by Ernie Moss, Colin Tartt and John Ridley.

In exchange for Henderson, Chesterfield received Bob Newton and £8,000. They had much the better of the deal. After one season at Vale Park, Henderson failed to report back for training, and on having his contract cancelled he went out of the League with Spalding United. Newton, who was born at Chesterfield, had been Vale's top scorer in their Fourth Division promotion season of 1982-83, and he was also his home club's main marksman in each of the two seasons he spent at Saltergate, totalling 29 goals in 78 League games, before returning to Hartlepool United in the summer of 1985 for a fee of £17,500 decided by tribunal. He first joined Hartlepool from Huddersfield Town, where he began his senior career in 1973 after being named as the most valuable player in a world youth competition at the age of seventeen.

Two severe injuries kept Newton out of action for more than two years while with Huddersfield, however, and his first spell at Hartlepool was split in 1978 following a car accident in which his passenger, teammate Dave Wiggett, a Sheffield-born full-back, was fatally injured. After that tragedy Newton played in the North American League with the Jacksonville Tea Men before resuming a Hartlepool strike partnership with Keith Houchen, a former youth player at Chesterfield, that produced more than 100 goals, fairly evenly divided, before both left in 1982.

Houchen moved to Orient six months before Newton joined Port Vale, but he is best remembered for the spectacular diving header in Coventry City's unexpected victory over Tottenham Hotspur in the 1987 FA Cup final. It earned him Match of the Day's Goal of the Season award.

Newton's return to Hartlepool was short-lived, released after being loaned to Stockport, but he was later voted the North-East club's Player of the 1980s on the strength of what he had achieved for them earlier. He ended his League career with Bristol Rovers, and subsequently played in Cyprus and Hong Kong before coming back to England and joining the Chesterfield-based KSPO team. Alfreton Town were among the non-League clubs for which he finally played, since when he has been involved in various charity causes.

Chesterfield's loss of John Ridley, who was described on the club's website as 'a powerful dominating type who nevertheless had a calming influence and elegant touch to his play', was a particularly severe blow. He had been Port Vale's Player of the Year before moving to Leicester, and after forming an impressive centre-back partnership with Bill Green for Chesterfield he helped the Potteries club to promotion from the Fourth Division in his second spell at Vale Park (although they were promptly relegated).

On ending a Football League career of more than 400 games, Ridley joined Stafford Rangers as player-coach for a fee of £700 decided by a tribunal, and they were promptly promoted to the Alliance Premier League. After that he coached at Matlock Town and Newcastle Town besides Stafford, and also returned to teaching mathematics, for which he had qualified before becoming a professional footballer.

It was while Ridley was with Chesterfield that Arthur Sutherland, who had been with the club for 45 years as player (half-back), clerk, secretary and general manager, announced his retirement at the age of 66 in May 1981. He could certainly have wished to be leaving with the club thriving instead of heading towards a situation in which the latest chairman, Ian Gaunt, could see scant hope for the future.

From the financially crippling promotion near-misses under Arthur Cox's direction (a loss of £13,608 announced in February 1983 pushed the overall deficit to nearly £360,000), the team plummeted back into Division Four in the 1982-83 season, finishing a very poor last with only eight wins to set against 25 defeats. Their 37 points left them seventeen adrift of Wigan, Exeter and Orient, the clubs immediately above the four that went down. These were the final positions at the bottom of the table:

Season 1982-83	P	W	D	L	F	A	Pts
18. Wigan	46	15	9	22	60	72	54
19. Exeter	46	14	12	20	81	104	54
20. Orient	46	15	9	22	64	88	54
21. Reading	46	12	17	17	64	79	53
22. Wrexham	46	12	15	19	56	76	51
23. Doncaster	46	9	11	26	57	97	38
24. Chesterfield	46	8	13	25	43	68	37

The alarm signals were flying for Chesterfield right from a depressing start of three successive defeats, and then two draws, in which the club's only goal was scored by Danny Wilson at home to Orient on the opening day. The finish was even worse, with no goals and just one point in the last five games. In between, the team's highest position was sixteenth, held for a few weeks in October during which two victories were strung together for the only time. January brought the sudden and lone highlight of a 5-1 home win against Wrexham, though that was also the month in which Chesterfield first sank into the drop zone. Only 2,805 were there to see the eclipse of those relegation companions-to-be, but even that was not the smallest gate of the season for a League match at Saltergate. Indeed, there were as many as fifteen fewer, the lowest 1,645 for the visit of Newport County on the first day of February.

And there were two still lower than that, both in the group stages of the League Trophy competition – 1,149 for a drawn game with Chester, 1,177 for a 1-0 win against Shrewsbury Town. Chesterfield drew their other group match, away to Tranmere Rovers, yet failed to qualify for the quarter-finals. They also made early exits from the League Cup and FA Cup, in respective first-round replays against Fourth Division clubs at Peterborough and, after extra-time, Hartlepool.

The total of 37 League points, meagre though it was, bettered by five the number scraped together, also from 46 games, when Chesterfield had been demoted to Division Four in 1960-61, but two points had then been awarded for a win instead of the three that came into force for the 1981-82 season. The club's lowest total of all, 23, dated back to 1907-08, when only six wins were gained from 38 matches.

As few as 43 goals had previously been scored in a League season by Chesterfield in the 42 games of 1949-50, the season before relegation from the Second Division, and in the 46 matches of 1968-69, when there had been a close brush with having to seek re-election. There had been three totals below that – 37 from 34 games in 1903-04, and from 38 in 1908-09 (after which Lincoln City had been elected in Chesterfield's place), and 40 from 38 games in 1905-06. Martin Henderson was the team's leading scorer in 1982-83 with ten goals, followed by Dave Windridge (eight) and Calvin Plummer, four of whose seven were penalties. Windridge was another signing from Sheffield United, but he did not play in the Blades' League side. After about 80 games for Chesterfield he just exceeded 100, including substitutions, with Blackpool.

Only five players made 40 or more League appearances during the season in which the Spireites fell back into Division Four for the second time – Bill Green (44), Gary Bellamy, a defender who had joined the club as an apprentice, and Andy Kowalski (both 42), Henderson and Windridge (both 40). Frank Barlow altogether called on 28 players, hamstrung in his attempts to field a settled side by having to bring in players on loan after his enforced loss of Phil Bonnyman to Grimsby and John Ridley to Port Vale before the season started, and of Phil Walker to Rotherham and Danny Wilson to Nottingham Forest during it.

In those difficult circumstances, Barlow did not have to shoulder too much of the blame for the failure to avoid the drop, and he left with his self-respect intact after declining the chance to remain at Saltergate as assistant manager when John Duncan took his place in June 1983. With Barrie Hubbard, a local businessman, now the chairman again, the club faced being wound up in the High Court in London. The Inland Revenue and Customs and Excise were owed £91,000, so Bob Pepper, a future Chesterfield director who had come from Stafford Rangers as Arthur Sutherland's secretarial successor, and the club's solicitor, Roger Woodhead, approached snooker entrepreneur Mike Watterson, a Chesterfield man, and enquired whether there was anything he could do to help.

Watterson had only recently given up the chairmanship of Derby County, disillusioned by boardroom disharmony, hooliganism among fans, and lack of success on the field, but he saved the day for his home club by signing cheques from a couple of his accounts for presentation at the Court. Watterson, who filed writs to recover £33,000 in loans to Derby, then became Chesterfield's vice-chairman, but only until November that year.

'I believe it would be wrong of me to continue putting Chesterfield in an embarrassing position,' said Watterson, 'and since I do not seem to be able to stop speculation about me I have no honourable alternative but to resign.' But he rejoined the Chesterfield board in July 1984, having recently transferred his shareholding at Derby to the Rams' new chairman, Stuart Webb. The accounts that County published that September showed that Watterson had been paid a consultancy fee of £18,000. In

May 1986, Watterson took over as Chesterfield's chairman and majority shareholder in a boardroom move to save the club from another threat of closure. They were then losing £3,000 a week and had debts of more than £650,000. Those desperate days of the 1980s had already compelled the club's very reluctant sale for housing of their excellent training facilities at Pitt Street in Eckington.

Watterson's takeover was soon followed by the resignation of Norman Lea, a former Mansfield Town director who had been on Chesterfield's board for sixteen months. Lea gave no reason, but was believed to be unhappy with Watterson's taking a majority shareholding. Ken Unwin, who had been chairman since the previous autumn, became managing director. He insisted there had been no bitterness in the takeover, but, speaking a week before Lea quit, he proved too optimistic in adding: 'We are all quite happy with the deal, and all the existing members of the board will be staying together.' Neither did Watterson remain for long. He planned a series of cost-cutting measures, but stepped down just over a year later, fed up with football in general. D P Kelly moved up from vice-chairman.

Fortunately, however, the appointment of John Duncan as manager had soon produced the desired effect of bringing about an improvement on the pitch to compensate for the financial worries off it. Duncan, who had been a Scottish League Cup winner with Dundee in 1974 and Tottenham's leading scorer when they were promoted to Division One in 1978, began his managerial career with Scunthorpe United in 1981. He had played the last few of his 269 Scottish and Football League games (129 goals) for the Lincolnshire club after joining them from Derby County, whose £150,000 investment in September 1978 had been jeopardised by the back injury he had first suffered while still with Spurs. He was out of action at Derby for as long as fifteen months, also troubled by thigh and Achilles tendon injuries. 'Everyone reckons I'm injury prone,' he said, but over-optimistically added: 'Everything is fine now, thanks to a second ankle operation.'

Scunthorpe had to seek re-election to the League at the end of Duncan's first season as their manager, but there was such a boost in the next one, with a strong challenge being made for the Fourth Division title, that it caused quite a stir when he was controversially sacked in February 1983. There were allegations that he had been in talks about the manager's job at Grimsby Town, and that Scunthorpe's chairman wanted him out so that he could install his friend Allan Clarke in his place. Confirmation that Duncan had reorganised along the right lines came when the fourth promotion place was clinched under the direction of

Clarke, but then came the immediate relegation that brought Clarke's replacement by Frank Barlow.

Six weeks after being dismissed by Scunthorpe, Duncan accepted an invitation to become Hartlepool United's interim manager between the departure of Billy Horner, a former Middlesbrough wing-half, and the appointment of Michael Docherty, son of Tommy, that man of many clubs who had signed Duncan for Derby. Hartlepool were at the bottom of Division Four when Duncan took over in April 1983, and there was insufficient time for him to bring about a remarkable rescue act. He did well to see them rise two places, though that still made him a manager who had to spend a second successive year watching his club apply (successfully) for re-election – in Hartlepool's case for a record fourteenth time.

Even so, Duncan was offered the chance to stay on as manager, but he turned it down in favour of joining Chesterfield. It was a wise decision. In the following December, Hartlepool were back at the bottom of the table, with only one win in 23 games, and Horner was brought back to replace the dismissed Docherty. Meanwhile, Chesterfield ended Duncan's first season at Saltergate in mid-table, but in the following one, 1984-85, he steered them to promotion as Fourth Division champions.

13

Another promotion, under John Duncan's direction

Of the 28 players who turned out for Chesterfield in their relegation season of 1982-83, only four were among the twenty used when the Fourth Division championship was won in 1984-85. And of those four only two, Steve Kendal (43 games) and 'Sean' O'Neill (41), were regular members of the title-winning side.

There would almost certainly have been a third, but Gary Bellamy (22 games) was injured during a 0-4 defeat at Swindon on New Year's Day in 1985 and did not reappear in the team for nearly fifteen months, until 18 March 1986, when Plymouth were 2-1 winners at Saltergate. The fourth man was Phil Brown (27 games), who only just qualified with one appearance, and that as a substitute, when the club went down from Division Three in 1983.

Bellamy might have had a career as a cricketer instead as a footballer, for he had a spell with his home county, Nottinghamshire (he was born at Worksop), while in his teens. He decided, however, that he would have a better chance of making progress in the winter game, and he joined Chesterfield as an apprentice after leaving school in July 1978. He became a full-time professional two years later, and broke into the first team at full-back, originally as a substitute, for the last three matches of the 1980-81 season. He went on to make more than 200 appearances, also in the half-back line, before Wolves signed him in July 1987 for a fee of £17,000 that made him as big a bargain for them as he had been for Chesterfield. He was a key defensive figure in the Molineux club's teams that won promotion from the Fourth Division to Second in successive seasons, 1987-89, and carried off the Sherpa Van Trophy at Wembley in 1988.

After 165 games for Wolves, whom he captained, and nine on loan to Cardiff City, Bellamy moved to Leyton Orient in September 1992 and repaid their £30,000 investment with four seasons as a first choice. His next move took him to Chelmsford City, and during his five years as their joint manager they gained promotion to the Premier Division of the Dr Martens League as runners-up to Newport (Isle of Wight) in 2001. The Essex club thought they had qualified for a rise in 1998, but at that time their ground had not met the requirements of the higher division. Unfortunately, Bellamy's subsequent experience of management with

Dover Athletic and Braintree Town did not meet with similar success. He was sacked by both.

Bellamy was one of only three players (along with O'Neill and Martin Henderson) who were not new signings in the first team Chesterfield fielded after John Duncan's arrival as manager in mid-June 1983. Strictly speaking, two of the eight others were not exactly new, but were returning for a second stint with the club – Jim Brown, who had been with Cardiff City and Kettering the previous season, and Alan Birch, back from Barnsley. This was the line-up for the home match in which Swindon Town were beaten by a Birch goal on 27 August 1983: Brown; Scrimgeour, O'Neill; Klug, Baines, Bellamy; Birch, Spooner, Bell, Henderson, Waddington.

One of the most urgent tasks in preparation for that season was to find a suitable replacement at centre-half for Bill Green, the Geordie who was given a free transfer to Doncaster Rovers a few days after Duncan's appointment. Of his nearly 500 League games, from 1969 to 1984, Green played in most (160) for Chesterfield, though he had previously exceeded the century with Hartlepool United, whom he joined straight from school, and Carlisle United. He was also with West Ham and Peterborough before his move to Saltergate.

Green's venture into management with Scunthorpe United in 1991 ended two years later when he was unable to sustain hopes of promotion that had been boosted by a fifth-place finish, and failure only on penalties in a Fourth Division play-off final against Blackpool at Wembley, in his first season on south Humberside. After that he was caretaker manager of Sheffield Wednesday for just one match (lost) before being a European scout, in turn, with Wigan Athletic, Derby County and Bolton Wanderers. Six months with Southampton followed, and Green was then on the staff that Sven Goran Eriksson assembled for the former England manager's short-lived reign at Leicester.

The choice of the man to fill the gap left by Green at the centre of Chesterfield's defence was most adequately filled, for a bargain fee of £5,000 paid to Scunthorpe, by Steve Baines, a veteran of more than 300 League games with six previous clubs. This Newark-born defender made over a third of those appearances for Huddersfield after starting out with Nottingham Forest in April 1973, but, like Green, he most regularly played for Chesterfield in raising his overall total to almost 450 in a stay that lasted until 1987. During that time he served the Spireites as player-coach and latterly as assistant manager to John Duncan as well as coach.

On rounding off his playing career out of the Football League, Baines remained in Chesterfield, working in insurance. He also did something very rare for a former player by taking up refereeing. Indeed, he went on to become the only referee in Football League history to have had a significant career as a professional footballer. Only two other top referees, Bob Matthewson and John Lloyd, had gained previous professional playing experience – but with only five League appearances between them. Matthewson, who made three at centre-half for Bolton Wanderers, was the referee who sent off Billy Bremner and Kevin Keegan for fighting in the 1974 FA Charity Shield match between Leeds United and Liverpool, and he ended his nine years with the whistle back at Wembley for the 1977 FA Cup final in which Liverpool lost to Manchester United. Lloyd, a leading referee from 1985 to 1996, played twice on the right wing for Wrexham.

Baines, who also played for Bradford City, Walsall and Bury before making Chesterfield his last club, took less than ten years to reach the League's referees list in 1995, only one year after graduating as an assistant. He remained on that list for eight seasons. Just one referee had been promoted more quickly; that was Joe Timmons, in the Scottish League in 1987.

As a player, Baines was so consistently dependable (and injury-free) for Chesterfield that he missed only one match in his first season at Saltergate and was an ever-present when promotion was clinched the following year. Of his fellow newcomers, the most appearances in 1983-84 were made by Brian Scrimgeour, for whom Duncan looked back to Dundee. Scrimgeour, who, like the manager, was born in that Scottish city, demonstrated his versatility by playing at right-half, outside-left and inside-right in addition to right-back in his 41 games. Before returning to Scotland with Falkirk in January 1987 (and later Partick Thistle) he also turned out at centre-half and centre-forward in totalling almost 150 League and Cup games.

Steve Spooner also got into three figures for appearances with Chesterfield, the majority of them in his first spell with the club that began with his transfer from Halifax Town in July 1983, the month in which Baines was signed, and ended with his move to Hereford United at the beginning of August in 1986, just over five months before Scrimgeour left. Spooner's League career of 420 games, which also took in York, Rotherham, Mansfield and Blackpool, stretched from 1979, when he made his debut for Derby, to 1994, back with Chesterfield. He was finally with two clubs who were later admitted to the League, Rushden & Diamonds (who were soon demoted from it) and Burton Albion, before turning to coaching.

The three other new men for Chesterfield's first match with John

Duncan as manager were soon on their way out. Derek Bell, who, like Spooner, had started with Derby, as an apprentice, and played for Halifax, cost £8,500 from Lincoln City in August 1983, but was offloaded to Scunthorpe the following January. He had been bedevilled with injury problems since breaking a leg in his second season with Lincoln, who had paid their then record fee of £34,000 to sign him from Barnsley.

Steve Waddington, son of the then Stoke manager, came the month before Bell on a free transfer from Port Vale, for whom he had played only one League game after totting up nearly 200 with Stoke and Walsall. He joined Macclesfield Town on having his Chesterfield contract cancelled in April 1984.

Bryan Klug, another free signing, ended a year's stay four months later by going to Peterborough. He had played his few League games on loan to Wimbledon before moving to Saltergate, originally on loan, from Ipswich Town. After going out of the League with Chelmsford City, he rejoined Ipswich as head of their academy, also serving the Suffolk club as assistant manager and, for one match, caretaker manager. Soon after the turn into the 21st century he became assistant academy manager and head of player development at Tottenham.

Although Martin Henderson, like Alan Birch, also left before promotion was achieved, Chesterfield still had a Henderson in the team that topped the Fourth Division in 1986. This was Mick Henderson, yet another signing from Sheffield United and a product of the North-East. Gosforth-born, this defender turned midfielder joined Sunderland from school and was among the players they used in getting out of the Second Division as champions in the 1975-76 season.

Watford paid £120,000 for Henderson in 1979, but he failed to hold a regular place when they reached the First Division for the first time as runners-up to Luton in 1982, and found more opportunities with Sheffield United after a short stay at Cardiff. Towards the end of his four years with Chesterfield, during which he made some 150 appearances, he combined playing with coaching, then was with Matlock Town before becoming a policeman.

In addition to Bob Newton's arrival in October in exchange for Martin Henderson, and Les Hunter's return from Scunthorpe, other additions to Chesterfield's playing strength in Duncan's first season as manager included Barrie Stimpson, a full-back from Hartlepool United, and John Clayton, a Scottish striker who had been with the Bulova club in Hong Kong after starting out as a Derby County apprentice. Both also left before promotion, Stimpson returning to Hartlepool and Clayton joining Tranmere Rovers.

Towards the end of 2006 Stimpson made another return by taking over as manager of Lancaster City, a hard-up club with which he had previously been assistant manager. They were rooted to the foot of the Nationwide Conference North table, and he had the mortification of seeing them finish the season with one paltry point, 44 adrift, after having ten deducted for going into administration.

Clayton, in contrast, prospered after scoring only five goals for Chesterfield. He found his shooting boots with 35 for Tranmere in the 1984-85 season, and in the following one he repaid Plymouth's £25,000 investment by helping them to promotion from Division Three as runners-up to Reading.

Chesterfield's own promotion looked like coming a year earlier than it did when they rose to fourth on 15 October 1983 with a 4-2 win at Rochdale, in which Bob Newton scored two of the seventeen goals that made him Chesterfield's highest scorer of the first season under Duncan's direction. At that stage the Spireites had lost only once in their first ten League games, narrowly at Crewe on the second Saturday, but after extending their unbeaten run with a draw at home to Doncaster they then went eight games without a win, dropping to eighteenth before a 1-0 victory at Mansfield on Boxing Day. Next day they suffered their heaviest defeat of the season, by 1-5 at home to Bury, and they sank to their lowest position, nineteenth, after Crewe's completion of the double early in January. They ended thirteenth after only one defeat in six matches had hoisted them to mid-table, a sequence that included a 3-2 home win against Torquay United in their first Sunday fixture.

Sunday soccer had first been allowed in the Football League from January to March in 1974 owing to the imposition of a three-day week that arose from a power crisis, but the FA remained firmly opposed to it, and Fulham's proposal for games to be played regularly on that day was rejected at the League's annual meeting in 1979. It was not permitted again until February 1981, for Darlington's match with Mansfield, and for the rest of that season the change applied only to the three lower divisions of the League.

Chesterfield spurned Sunday football at that time. A snap poll among their first-team players rejected Walsall's request for the clubs' game at Fellows Park to be played on the Sabbath. Two of the players objected on religious grounds. Frank Barlow, then the manager, said that 'like most clubs we have conscience clauses in players' contracts which allow them the right to withdraw their labour on a Sunday. I agree with them that Sunday is the only day of the week when I can put my family first instead of my job'. How different are attitudes to this subject these days.

Chesterfield's changed view about Sunday play was not the only innovation they were involved with in the 1983-84 season. The Associate Members' Cup was introduced to give the 48 clubs in the Third and Fourth divisions a midwinter fillip. It was the descendant of the Anglo-Scottish Cup that had replaced the Texaco Cup in which teams from Northern Ireland had been included as well as those from England and Scotland.

Gordon Taylor, the PFA secretary, believed this new competition to be a mistake. 'Clubs are going too often to the well,' he said. 'They are not only asking a diminishing band of fans to turn out too often. They are also asking players to fulfil two or three fixtures a week from squads that have been cut to the bone. Squads of fifteen or sixteen players are being asked to cover more games than were handled by twenty and above last season. I honestly think there is a grave danger of this competition being counter-productive.'

Fears for its future were confirmed after only one season, but in name only. It continued for the next three seasons as the Freight Rover Trophy, and there have since been six more name changes under sponsorship – plus another when it was known as the Football League Trophy for 2005-06 before Johnstone's Paint first put their trophy at stake. And since the first final in which Bournemouth beat Hull on Humberside before a crowd of only just over 6,500, the old and new Wembleys have been the crowning venues either side of the seven years of the switch to the Millennium Stadium in Cardiff, with an attendance as high as 80,841 in 1988, when Wolves beat Burnley for the Sherpa Van Trophy.

Chesterfield, unfortunately, have not had their resources stretched by this competition to the extent Gordon Taylor suspected. Not until its tenth season did they get as far as the Northern semi-final, then losing by the odd goal of three to Stockport County, who went on to be runners-up to Port Vale for the Autoglass Trophy. And not until its 29th season did Chesterfield finally carry off the (Johnstone's Paint) trophy by defeating Swindon Town on their first visit to the new Wembley. More about that later.

Another memorable game in this competition was played against Sheffield Wednesday in 2010, Chesterfield going out 7-8 on penalties after a 2-2 extra-time draw in the second round at Hillsborough. At the same stage in 2001, when the the LDV Vans Trophy was the prize, the deadlock was decided by sudden death, Chesterfield defeating Kidderminster Harriers with a 93rd-minute goal from Dave Reeves, only then to go out at the quarter-final stage to Blackpool, who went on to become the new holders. Reeves, whose twin brother Alan was also a professional footballer, was another of the players who had two spells with Chesterfield. He joined them first from Preston North End in 1997, in part exchange for Tony Lormor, then from Oldham Athletic in 2002.

Reeves and Lormor had something else in common. Both played for thirteen clubs. Lormor, in fact, could claim to have been with one more, but neither he nor Andy Fensome made a first-team appearance while on their loan swap between Newcastle and Norwich. Lormor, yet another product of that North-East soccer hot-bed Ashington, joined Newcastle as a youth trainee from Wallsend Boys Club, but first made his mark with Lincoln City, who paid £25,000 for him in January 1990. He scored the winner on his debut for the Imps, and was their top scorer for two successive seasons before missing the whole of the next one, 1992-93, with a cruciate injury. He then went on loan to Halifax in the Conference before regaining form and fitness with Peterborough United, the club from which he moved to Chesterfield on a free transfer in December 1994. The Spireites went unbeaten through their first 21 games with Lormor in their attack (it could have been 22 if he had not then missed a penalty in a 1-2 home defeat by Carlisle), and, as we shall be coming to in its proper turn, he was to play an important part on another of the Derbyshire club's big days before his departure to Preston.

Dave Reeves's playing career began with Sheffield Wednesday as a teenager, and was afterwards coach and assistant manager at Gainsborough. With Trinity he linked up again on the coaching staff with Steve Blatherwick, whose career as a Chesterfield defender had been ended by a back injury, and in August 2009 they were made the Lincolnshire club's joint caretaker managers – for just one match. They subsequently went into business together.

In 1983-84, Chesterfield's immediate exit from the inaugural competition for clubs below the League's top two divisions, added to their failure to progress far in the Milk Cup and FA Cup, and their mid-table finish 22 points off the fourth promotion place in Division Four, gave no indication of the transformation in their fortunes that (as in 1969-70) was so swiftly to come.

In 1984-85 they were again quickly dismissed from all three knock-out competitions, but in the League they lost only once, by a lone goal at Hartlepool, in their first eighteen games and were never lower than sixth before getting back to the top to stay with a home win against Swindon in April. They were beaten only at Wrexham in their remaining eight matches and ended five points clear of runners-up Blackpool with a credit goal-difference of 29. These were the final leading positions, the top four promoted:

Season 1984-85	P	W	D	L	F	A	Pts
1. Chesterfield	46	26	13	7	64	35	91
2. Blackpool	46	24	14	8	73	39	86
3. Darlington	46	24	13	9	66	49	85
4. Bury	46	24	12	10	76	50	84
5. Hereford	46	22	11	13	65	47	77
6. Tranmere	46	24	3	19	83	66	75

Bury, Darlington and Hereford had turns at the top before Chesterfield established themselves there. Hereford were early pacesetters despite being under the threat of liquidation until settling their debts at the end of September, and they did not concede a goal in their first seven games before letting in three at Saltergate on the first Tuesday of October. Chesterfield took over the leadership with their biggest win of the season on the penultimate Saturday of that month, by 5-1 at home to Exeter City, but had to hand it back to Hereford in dropping a point at Chester a week later. Another draw, with visitors from Colchester, kept Chesterfield in second place when Bury led for the first time with a win at Northampton on the first Saturday of November, but Duncan's men promptly reclaimed first place by beating Tranmere 4-2, and they held it until suffering only their second League defeat, by 1-3 at Rochdale, a few days before Christmas.

Not until late in March, when they won 3-1 at Darlington, did Chesterfield head the table again, but they stayed there until the end of the season apart from a week in early April when a scoreless draw at Mansfield returned them to second place behind Darlington. A home victory against Swindon three days later put Chesterfield back on course for the title, and avenged the heaviest defeat they had suffered in conceding four goals without reply at the County Ground in Wiltshire on New Year's Day. Bury, who also took a point off Chesterfield at Gigg Lane, were the only League winners at Saltergate that season, though Halifax, who had to seek re-election to Division Four, were successful there in the Milk Cup's first round.

Bob Newton was Chesterfield's top scorer for the second successive season, with fifteen goals in the League, two in the Milk Cup and one in an FA Cup win at Whitby before a second round exit at Walsall. Ernie Moss, back from Doncaster for his third spell with the club, contributed a dozen, and Phil Brown weighed in with nine. Generally, however, defence was Chesterfield's strongest suit, with no goals conceded in 21 of their 46 League matches. Neither side scored in nine of those games, including the last two of the season when promotion was already assured.

Eight of the players who had taken part in the first match of the season also appeared in the last one, at home to Rochdale. They were ever-presents Baines and Hunter, Newton, who was absent only once, Kendal, O'Neill, Moss, Spooner and Matthews. Spooner, who had been sent on as substitute for Scrimgeour on the opening day, was on the right wing in place of Phil Brown. John Matthews, a Londoner whose career as a mid-fielder with Arsenal had been blighted by a broken leg, was yet another Chesterfield player who had worn Sheffield United's red and white stripes. The Blades paid the Gunners £90,000 for him in August 1978, and he was with them for four years before being given a free transfer to Mansfield Town. No fee was again involved when he moved from there to Chesterfield in August 1984, nor when he left for Plymouth a year later. With Argyle he was again a first-season promotion winner, helping them out of the Third Division as runners-up to Reading.

The three members of Chesterfield's promoted side who did not play in the club's opening match were Chris Marples, in goal for Jim Brown, who had his work as commercial manager to concentrate upon, Brian Ferguson, a signing from Southend who replaced the injury-hit Burgess at right-back, and Mick Henderson, who partnered Kendal at inside-left. Chesterfield were Ferguson's last League club, and his move to Skegness Town after that season left him just four short of 100 appearances at that level. He had previously played for Newcastle and Hull after starting as a Mansfield apprentice, then had briefly been out of the League with Goole Town before joining Southend.

To finish with two scoreless draws came as something as an anti-climax, but that was not the reason why Chesterfield's promotion celebrations fizzled out. Indeed, nobody in the country was in the mood to celebrate anything, for it was on the last day of the season, 11 May 1985, that a flash fire consumed one side of Bradford City's Valley Parade stadium. The death toll rose to 56 and more than 260 were injured. Bradford City, too, would have been celebrating promotion but for the disaster. In their penultimate match on the Monday of that week they had made sure of the Third Division title with a 2-0 win at Bolton. They were back in the second flight of League football for the first time since 1937.

A tragedy on that horrendous scale put into proper prospective the trials and tribulations clubs such as Chesterfield have to endure.

14

Record 0-10 defeat at Gillingham and relegated again

Only four seasons went by before Chesterfield dropped back into Division Four. During that period, from 1985 to 1989, they had three managers, attracted their smallest home attendance since their readmission to the Football League as founder members of the Third Division North in 1921, and suffered their biggest defeat.

The three managers were John Duncan, Kevin Randall and Paul Hart. Randall stepped up from assistant manager when Duncan was lured away by Ipswich's better offer in June 1987, but he was sacked in October 1988 after eight defeats in the first ten games of the season had dumped the club next to the bottom of the Third Division. In all but one of those defeats Chesterfield failed to score, and after a misleading 2-1 home win on the opening day against Aldershot, a club destined for the final last place, they had only two goals to set against the 26 conceded. They lost by five to Port Vale, who went on to gain promotion via the play-offs, by four to Bristol City and Notts County, by three to Wolves (the coming champions), Northampton Town and Preston North End, and by two to Blackpool. They mustered one response to the couple also scored by Bury, and netted their other goal of that depressing spell in winning away to Gillingham, who ended the season just below them next to last.

At Ipswich, Duncan succeeded Bobby Ferguson, a former Derby County full-back, who was cast aside for failing to regain First Division status – a fate that also befell John Duncan after three mid-table seasons at Portman Road (though in the middle one they missed the play-offs by just three points). It would be back with Chesterfield that Duncan again achieved promotion (and some Cup glory too) after his return from a spell out of football as a schoolteacher in Suffolk.

Paul Hart entered management with Chesterfield in November 1988 from Notts County, with whom, as player-coach, he made the last 23 of his 567 League appearances. That was almost 400 more than his father made in almost two decades as a Manchester City inside-forward. Johnny Hart was most unfortunate with injuries, most notably when he broke a leg in a match at Huddersfield shortly before City met Newcastle in the 1955 FA Cup final. He was also unlucky as a manager, forced to resign because of ill health only six months after being the Manchester club's surprise choice following the departure of Malcolm Allison, but he served for ten more years as coach and later worked on the promotional side at Maine Road.

Like his father, Paul Hart was born at Golborne, a centre of coalmining, textiles and engineering in the Greater Manchester area a few miles north of Warrington. He was signed by Stockport County as an apprentice at the age of seventeen in September 1970 after attracting attention in the Manchester Boys team. Just under three years later, having developed into a well-built 6ft 2in central defender, skilful enough also to be a competent midfielder, in the course of almost 100 first-team games for the Cheshire club, he moved to Blackpool for £25,000. With the Seasiders he made 156 League and Cup appearances, building further on his reputation to such an extent that, even though in a side heading for relegation to Division Three, his value had risen to £300,000 by the time Leeds United came for him in March 1978 to fill the gap left by Scottish international Gordon McQueen's transfer to Manchester United.

After a shaky start at Elland Road, Hart settled down to become the defensive strongman in more than 200 matches, including cup-ties, and he was tipped for the international honours which, however, never came his way. The only Leeds player named Hart to play for England was Ernie, a burly former miner who was the club's centre-half in over 470 games between the two world wars.

In May 1983, the month of his 30th birthday, Paul Hart went to Nottingham Forest for £40,000 as replacement for Willie Young, who had left for Norwich City. Nearly 100 more games were added to his tally for Forest, among them a controversial UEFA Cup semi-final against Anderlecht in which he had a goal ruled out for no apparent reason (the official was alleged to have been bribed) as a 2-0 lead gained in the first leg in Nottingham was wiped out by a 0-3 defeat in the second in Belgium.

The other League clubs for which Hart played before Notts County were Sheffield Wednesday and Birmingham City. He exceeded 50 first-team games for the Owls, but broke a leg in his only one for Birmingham – a 3-2 home win against Plymouth on New Year's Day in 1987.

In common with so many of his predecessors, Hart found himself seriously handicapped by Chesterfield's financial problems. These had already caused Chesterfield Borough Council to bail out the club, and forced the training ground to be sold. John Duncan helped to reduce the overdraft with £3,000 he raised through a sponsored walk to a match at Rotherham in December 1985 (won 2-1 with goals from Mick Henderson and Steve Spooner), but the difficulties were intensified by boardroom squabbles arising from the cash constraints that prevented team strengthening. This, combined with the consequent lack of success on the field, had a considerable adverse effect on support, culminating in Saltergate's smallest attendance for a League match since just after the First World War.

On 4 May 1987, only 1,435 turned up for the match in which Darlington were beaten by a goal scored by Glaswegian Tony Coyle, a winger who was with Stockport County either side of his two seasons at Chesterfield. Down to Division Four went Darlington – and with them went Carlisle, who had only one spectator more than that all-time Saltergate low for their home game against Chesterfield at the season's end a few days later.

Chesterfield's home gates in 1986-87 averaged 2,575, a drop of 636 on the previous season. They had fewer than 2,000 for four other League games, and for the first leg of a Littlewoods Cup-tie in which they were defeated by Wrexham. Only twice did they have more than 4,000 – and then only just, for the visits of Mansfield and promoted Middlesbrough. One of the best of their other home attendances, 3,810, was for a match with Swindon to which admission was free. That was in response to spectators asking for their money back after the game had been called off the previous day, an hour after the kick-off, when electricians had failed to repair the floodlights in time for it to continue. Swindon, promoted the previous season, won the replay 3-1.

The match in which Chesterfield crashed to their record defeat, conceding five goals in each half without reply, was played at Gillingham on 5 September 1987. It replaced the 1-9 Second Division trouncing to which Port Vale's Stewart Littlewood had contributed six goals on 24 September 1932.

The Gillingham game was the 61st in Football League history with a double-figure score – and the only one in which no player did the hat-trick. Howard Pritchard, Dave Shearer, George Shipley and Karl Elsey each scored twice, Dave Smith and Colin Greenall once. The big surprise about that list was that it did not include Steve Lovell, a Welsh international who led the home attack (but was substituted). It was not just that he was the Kent club's leading scorer for four consecutive seasons. At the same ground the previous Saturday he had bagged half Gillingham's goals in the 8-1 eclipse of Southend United that had also come as quite a surprise. The Gills had gone goalless in picking up a mere point from their first two games of the season, at home to Blackpool and away to Grimsby, and they then netted only once in a midweek draw at Wigan before getting into double figures against Chesterfield.

Gillingham's record victory, narrowly replacing their 10-1 demolition of Gorleston in a 1957 FA Cup-tie (though they had beaten Gloucester City 12-1 in the Southern League in 1946), was all the more amazing for the fact that the Spireites went into the match as the only club in the whole League not to have had a goal scored against them that season. In their previous four games Chesterfield had won 1-0 at Preston and Mansfield, and at home to Bury, and drawn 0-0 with visitors from Brighton who would go on to earn promotion as runners-up to Sunderland. Gillingham, for whom Lovell did the hat-trick in a 4-1 victory in the return match at Saltergate in February, finished the season thirteenth five places and four points above Chesterfield.

The team that tumbled to that thrashing at the Priestfield Stadium was: Jim Brown; Lee Rogers, Mick Henderson; Darren Bradshaw, Tristan Benjamin, David Travis; Kevin Eley (Jamie Hewitt), Pat McGeeney, Dave Waller, Andy Taylor, Bob Bloomer. Of those players, Hewitt, though then a substitute, is the one who has become another of the iconic figures of Chesterfield soccer. In two spells with his home club (he was born in the town on 17 May 1968), he amassed 585 appearances, 506 of them in the League. This took him to second place in the Spireites' all-time list behind Dave Blakey, followed by Ernie Moss,. Albert Holmes, Ron Powell and Sean O'Neill, the others who, in that order, have exceeded 500 games for Chesterfield. With the inclusion of his appearances during his break of just over a season at Doncaster in the early 1990s, Hewitt ended only 35 games behind Blakey's 658 overall. And after finally ending his playing career in 2002 he continued with Chesterfield as physiotherapist.

The only other member of the side humbled at Gillingham to play in more than 300 matches for Chesterfield was Hewitt's fellow defender Lee Rogers, who was signed from Doncaster. Rogers went close to 350 in Cup and League before leaving for Gainsborough Trinity, the club to which Eley, Travis and McGeeney also moved. Eley was formerly with Rotherham United, having become their youngest player at the age of sixteen years 71 days on his debut day as a substitute in their final match of the 1983-84 season. McGeeney was yet another of Chesterfield's former Sheffield United players; Bloomer, like Taylor a product of the junior side at Saltergate, and Bradshaw, who played most of his 261 League games for other clubs, were born in the Yorkshire city. Bloomer, who was spotted playing for Harrow United, a Sheffield junior side, and Waller both turned out more than 100 times for Chesterfield. Waller repeated what he had done for Crewe, exceed 50 goals, between his arrival from Shrewsbury Town and departure to Worksop. Benjamin, a West Indian from St Kitts, took his total of League appearances to almost 345 (all but 34 of them for Notts County) before joining the Leicestershire club Shepshed Charterhouse.

After finishing seventeenth in both their first two seasons back in the Third Division, Chesterfield slipped down another place in 1987-88, then failed to escape relegation a season later. In each of those four campaigns they also fell at the first fence in both the League and FA Cup competitions. With Bob Newton having returned to Hartlepool, Ernie Moss again took over as the club's leading scorer in 1985-86, his seventeen goals including three in the Milk Cup and his 250th in a 2-2 draw with Notts County. And when Moss finally left for Stockport in December 1986 Waller was preceded as the chief goal-getter (though with only fourteen that season) by David Caldwell, a tempestuous Scot who cost £12,000 after scoring 57 goals in 157 League appearances for Mansfield.

Caldwell was put on the transfer list by the Stags' manager, former Manchester United defender Ian Greaves, after twice being sent off – and he stayed on it despite scoring four times against Hartlepool in the next game. He was then loaned to Carlisle and Swindon before joining Chesterfield, who recouped £7,000 from selling him to Torquay United, with whom he had mixed fortunes in the 1987-88 season. He was ordered off three more times, but helped the Devon club to a Fourth Division play-off final in which they lost 4-5 to Swansea over two legs.

In the following August the Belgian club KVV Overpelt paid £13,000 for Caldwell, and after he had been loaned back to Torquay just over a year later, and then played in South Africa, they made a profit of £1,500 in returning him to Chesterfield in October 1990, having retained his registration. A cartilage injury cut short his second Saltergate spell of four goals and a dozen games, after which he went back to Scotland with Inverness Caledonian, the club from which he had joined Mansfield. In 1994 he moved to a Highland League team based in Aberdeen and began working as a sales executive for a company in the office equipment business. He then combined that job with being part-time manager of another Highland League club, Lossiemouth, until the end of the 1998-99 season, when he accepted an offer as group sales manager of a firm in Edinburgh.

In addition to the defensive shortcomings to cruelly exposed in the grilling at Gillingham, there were two main reasons why the warning signals flashed with alarming clarity for Chesterfield in the 1987-88 season that preceded relegation. One was that their goals total of 41 in the League (25 at home, sixteen away) was their lowest-ever for 46 matches, in twenty of which they failed to score, and, indeed, their lowest since the

37 from the 38 games of the 1908-09 season that had led to their loss of League status to Lincoln. The other was their over-reliance on the finishing power of Dave Waller. He netted nineteen times, plus three in the knock-out competitions. The club's next highest scorer, with just three, was Les Hunter, who was chiefly concerned with preventing goals rather than getting them, and, in any case, did not make his second return to Saltergate until the season was almost half over. Chesterfield were in the relegation zone until mid-April, then pulled three points clear by losing only one of their last six matches – and that by an only goal at Blackpool.

Ironically, it was when Waller had better scoring support that the Spireites found relegation inescapable. In 1988-89 his eighteen League goals were backed up by Bob Bloomer's ten (though six of them were penalties) and nine from Andy Morris, a newcomer from Rotherham whose transfer fee was said to be £500 and a bag of footballs. The Sheffield-born Morris, who also scored four Cup goals to Waller's one that season, became a big favourite of fans who nicknamed him Bruno because of some resemblance to the British boxer Frank Bruno. He played in more than 200 games for the club before persistent injury problems resulted in his departure in 1998, shortly after being granted a testimonial match against Nottingham Forest. On ending his League career with Rochdale he finally retired as a Hucknall Town player, and in the summer of 2000 he rejoined Chesterfield as their Football in the Community manager.

There was another ironic twist to Chesterfield's relegation season of 1988-89 when the only win they added to that of the opening day in the thirteen games before Paul Hart's appointment as manager was gained at Gillingham, scene of that whipping the year before. As already recalled, this time there was only one goal, scored by Steve Prindiville, a full-back who had made only one League appearance for Leicester City but was Chesterfield's most-used player in what would be his only season at Saltergate before moving on to Mansfield. Signed from the Foxes three League games into the season, he played in the remaining 43 – one more than Morris, who had not been given even one League chance by Rotherham.

With Hart at the helm, and a backroom staff of Chris McMenemy as assistant manager, Mick Henderson coach and Dave Rushbury physio, Chesterfield went right to the very end of the year before gaining their third League victory, by 4-1 at home to Fulham. One of their scorers that last December day was Dubliner Tony Brien, another recruit from Leicester who was the new manager's first signing to cost money. And what money! After several loan deals in keeping with the club's parlous financial situation, Brien was brought in for what was described at the time as a jaw-dropping £90,000.

This former Irish youth international had something of the swagger about him, and for the first two of the five seasons he spent in completing a double century of appearances for Chesterfield he played the best football of his career in the central defensive position of which his manager had the specialist knowledge to recognise exceptional ability. During that period Brien looked a strong contender for a full cap, also likely to be the target for a bigger club, but his form then fell away inexplicably. Even so, he remained a regular choice until his transfer to Rotherham United early in October 1993, though he did not stay long at either that club or the four others (two of them on loan) for which he played before going out of the League with Stalybridge Celtic.

Hart's other main signing during 1988-89 was Mick Leonard, a goalkeeper who had exceeded 250 games for Notts County since joining them from Halifax. Leonard neared another double century of games for Chesterfield before going in 1994 to Hong Kong, where he represented two of the leading clubs until injury forced him into retirement in 2000. Chesterfield had recently suffered their heaviest defeat of the season, by six goals at Preston, when Leonard joined them at the beginning of March 1989, but they then enjoyed a short spell of comparative success that hoisted them clear of the dreaded last four places by the end of that month. It included their completion of a prized double over Sheffield United, who were heading for automatic promotion with Wolves, and their biggest win of that sad season, at home to Cardiff. Morris scored three of the four goals the Welsh club conceded without reply.

But only two more victories were gained in the remaining ten matches after the Blades' unsuccessful visit to Saltergate, despite Waller's equalling a club record by scoring in eight of them in succession. One of those Waller goals, the winner of the return game in Cardiff, raised the last lingering hopes of avoiding the drop, only for defeats in the last two matches, at Mansfield and at home to Reading, to plunge the team back into the relegation mire. These were the final positions at the bottom:

Season 1988-89	P	W	D	L	F	A	Pts
19. Blackpool	46	14	13	19	56	59	54
20. Northampton	46	16	6	24	66	76	54
21. Southend	46	13	15	18	56	75	54
22. Chesterfield	46	14	7	25	51	86	49
23. Gillingham	46	12	4	30	47	81	40
24. Aldershot	46	8	13	25	48	78	37

Birmingham and Walsall, both relegated from Division Two, had worse goal-difference figures than Chesterfield, but the Derbyshire club, once so renowned for defensive strength, had the highest goals-against total in the whole League.

Team strengthening at Saltergate was obviously urgently needed, and Paul Hart sought to implement it in defence by bringing in a new full-back pairing, Bryn Gunn from Peterborough and John Ryan from Mansfield, though both were switched to other positions after a few months in being regular members of the team during the 1989-90 season in which promotion was almost immediately secured. Gunn, whose daughter Jenny was in the England women's Ashes-winning cricket team in 2005, had come to the fore with Nottingham Forest, whom he had helped, as a substitute, to win the European Cup in 1980.

Hart also brought back Calvin Plummer, for whom life had been unhappily eventful before first being with Chesterfield, and very varied since leaving them for Derby County. In 1982, the year he had ended by originally moving from Forest to Saltergate on loan, Plummer's inclusion in an unofficial tour of South Africa had provoked accusations of tokenism for not only being the youngest member of a squad largely made up of players nearing the end of their careers but also, and most damaging, because he was the only black player among those initially invited. The tour had been a public relations flop, and Plummer deemed naïve.

Derby paid Chesterfield £10,000 for Plummer in August 1983, but had to sell him to Barnsley the following March, along with centre-half Paul Futcher, to ease their own desperate financial plight. He was later back with Forest in the First Division between playing in Finland for Lahden Reipas and the Republic of Ireland for Derry City, then found his way back to Chesterfield via Plymouth. Another Spireites player with overseas experience around that time was Kevin Arnott, a Gateshead-born midfielder who had played regularly in Sunderland's Second Division promotion-winning side of 1979-80 before spending five seasons with Sheffield United. He saw out his League career with Chesterfield, for whom he made just over 70 of more than 360 appearances, after being with the Swedish club Vasalund.

Eight players made more than 40 League appearances for Chesterfield in the 1989-90 season, though goalkeeper Leonard, an ever-present with Gunn, was the only one not to have a change of position. The others were Plummer, who played in all but two of the 46 games, Brien, Ryan and Waller (each 43), Hewitt (42) and Morris (41, and two as substitute). Waller was again the leading scorer, with sixteen goals – plus two in the

Cup competitions. The conversion of seven penalties enabled Gunn to share second place with Plummer on eight goals, and he put away another spot-kick in a first-round FA Cup win at Shrewsbury in which Plummer also scored. A home defeat by Huddersfield in the second round left Chesterfield clear to concentrate on the League, early exits having already been made from the Littlewoods Cup and Leyland Daf Cup.

From sinking to their lowest position of 21st out of 24 at the beginning of September, Chesterfield climbed to ninth by losing only once in the next six matches, then ended the year fourth with an unbeaten run of nine. There was a setback when a deal broke down for a player who had been lined up to replace Bob Bloomer, surprisingly sold to Bristol Rovers on transfer deadline day, but by early April the Spireites were up to the third automatic promotion place. Their hopes of a prompt escape from Division Four were boosted by the bolstering of their defence by Sean Dyche, and of their attack by John Chiedozie.

Dyche would become the strong man of some 250 games for Chesterfield, rising to the captaincy, but he arrived from Nottingham Forest, at first on loan, without any League experience despite having shown promising form in their youth team. He had even been employed by manager Clough as a part-time gardener while a trainee. Chiedozie, a Nigerian international who had commanded about £1m in transfer fees, came free from Notts County, without a contract, as the veteran of well over 300 League and Cup games that had also been chiefly shared between Leyton Orient and Tottenham, but he only just got into double figures for Chesterfield before going into the Hampshire League.

The infusion of new blood helped Chesterfield to a sequence of seven games without defeat, but this was followed by seven without a win, pitching them down to ninth with only one match left. Their heaviest defeat of the season came during that late slump, by four goals away to a York City team that included two former Chesterfield players – goalkeeper Chris Marples and inside-left Steve Spooner, one of the scorers. With only two points taken from the next three matches after that setback, Hart's men went into their final one on 5 May, at home to a Grimsby side already assured of automatic promotion, clinging to the faintest of hopes that they could still scrape into the last play-off place. And, wonder of wonders, those hopes were realised as results went their way.

Goal-difference of a dozen was the decider. Victory with two Ryan goals raised Chesterfield (plus thirteen) to 71 points, the number at which Carlisle United (plus one) stuck to their detriment in losing 2-5 at

Maidstone. Carlisle, one of whose goals was scored by another ex-Chesterfield player, Keith Walwyn, had topped the table during January and February, and until that fateful last day they had not been out of the top six since late October. These were the final positions:

Season 1989-90	P	W	D	L	F	A	Pts
1. Exeter	46	28	5	13	83	48	89
2. Grimsby	46	22	13	11	70	47	79
3. Southend	46	22	9	15	61	48	75
4. Stockport	46	21	11	14	68	62	74
5. Maidstone	46	22	7	17	77	61	73
6. Cambridge	46	21	10	15	76	66	73
7. Chesterfield	46	19	14	13	63	50	71
8. Carlisle	46	21	8	17	61	60	71

The signs were not good when the play-offs pitted Chesterfield against Stockport, who had taken a point at Saltergate and won the return game 3-1 at the end of April. But what a reversal of form there now was. The outcome of their semi-final was as good as put beyond doubt when a crowd of 8,277 (the average at Saltergate that season was 4,181) saw Chesterfield win the home leg 4-0, Plummer doing the hat-trick. And goals by Plummer and Chiedozie at Edgeley Park, again without reply, completed an emphatic triumph that enabled 'unfashionable' Chesterfield to chalk up another first, though this was one they had to share, and the desired outcome eluded them. It took them to the first play-off final to be staged at Wembley. Until then the finals had been staged over two legs since their introduction in 1987 – home and away at the grounds of the clubs involved, but with a neutral venue needed for a tie-breaker on three occasions.

In the other semi-final of 1990, Cambridge United accounted by 3-1 on aggregate for Maidstone, who were in their first Football League season after winning the GM Vauxhall Conference championship from Kettering Town by a record eight points. Maidstone, who shared Dartford's ground, had displaced Darlington, among whose players was one Phil Bonnyman. Cambridge, however, got through to meet Chesterfield only after extra-time in the second leg in Kent, and with the aid of two penalties. Play-off form therefore strongly favoured the Derbyshire club, plus the fact that they had won at Cambridge in the League and shared the points with United in the return game.

But it was not to be. Fate decreed that the team finishing sixth in the Fourth Division would go up for the fourth year in succession. The only goal was scored in the 77th minute by Dion Dublin, a centre-half turned striker who would also help Cambridge to another promotion a year later (but miss a third through the play-offs in 1991-92), and play for England after being transferred to Manchester United for £1 million.

Chesterfield's team in the play-offs included another newcomer, Lee Francis, a full-back taken on loan from Arsenal in time to partner Ryan in the last two matches of the League season. Francis therefore made only his fifth appearance for the club in the final, but there were 68 more to come after his free transfer the following summer. The team fielded at Wembley was: Leonard; Francis, Ryan; Dyche, Brien, Gunn; Plummer, Hewitt, Chiedozie, Rogers, Morris. Waller was sent on as substitute for Plummer in the second leg of the semi-final, and for Chiedozie in the final (the Nigerian's tenth and last game for the Spireites).

Attendances were disappointing for Chesterfield's play-off final (26,404) on 16 May, and for the Division Three final (29,252) in which Notts County defeated Tranmere 2-0 on 27 May. Next day, however, there was a 72,873 sell-out for the match in which Swindon would have reached the First Division with a 1-0 win over Sunderland but for their admission of 36 breaches of Football League rules, all but one of them involving illegal payments to players. The Wiltshire club were at first relegated to Division Three, with Sunderland promoted in their place and Tranmere moving up with Notts County, but Tranmere, much to their mortification, were kept down when an FA appeal panel allowed Swindon to stay in Division Two. The League continued their investigation, however, and Swindon were ordered to pay £67,000 additional transfer fees for some previous deals.

Though Chesterfield were also denied promotion, such a close approach as the one they made to it might well have been expected to keep Paul Hart firmly installed in his job with the prospect of further improvement. Not so!

15

Shakers shaken in play-off final at Wembley

Chesterfield were about halfway through the 1990-91 season, hopes of building on the promotion near-miss of the past campaign dashed by a descent into the relegation region, when they parted company with manager Paul Hart. It was their second loss of Hart around that time, for Nigel, a full-back or wing-half who had been recruited from Stockport County by his elder brother (by some 5½ years) early the previous season, was also shown the exit. Paul, whose differences with directors precipitated his departure as well as the struggles of his team, at first went back to playing, for Grantham. Nigel was transferred to York City, with whom he was substituted in his only first-team appearance before also going out of the Football League, with Droylesden. Of his eight League clubs, Nigel played most of his 300 or so games for Crewe.

The switch Paul Hart soon made to youth coaching did not take long to bear fruit. After starting out with Nottingham Forest, he was put in charge of Leeds United's academy, and his proteges not only won the FA Youth Cup in 1993 and 1997, but also formed the nucleus of the Yorkshire club's team that reached the Champions League semi-finals in 2000-01.

However, Hart fell out with manager George Graham through a difference of opinion about Jonathan Woodgate, a gifted but injury-troubled centre-back who was sold to Newcastle to ease Leeds' financial problems. As a result, Hart returned to Forest to supervise their academy, and the success he achieved with the Under-19 side, winners of their group in the FA Academy League of 1999-2000, led to his taking over as manager when David Platt left to supervise the England Under-21 team in the summer of 2001.

As at Chesterfield, however, Hart went with Forest from a narrow play-off defeat (by Sheffield United in a Division One semi-final in 2003) to dismissal when there was a dramatic slump (fourteen League games without a win; the last seven of them without a goal). His subsequent managerial posts took him from Barnsley to Swindon by way of Rushden & Diamonds, Portsmouth, QPR and Crystal Palace.

At Saltergate, Hart was frustrated in being limited to signings either on loan, free or for 'nominal' fees in his efforts to gain promotion. The biggest name among those registered through such arrangements was that of Arthur Albiston. The former Manchester United and Scotland full-back played only three times, but scored one of his rare goals to earn a home point against Gillingham. Others included midfielder Paul Lemon, signed from Sunderland for the mysterious nominal fee after being on loan, Lee Francis, a defender taken on a free transfer from Arsenal following his loan, and Steve Williams, brought back into the League from Eastwood Town after being given only four starts by his home club, Mansfield Town.

Williams, known as 'George' because of his resemblance to actor Brian Murphy's character in the TV sitcom *George and Mildred*, was seen at his best after switching to the left wing-back position following an impressive try-out there in a pre-season friendly in 1991, but Dame Fortune deserted him both on and off the field. He broke a leg twice – first in a home match with York on the Saturday before Christmas in 1989, then during his comeback with the Reserves in February 1994. While recovering from the first break he was knocked off his bicycle and damaged his back. Then, in the summer of 1993, he ruptured an Achilles tendon while walking upstairs at home. After the second break, he had to abandon a second comeback he attempted in a few reserve games towards the end of the 1994-95 season. He then helped with coaching the youth team before going out of the League with Ilkeston Town, and becoming a postman. For all his misfortunes, he still completed a century of first-team appearances for Chesterfield.

Tight though the purse strings had been kept, they were slackened the month after Paul Hart's departure. In February 1991, hey presto, Glaswegian Paul McGugan was signed from Barnsley for £15,000, and North-Easterner Lee Turnbull from Doncaster Rovers for £35,000. McGugan, a central defender, came with the experience of 98 League matches, exactly divided between Glasgow Celtic and Barnsley. He would play in 77 more for Chesterfield before retiring. Turnbull, a forward or midfielder, began as an apprentice with his home club, Middlesbrough. From there he went to Aston Villa, but did not appear in their League side before his transfer to Doncaster, for whom he achieved a rare hat-trick of headers in a home win against Aldershot. With Chesterfield he took his career total of appearances beyond 200, then went back to Doncaster in exchange for midfielder David Moss, and edged past 300 in also playing for Wycombe Wanderers, Scunthorpe (the club to which Moss moved from Chesterfield in 1996) and Darlington. After that Turnbull was manager of Barrow, assistant manager of Southport, and back with Scunthorpe as chief scout.

Chris McMenemy, whose father Lawrie (remembered best for piloting Southampton to an FA Cup final victory over Manchester United) had recently been appointed England manager Graham Taylor's No 2, moved up to manage Chesterfield when Paul Hart left, but his appointment was not officially confirmed until the following April – the month during which a future Chesterfield manager, John Sheridan, won the Rumbelows Cup for Sheffield Wednesday with an opportunist goal near the end of the final against Manchester United.

Other notable newcomers after Paul Hart's replacement included Trevor Hebberd, Dave Lancaster, Steve Norris, Cliff Carr, Stuart Cash and Mick Kennedy. There was also a recall for goalkeeper Chris Marples, on a free from York after a spell on loan.

Hebberd, a former Southampton midfielder, had played – as also had ex-Chesterfield goalkeeper Steve Hardwick – in all 88 of Oxford United's League matches in their rocket-like rise as double champions from Third Division to First in successive seasons, 1983-85. Hebberd had also been Man of the Match in Oxford's Milk (League) Cup win at Wembley in 1986, augmenting his scheming by scoring the first goal in the 3-0 defeat of QPR. The versatile Stuart Cash came from Nottingham Forest, full-back Carr from Mansfield Town, Kennedy, a left-sided midfielder twice capped by the Republic of Ireland, from Stoke City. Cash had been a member of Wycombe Wanderers' FA Trophy-winning side of 1991 while on loan from Forest.

Lancaster, originally on loan from Blackpool, was signed, reportedly for as much as £70,000, a few days into the 1991-92 season. And in the following February just over £30,000 was needed to bring in Norris from Halifax, also after being on loan. This pair featured prominently in the most memorable match of McMenemy's tenure – an epic 4-4 draw with Liverpool at Anfield in the first leg of the Coca-Cola (League) Cup's second round on 22 September 1992. Norris gave Chesterfield the lead after only seven minutes, Lancaster increased it on the half-hour, and Norris made it 3-0 three minutes after the interval. That shock margin was reduced by Ronny Rosenthal in the 51st minute and Don Hutchison (his first goal for the club) in the 58th, but Norris scored again after 69. Two Marks then made their mark in coming to the rescue of the Merseysiders. Mark Walters gave them new hope of avoiding a big upset after 72 minutes; Mark Wright, an England centre-half, snatched an 85th-minute equaliser. 'We thought there could be as many as eight goals in it,' said Lancaster, 'but we didn't think we'd get four of 'em!'

Admittedly, Liverpool's line-up was not all that star-studded, with several first choices out injured, but they were the current holders of the FA

Cup and among the leading clubs in that inaugural season of the FA Premier League. Their team was: James; Marsh, Burrows, Tanner, Redknapp, Wright, Rosenthal, Charnock (Kozma), Hutchison, Molby, Walters. Chesterfield fielded: Leonard; Lemon, Carr, Williams, Brien, Rogers, Cash, Norris (Turnbull), Morris, Lancaster (Kennedy), Hebberd.

For the second leg at Saltergate Liverpool's goal was guarded by the South Africa-born Bruce Grobbelaar, who had played for Rhodesia (now Zimbabwe). He was nearing the end of his long reign following the arrival of David James from Watford, and later that season was loaned out to Stoke City. Two internationals, Steve Nicol of Scotland and Welshman Ian Rush, and a coming England one, Steve McManaman, were also back in the side. Another alteration brought in the newly signed Torban Piechnik, a £500,000 defender from Copenhagen. Chesterfield were unchanged, but with Turnbull this time substituting for Morris, and the disappointing Kennedy not required.

Home advantage counted for nothing as Liverpool swept to a 4-1 victory that took them into the third round by 8-5 on aggregate. Hebberd made the lone reply to first-half goals from Hutchison, Redknapp and Walters, and Rush rounded off the scoring. Liverpool next knocked out Sheffield United, in a replay after a scoreless draw at Bramall Lane, but then lost another replay following a home draw with Crystal Palace, who fell to Arsenal, eventual winners of the trophy, in the semi-finals and ended the season relegated from the First Division.

It was also a disappointing finish for Chesterfield and Liverpool. The Spireites went straight out of the FA Cup, beaten 2-3 on penalties after twice being held to a draw by Macclesfield Town, a lowly team from the GM Vauxhall Conference, lost to Stockport in a North semi-final of the Autoglass Trophy, and occupied a final twelfth place, seven points outside the play-offs, in the Third Division (as the Fourth had become with the formation of the FA Premier League and the reduction of the Barclays League to three sections). Liverpool had no trophy to show for their efforts, and they were left without any European football for the 1993-94 season in finishing sixth in the Premier League

For Chris McMenemy, time ran out only four months after that dramatic draw at Anfield. Chesterfield sacked him on 17 February 1993 – and back in his place came John Duncan, with Kevin Randall also recalled, from Mansfield, as his assistant. Duncan had been out of management for nearly three years since being dismissed by Ipswich in May 1990. The Suffolk club had missed the play-offs by three points in his second season with them, but they had started the next one badly and some good results towards the end of it had not been enough to make a realistic push for promotion. While out of the game Duncan talked about it on radio and went into teaching at a school in Suffolk, but Graham Taylor enabled him to keep in some sort of touch by making him one of his 'observers' for the England team.

In Duncan's second full season back at Saltergate, 1993-94, the Football League's first under the sponsorship of the Gloucester-based Endsleigh Insurance company), Chesterfield were just one victory short of qualifying for the play-offs. In the next one they not only qualified, after starting with three of the seven defeats they were to suffer, but also won the Wembley final. The need for some of the now unrequired players signed by McMenemy to see out their contracts slowed Duncan's rebuilding of the team until the summer of 1993, when he made three significant signings.

Darren Carr, a defender, came from Crewe after previously being with Bristol Rovers (his home club), Newport County and Sheffield United; Mark Jules arrived from Scarborough, for whom his lively display had inspired a 3-0 defeat of Chesterfield on a day when an unhappy switch to centre-half had made Dave Lancaster somewhat unfortunate to be among the cast-offs of the new regime, to Rochdale, soon afterwards; Tom Curtis, a midfielder who in seven years with Chesterfield would make more than 250 of the 400-plus appearances he totalled in subsequently playing for six other League clubs, was snapped up while on a university course. Curtis was later Loughborough University's head football coach, and assistant coach to the English Universities squad, before being appointed Technical Director and head coach by the Antigua and Barbuda FA in 2011.

Duncan continued to make up for lost time with more transfer activity in the third month of the 1993-94 season. He was particularly busy on 8 October. That was the day he signed Nicky Law from Rotherham, with Tony Brien joining the Millers as part of the deal, and also arranged the exchange of Lee Turnbull for David Moss with Doncaster Rovers. Later that month Jamie Hewitt, who had been freed under McMenemy's management, was brought back from Doncaster, and the experience of more than 450 League games came with Lawrie Madden when he made Chesterfield his eighth and last senior club. Most of those Madden matches were played for Sheffield Wednesday, with whom he was a Rumbelows Cup winner, as a substitute, in the 1991 final.

At the age of almost 38, Madden could be nothing more than a short-term signing by the Spireites, but he increased his League appearances to within six of 500 before turning to freelance journalism after leaving Saltergate towards the end of 1995-96. If he had seen that season out as a first-team regular he would have been close to challenging Billy Kidd as the club's oldest player, having been born on 28 September 1955, but his last League game was on the opening day, 12 August 1995.

Law was also getting on a bit, just a few weeks short of his 32nd birthday, but his acquisition was to have a bigger influence – as player, captain, and finally manager. This central defender, capped by England at schoolboy level, began with Arsenal as an apprentice, but it was not until he moved to Barnsley that he made the first of the 405 League appearances he stacked up before joining Chesterfield. Between being with Barnsley and Rotherham, for both of whom he exceeded 100 games, he played for Blackpool, Plymouth, Notts County and, on loan, Scarborough. For Chesterfield he clocked up another century of matches despite being latterly dogged by injury, then wound down with Hereford before returning to Saltergate as Football in the Community officer.

In 1994, Chesterfield just missed the play-offs because they had too many draws – fourteen of them, six in the last eight games. A 4-0 home win against Northampton on the final day came too late to overtake Carlisle, whose finishing burst of four consecutive victories, with only one goal conceded, swept them up from twelfth to seventh, the last play-off place. They had 64 points to Chesterfield's 62, and a superior goal-difference of plus fifteen to plus seven. So, besides the draws, Chesterfield had reason to rue letting in five goals at Rochdale (in the first half), four at Preston, and three at Chester, Carlisle and at home to Wycombe – all in the first ten games of the season before the improvement that produced fourteen clean sheets.

Northampton's defeat at Saltergate dumped them at the foot of the table in place of Darlington, who pulled three points clear by beating Bury on the same day, and the Cobblers would have been condemned to non-League football if Kidderminster Harriers, the GM Vauxhall Conference champions, had not been denied promotion by their failure to complete ground improvements in time.

It was during the 1993-94 season that Chesterfield introduced into their team a forward who was to rise to prominence in the Premiership and play for England. Kevin Davies, who had been released by his home club, Sheffield United, at the age of fifteen, became the Spireites' second youngest first-team player (after Dennis Thompson) when he was sent on as a substitute during a home match with Walsall on 18 September. Four days later, again as a sub, he became the youngest of any club, at sixteen – he was born on 26 March 1977 – to make his debut in the Coca-Cola Cup, in a second-round tie at West Ham. His international call-up put him at the other end of the footballing time scale. When, at 33, he played, once more as a sub, in a European qualifying game against Montenegro on 12 October 2010, he became the oldest England newcomer since 38-year-old Leslie Compton made his full debut against Wales in 1950.

Davies was on the losing side in both his first two games for Chesterfield, Walsall winning 1-0 and the Hammers 5-1, but, well built and strong for a teenager, he settled regularly into the side soon after Christmas and he was so obviously a cut above the ordinary that Chesterfield were fortunate to hang on to him for as long as they did – until May 1977, when their biggest incoming fee was raised to £750,000 by his sale to Southampton. Ten days after the deal was completed the manager who had signed him, Graeme Souness, the former Scottish international who had captained Liverpool, resigned – allegedly, and ironically, after a disagreement with the Saints' new chairman, Rupert Lowe, about money for new players. At the same time, Lawrie McMenemy stood down as the club's Director of Football.

Just over a year later, Davies moved to Blackburn, with fellow striker James Beattie going the opposite way. The fee this time was said to be £7.25 million, a record for both clubs. Chesterfield missed a trick there, having omitted to negotiate a sell-on clause. Again, the manager who did the deal, Rovers' Roy Hodgson, was soon on his way out, dismissed in November 1998, only sixteen months after this future England manager's appointment, following a home defeat by, of all clubs, Southampton, that sank Rovers to the bottom of the table. Davies, too, did not last long at Ewood Park. He scored just one goal in 21 Premiership appearances, a dozen of them as substitute, as Blackburn plunged to relegation only four years after becoming champions. It was a fate narrowly averted by Southampton, to whom Davies returned in August 1999 in a deal, involving the exchange of Norwegian Egil Ostenstad, valued at £1.25 million.

It was not a happy return. In only the second Premiership appearance of his second coming, as a substitute for Mark Hughes in a defeat at Leicester, Davies was one of fourteen players sent off that day in England (and a dozen more in Scotland). Yet again there was soon a change of manager. Glenn Hoddle, of Tottenham and England fame, was brought in during January 2000, originally as caretaker, when Dave Jones was given leave on full pay to concentrate on facing child abuse charges, of which he was completely cleared, that arose from his work at a children's home at Formby, on Merseyside, ten years before

Davies served under two other managers, Stuart Gray and Gordon Strachan, during the four years he spent back at Southampton – too often for his liking as a substitute, and partly on loan to Millwall – before making the move in the summer of 2003 to Bolton, where he rediscovered his best form. With Wanderers he has added steel to the skill that brought him to the fore at Chesterfield – no doubt rather too much in some eyes considering that in September 2011 he received his 100th yellow card (a number then exceeded only by Lee Bowyer), though he had himself been regularly fouled. He completed a more acceptable century when he took his total of career goals into three figures with the winner against West Ham in April 2008 – after dislocating a finger and playing on with it painfully placed back into its socket.

Scoring was not Davies's main attribute while with Chesterfield, for whom he operated mostly wide in midfield, though he was the club's leading marksman with eleven goals (and another in the Coca-Cola Cup) when promotion was won in 1994-95. That was his most successful Spireites season as a scorer. Gifted as he was, he was not suited to lead the attack, so it was towards the end of 1994 that Duncan pulled off a real bargain with the free transfer of Tony Lormor from Peterborough. Another astute deal that December landed Phil Robinson, an absolute 'steal' at £15,000 from Huddersfield Town. Two Robinson goals won the points when, as already recalled, Lormor made his debut at Doncaster on Boxing Day in the first of 21 games unbeaten. That club record run (the old one was broken at fourteen) spurred Chesterfield from seventh to second, an automatic promotion position they held until a defeat by Carlisle and draw with Colchester, both at home, in their last two matches dropped them to third as top qualifiers for the play-offs. It was their failure to take all three points from Colchester on the final day that proved so costly – and they needed a penalty to take just the one.

The increase to 22 clean sheets had a big bearing on the progress made by Duncan's men. Half of them came while Chris Marples was in goal up to mid-January, the other half after the introduction from Doncaster of Andy Beasley, who had twice been a promotion winner with Mansfield. The rearguard had a very settled look, with Jamie Hewitt and Lee Rogers at full-back, and Darren Carr and Nicky Law the regulars in central defence. Up front, three players (Lormor and David Moss besides Davies) got into double figures, and Robinson was just two short.

Walsall, from whom Chesterfield had taken only one point (in a scoreless home draw back in September) nipped in to snatch second place behind Carlisle by rounding off an undefeated six-game finish with a win at lowly Scarborough and draw at fourth-placed Bury. Scarborough, who won at Chesterfield on the opening day, and also knocked them out of the FA Cup despite being halfway through sixteen League matches without a victory, escaped ending up last only through having a better inferior goal-difference than Exeter, but there was again no demotion to the

Conference in any case. Like Kiddermister before them, Macclesfield were kept waiting for League status because their ground did not then meet requirements, a rather surprising decision in view of the fact that they had provided Chester with a temporary home two years earlier.

These were the final leading positions in Division Three of the Endsleigh Insurance League:

Season 1994-95	P	W	D	L	F	A	Pts
1. Carlisle	42	27	10	5	67	31	91
2. Walsall	42	24	11	7	75	40	83
3. Chesterfield	42	23	12	7	62	37	81
4. Bury	42	23	11	8	73	36	80
5. Preston	42	19	10	13	58	41	67
6. Mansfield	42	18	11	13	84	59	65
7. Fulham	42	16	14	12	60	54	62
8. Scunthorpe	42	18	8	16	68	63	62

Disappointment at having to endure the torment of the play-offs after being a last-day victory short of prompt promotion was dispelled to some extent when Chesterfield reached Wembley again by beating Mansfield, if only after losing the lead in the drawn away leg of their semi-final, and then having to overcome a half-time deficit and needing extra-time against a team that had two players sent off in the return game at Saltergate. Mansfield had been third in the table after hitting Lincoln for six during March, but the defensive flaws that had then weakened their challenge were clearly evident when they conceded three goals during the added period as Chesterfield triumphed 5-2 for a 6-3 aggregate victory.

Chesterfield's starting line-up at Field Mill included a former Mansfield player, Nottingham-born Chris Perkins, who had taken over from Sean Dyche on the left side of midfield for the last half-dozen League matches after making only intermittent appearances since the start of the season. This was the team: Beasley; Hewitt, Rogers; Curtis, Carr, Law (capt), Robinson, Davies, Lormor, Moss, Perkins. Jon Howard, who had been signed midway through the season from Rotherham, went on as substitute for the injured Davies. For the second leg, which produced the club's record receipts of £45,000 from a gate of 8,165, Howard was on from the start, adding a goal to those netted by Lormor, Robinson (who had been on target at Mansfield) and Law, whose couple included a penalty. Howard took the place of Perkins, who subbed for Davies's deputy Des Hazel, another former Rotherham player. A further change brought back Morris for Moss, and a sub also had to be used when Beasley handed over to Liverpudlian Billy Stewart, who had made only one League appearance, in a goalless home game with Wigan, one of his former clubs, since being taken on loan from Northampton.

Hazel, who was born at Bradford and had previously played for Sheffield Wednesday and, on loan, Grimsby Town, later represented St Kitts and Nevis in international football, but he did not stay with Chesterfield for long before going to Australia. Howard, on the other hand, played more than 200 times for the Spireites and, as we shall be coming to in the next chapter, he was a central figure in the club's most famous FA Cup exploit.

For the play-off final on 27 May 1995, Chesterfield fielded: Stewart; Hewitt, Rogers; Curtis, Carr, Law, Robinson, Hazel, Lormor (Davies, 85 mins), Morris, Howard (Perkins, 77 mins). It was quite an experience for Stewart, who was Man of the Match in only his second, and last, full first-team appearance for the club. He left for a second spell with Chester City that summer. And Wembley had not seen the last of him. He would be back there in 1998 in the Southport side that lost by an only goal to Cheltenham Town in the FA Umbro Trophy final.

Bury, 1-0 winners of both legs in the other semi-final against Preston, were the team bang in form, having gone through their last eleven Third Division games unbeaten and not given a goal away in five of them. Their total of League clean sheets that season had been only one inferior to Chesterfield's, yet Preston, ironically, had inflicted their heaviest defeat in scoring five goals without reply immediately before that impressive run-in of eight wins and three draws.

But, Shakers though they were known, Bury were not to shake Chesterfield. Lormor gained the lead after 23 minutes and Robinson increased it four minutes from the interval. Mainly thanks to Stewart's heroics, Bury were denied even a consolation goal and joy was, as they say, unconfined among the Derbyshire club's followers in the crowd of 22,814.

Chairman Norton Lea and Barrie Hubbard, the vice-chairman, joined in the post-match lap of honour, and on the return to the dressing room John Duncan, who took it in good part, was thrown fully clothed into the bath. The decision to recall Duncan and Randall had been fully justified. 'People say "Never go back," but I came back into football,' said the manager, 'and I'm delighted that it has all worked out. I really enjoy working with Kevin. He's a true ambassador of all that's good in football, a consummate professional with vast experience and a phenomenal knowledge of the game.'

There was another success for Chesterfield that season. Their interest in the national knock-out competitions soon ended, but they won the Derbyshire FA Centenary Cup for the first time since its inception in 1983 to celebrate that milestone in the county association's history. Derby County, as Derbyshire's other League club, provided the opposition apart from the 2003-04 season, when the Rams declined to take part and were replaced by Alfreton Town, who won 2-0. Chesterfield lifted the trophy, by an only goal, at the thirteenth attempt, the year after suffering their biggest defeat in the series, by 2-7. They were twice beaten only after extra-time during the 1980s, and since then they have lost and won on penalty shoot-outs. From 2005-09 there was no contest, and it has again been discontinued since Derby won 2-1 the following season.

16

Into the FA Cup semi-finals for the first time

Chesterfield's Duncan-Randall managerial partnership continued to thrive for four more seasons after the promotion success of '95, with a further rise in status for some time a distinct possibility and unprecedented progress in the FA Cup, but a slump in form then gathered momentum at an increasingly alarming rate. Randall stayed on as assistant manager for a few years after Duncan's dismissal when relegation once more became inevitable, but he was also unceremoniously cast aside following another change of chairman that led to one of the most catastrophic periods in the club's history.

The Spireites ended 1995-96 just one point short of having the chance to reach the First Division of the Endsleigh Insurance League through the play-offs. They had a slightly better goal-difference than Bradford City, who squeezed into the sixth and last qualifying place with 73 points to Chesterfield's 72 and went on to go up with the top two, Swindon and Oxford. A marked falling-off in the Derbyshire club's scoring rate on the run-in, only eight goals in the last dozen games, undermined their challenge. They were in the play-off frame for five months from late November, but then suffered three successive defeats before winding up with two wins, both by an only goal, that failed to retrieve lost ground. Bradford City's three wins in their last four matches (the other was drawn) included a crucial one at home to Chesterfield after trailing at half-time to a goal scored by David McDougald, who was on loan from Brighton.

Duncan again placed much reliance on players who had featured prominently in the rise to Division Two. Curtis was the only ever-present, but Dyche, Lormor, Robinson and Law were not far behind him and Jules, Davies, Hewitt and Rogers also had good runs in the side. There were three notable newcomers, on whom more than £300,000 was spent if sums announced at the time are to be believed. First, the day before the 1995-96 season opened, came Mark Williams, a defender from Shrewsbury, at the bargain price of £20,000. Then, to fill the gap left by the injury that ended Andy Beasley's career, goalkeeper Billy Mercer was taken on loan from Sheffield United in September and signed for £100,000 three months later. The third man, Paul Holland, a combative midfielder, also arrived from Bramall Lane, the costliest at £200,000 early in January.

Mark Williams was second to Curtis for appearances that season, missing four matches. He had spent three seasons with Shrewsbury, helping them to the Third Division championship in the middle one of 1993-94. To just one short of 100 League games for the Shrews he added 168 for Chesterfield and won the first of his 36 Northern Ireland caps (he was born in England, at Stalybridge, but had an Irish ancestor) before moving in 1999 to Watford. He was the first to make his international debut while a Chesterfield player. Watford had just been promoted to the Premiership, but they were relegated straightaway, finishing last with only 24 points, and Williams was transferred to Wimbledon, another club that had just dropped out of the top flight. He was later on loan to Stoke, and turned out a few times for Columbus Crew and Stafford Rangers before making the last of nearly 400 League appearances in the 2004-05 season with Rushden & Diamonds.

Billy Mercer joined his home club, Liverpool, as a trainee, but had still to make his League debut when he was transferred to Rotherham in February 1989. Over the next 5½ years he guarded the Millers' goal in more than 100 League and Cup games before moving to Sheffield United. He was unable to stake a claim to a regular place with the Blades, but in his four seasons with Chesterfield he was first choice for 164 matches and brought in a fee of £300,000 when he left for Bristol City in October 1999. After retiring from playing early in 2003 he continued with the Ashton Gate club as goalkeeping coach, a role in which he subsequently also served Sheffield Wednesday and Burnley. For a few weeks between a change of manager in the autumn of 2006 he was Wednesday's caretaker assistant manager to the club's Academy head coach, Sean McAuley, a former St Johnstone full-back who had been on loan to Chesterfield in the mid-90s.

Paul Holland, an England Under-21 international, also exceeded a century of games with the clubs, Mansfield and Chesterfield, for which he played before and after having few opportunities with Sheffield United. He, too, left Saltergate for Bristol City, but he suffered a serious knee injury soon afterwards, and then was forced into playing retirement by a stress fracture of the kneecap. He returned to Mansfield Town as the youth team's coach in January 2002, and was their caretaker manager after the dismissal of first ex-Wednesday defender Peter Shirtliff and then former Chesterfield forward Billy Dearden, to both of whom he had been assistant. After his four matches in temporary charge following Dearden's departure, he was given the job until the end of the 2007-08 season. 'We have had three good performances out of four under Paul,' said Stephen Booth, the club's chief executive. 'I am confident in his abilities and hope everyone gets behind him.' But Holland was powerless to prevent relegation from the Football League, Mansfield dropping into the Blue Square Premier League with Wrexham, and he was promptly sacked.

Chesterfield's final League position of tenth in 1996-97, five points from the play-offs with inferior goal figures, was a disappointment after being as high as fourth during the early months, but that was emphatically offset by the mounting excitement of the FA Cup run which took them to the semi-finals for the first time – and with a bit more luck might have even seen them through to Wembley. It was because of the Cup, however, that the League challenge was weakened by having to fit in ten games besides the semi-final and its replay during April – two of them against clubs that gained promotion (they defeated Crewe but lost to Stockport), and two others that reached the play-offs (they were beaten by both Brentford and Bristol City).

The only goals Chesterfield conceded in the six games they played to reach the last four were scored by Bolton Wanderers, whose 2-3 defeat on their own ground in the fourth round was given extra gloss when the Trotters climbed into the Premiership as that season's champions of the Nationwide First Division. Kevin Davies' hat-trick that February day turned out to be something of a mixed blessing, boosting the attention that lost him to Southampton during the close season, though the record fee considerably softened the blow of his departure.

In each of the first three rounds Chesterfield were drawn at home, beginning with victory by a Mark Williams goal against Bury, another club heading for promotion as champions – and one that took all six points from Duncan's men in Division Two. Goals from Davies and Lormor then saw off Scarborough, a mid-table Third Division side, and a Howard double, after 69 and 88 minutes, accounted for Bristol City, who had recovered to draw on their League visit (and would win the return game 2-0). The Ashton Gate club lost in their play-off semi-final to Brentford, who failed against Crewe in the final.

Premiership opposition had to be faced after the beating of Bolton, but Nottingham Forest were far removed from those halcyon days of European, League and League Cup glory under the management of Brian Clough and his assistant Peter Taylor. That, indeed, was the season in which the Reds were relegated from the Premiership for the second time in five years, finishing a poor last. Chesterfield, again with home advantage, won by an only goal, scored by Curtis from the penalty-spot after 54 minutes. The attendance of 8,890 was almost double the season's

League average at Saltergate, but only 200 more than saw Stockport gain the win there in late April that clinched their promotion to the First Division as runners-up. Just 155 fewer than the gate against Forest turned up for the sixth-round clash at home to Wrexham, who went on to finish above Chesterfield in the League by the slender margin of the point they had prised on their visit a month earlier.

There had been no goals on that former occasion. This time only one sufficed. It was scored thirteen minutes into the second half by Chris Beaumont, a £30,000 signing from Stockport the previous summer, but the Man of the Match was Billy Mercer, who had to be at his brilliant best to preserve one of his twenty clean sheets of the season. There had been the intriguing prospect of an all-Derbyshire clash in the Cup semi-finals, or (wow!) even in the final, when the draw for the quarter-finals kept the Spireites and Derby County apart, but the Rams' run was then ended by Middlesbrough – and it was Boro who next stood between Chesterfield and Wembley.

It looked a formidable task for the Spireites against a team packed with costly talent from overseas: the Italians Gianluca Festa and Fabrizio Ravanelli, the Brazilians Emerson and Juninho, Mikkel Beck of Denmark, and Vladimir Kinder, a Slovak. But all was not well on Teesside. Three months earlier, on the very day in January when Festa made his £2.7 million move from Inter Milan, Middlesbrough had been docked three points and fined £50,000 for illegally calling off their game at Blackburn shortly before Christmas, at very short notice, because a few of their players had influenza. This left them trailing by four points at the bottom of the Premiership and at the season's end they were those three lost points short of staying up. Down they went with 39 points; Southampton and Coventry, the clubs immediately above the relegated three (the others were Sunderland and Forest) both had 41.

On either side of their FA Cup semi-final with Chesterfield at Old Trafford on 13 April, Boro also had the distraction of a Coca-Cola Cup final in which they met Leicester City on their first appearance at Wembley. Ravanelli gave them the lead in extra-time on 6 April, but Leicester grabbed an equaliser – and then won the replay 1-0 at Hillsborough on 16 April.

Cruel as that outcome was for Middlesbrough, it could not compare with the injustice that robbed Chesterfield of a definite chance of becoming the first club from the Third Division to reach the FA Cup final. True, Boro were reduced to ten men from near the end of a largely uneventful first half by the sending-off of Kinder for a second bookable offence – a blatant pulling back of Davies, who had been giving him a torrid time. And there were only just over ten minutes of extra-time left when Jamie Hewitt scored the goal that snatched a 3-3 draw and a replay. But, and it was a very big but, Chesterfield were denied a perfectly legitimate goal that would have put them 3-1 ahead shortly after the 70th minute in which Ravanelli bundled the ball past Mercer to halve the shock two-goal lead the Derbyshire club gained in the first fifteen minutes of the second half. Jon Howard found space in the six-yard box and from his shot the ball clearly dropped down inside the goal-line from the underside of the crossbar before bouncing out.

The linesman nearest the incident appeared to signal for the award of a goal, but referee David Elleray waved him aside. For what reason has remained unclear. Indeed, Elleray, a housemaster at Harrow, merely added to the mystery when consulted after the match. 'I saw an offence,' he said, 'but I cannot remember what it was. I honestly can't remember whether the offence occurred before or after the ball bounced over the line.' Elleray was generally acknowledged to be a firm, fair and consistent referee, but he was also involved in several other controversial incidents – notably when he awarded Manchester United a dubious penalty in 1994 FA Cup final. He admitted in his autobiography that he 'blew without thinking', adding that although he knew he had made a major mistake he could not change his mind.

Elleray awarded two penalties in the 1997 semi-final at Old Trafford. The first one, on the hour, deservedly enabled Chesterfield to increase the lead Andy Morris had given them six minutes earlier after goalkeeper Ben Roberts had parried a fierce shot from Davies straight to his feet for a straightforward finish. Morris was brought down by Roberts as he raced into the area, and Sean Dyche, neither a noted scorer nor the usual man on the spot, stepped up to smash the ball home straight down the middle. In contrast, the second penalty was another controversial award, deepening Chesterfield's sense of injustice only a minute after Ravanelli's goal. Juninho was fouled all right, but outside the area. Craig Hignett's shot from the spot just squeezed through beneath the diving Mercer to make the score 2-2.

So to extra-time, in which revitalised Boro took charge, inspired by the scheming of Juninho, who had hitherto been subdued by Mark Jules. It looked all over for Chesterfield when, from one of the chances created by the elusive Brazilian, Festa slammed the ball into the roof of their net in the 100th minute. Chesterfield fans, though resigned to defeat as the remaining twenty minutes ticked away, chanted 'We're Proud of You'. But there was still one final moment of high drama to come. In the 119th minute the ball, whipped across from the right, bounced into the Boro box and Hewitt, the only Chesterfield-born player in the team, popped up to direct a looping header beyond the despairing reach of the stranded Roberts. Pandemonium! Duncan's glasses were knocked off as those around him leaped in delight. Supporters went wild, their ecstasy soaring to a crescendo when the final whistle confirmed that their team had earned a second chance.

These were the teams that memorable day:

Chesterfield: Mercer; Hewitt, Jules, Curtis, Williams, Dyche, Holland (Beaumont), Davies, Morris, Howard, Perkins (Carr).

Middlesbrough: Roberts; Fleming, Kinder, Vickers, Festa, Mustoe, Emerson, Hignett (Moore), Beck (Blackmore), Juninho, Ravanelli.

Sadly, however, that dramatic equaliser merely delayed the ending of Chesterfield's Wembley dream. Boro strolled to victory in an anti-climax of a replay at Hillsborough nine days later. Three times without reply, through Beck (twelve minutes), Ravanelli (57) and Emerson (89), they put the ball past Mercer, who was back at Sheffield Wednesday's ground for the first time since, as a Liverpool fan, he had been in the upper tier at the Leppings Lane end on the afternoon of the disaster eight years before. Chesterfield fielded the same players, with Davies and Holland switching places, Carr this time substituting for Howard, but Beaumont not required. Boro had Neil Cox (for whom Derek Whyte substituted) and Clayton Blackmore at full-back, Nigel Pearson in place of Festa, and Phil Stamp on as sub for Juninho.

For Boro, the joy of again getting to Wembley lasted only until their defeat in the League Cup final replay four days later. And, after promising so much, their season disintegrated into a triple trip-up with their subsequent relegation from the Premiership and defeat by Chelsea in an FA Cup final that swung against them as early as the 43rd second in which Roberto Di Matteo scored the competition's fastest-ever goal at Wembley. For Chesterfield, there was some consolation from their share of the Cup run's receipts. Their combined semi-final attendances alone totalled almost 80,000; the others on the way to the last four added up to more than 43,000.

In all, about £2 million came into the club's coffers, but that sum also included income from the sale of players. The departure of Phil Robinson to Notts County had already brought in £80,000 on the eve of the 1996-97 season. Sean Dyche followed Kevin Davies out during the summer after it, transferred to Bristol City for £275,000. Dyche helped the Robins up to Division One in his first season (though they were immediately relegated), then was with Millwall when they also climbed out of the Second Division in 2001 – and almost went straight through to the Premiership, losing to Birmingham in the play-offs. After that, Dyche was with Watford, whom he captained before being involved in another promotion from Division Two with Northampton Town in 2005-06. On retiring from playing, he rejoined Watford as youth team coach, taking over as their manager in 2011 when Malky Mackay left for Cardiff City.

In preparation for the 1997-98 season, Chesterfield spent some £350,000 of their increased income on three players: Ian Breckin, a central defender from Rotherham, Roger Willis, a midfielder or forward from Peterborough United, and Steve Wilkinson, a striker from Preston North End. It was only a few months later that Preston also parted with Dave Reeves in the deal that took Tony Lormor to Deepdale.

Breckin, who had joined Rotherham, his home club, as a trainee, was another of the players to have more than one spell with Chesterfield. His first one lasted for five years and more than 200 games; for the other he returned as club captain from Nottingham Forest in 2009, and he increased his total of appearances for the Spireites to around 300 before being released at the end of the 2010-11 season. In between he was a key member of the Wigan side that won promotion to the Premiership in 2005, earning the nickname Breckinbauer in a reference to the German icon. He did not, however, stay to play at that top level, moving instead for £350,000 to Forest, whom he helped up to the Coca-Cola Championship with a club record of two dozen clean sheets in 2007-08.

Wilkinson began with Leicester City, but played only a few League games for them, and was loaned out to Crewe, before costing Mansfield £80,000 in September 1989. Late that season he scored all the Stags' five goals against Birmingham, and although they were relegated the next year he played a prominent part when they climbed straight back. Again they promptly went down, but he gave Chesterfield good cause to remember him by doing the hat-trick against them on the way to the play-offs of 1995 in which he also scored as Mansfield lost their semi-final with the Spireites. Preston stepped in first, however, for this third highest marksman in the Town's history (behind Harry Johnson and Ken Wagstaff with 91 League goals), and they showed a profit of £50,000 on their £100,000 outlay when he moved to Chesterfield after helping to win the Division Three title during his two seasons at Deepdale. With Chesterfield he spent three seasons, for the more modest return of fifteen goals in 75 League games before leaving for Kettering. From there he became head of the football development centre at Loughborough College.

The Sheffield-born Willis, generally known as Harry, came to the fore with Barnet, who paid Grimsby £10,000 for him after he had been loaned out to Boston United, then members of the GM Vauxhall Conference. In his first season with Barnet, 1990-91, they rose to the Football League as Conference champions, and in his second they lost only narrowly to Blackpool in a Division Four play-off semi-final, a penalty deciding the outcome over the two legs. That led to his £175,000 transfer to Watford, and a year later he was taken to Birmingham for £150,000 by Barry Fry, who had also been his manager at Barnet. After that Willis was with Southend United, then at Peterborough both before and after the five years in which Chesterfield were the only club for which he exceeded 100 appearances.

Other newcomers during the Duncan-Randall reign most notably included Jason Lee, a 6ft 3in striker whose transfer from Watford a few weeks into the 1998-99 season raised Chesterfield's record outgoing fee to £250,000 from the £150,000 paid to Carlisle for Phil Bonnyman back in 1980. But it was a deal that literally misfired. Lee came fresh from one of his most successful seasons as a scorer, if with a modest total of ten goals in Watford's winning of the Second Division championship, but for Chesterfield he netted only once in 28 League games before being offloaded to Peterborough United – first on loan, then for a cut-price £50,000. That was quite enough of a comedown for a player who had three times commanded six-figure fees (Nottingham Forest had recouped from Watford the £200,000 they had spent to sign him from Southend), yet he was reduced to being given a free transfer when he joined Northampton Town early in 2006. And by the time he began a second spell with Boston United in 2011, latterly as player-manager, he had plied his trade around almost twenty clubs since starting out with Charlton Athletic in 1989.

Lee attributed an undermining of his confidence to the lampooning of him by the comedians Frank Skinner and David Baddiel in their tele-vised football chat show. This arose from the nickname Pineapple Head he incurred while with Forest because of his distinctive tied-up dreadlock hairstyle. He suffered much abuse from fans on the terraces who repeat-edly chanted 'He's got a pineapple on his head' to the tune of 'He's got the whole world in his hands'. It reached such a pitch that he felt com-pelled to have the 'pineapple' shaved off.

With Lee fading from the Chesterfield scene, the main reliance for goals rested on David Reeves. In 1999-2000, he responded with fourteen in the Second Division, four of them penalties, and four more in knock-out competitions, but his lack of scoring support resulted in the club's lowest-ever total of 34 for a League season. Ryan Williams, an £80,000 signing from Tranmere Rovers, came next with five goals, followed by

Willis (four) and Steve Payne, a newcomer from Macclesfield, who scored three. This lack of punch not only made relegation inevitable but also brought FA Cup humiliation within three years of that semi-final glory. Chesterfield were beaten at home in the first round by Enfield, humble members of the Ryman League who had been going through lean times since being among the strongest sides in the Conference during the early 1980s. Midfielder Jamie Lomas, who had joined as a youth trainee, wiped out Enfield's first-half lead, but there were still more than twenty minutes to go when the winner was put past Mark Gayle, a goalkeeper of many clubs who had rejoined Chesterfield from Rushden & Diamonds after first being with them on loan from Crewe.

With Billy Mercer having followed Paul Holland to Bristol City, Gayle was Chesterfield's most-used goalkeeeer that sad season, but there were four others: Andy Leaning, Carl Muggleton, John Vaughan and Joel Armstrong. Leaning was at the tail-end of a career he had begun with York City in 1985 when he moved back into English football with Chesterfield from Dundee, and he soon turned to coaching – first at Saltergate, then with Sheffield United, York and Leeds United.

Muggleton, who had also had some experience of Scottish soccer, with Celtic, was in his second spell on loan to Chesterfield (from Stoke; previously from Leicester). In May 2002 he would be back for a third time, signed from Cheltenham and set for a four-year stay in which he played more than 120 games before rejoining Mansfield, one of the ten other clubs he had been with on loan. He also became a goalkeeping coach, part-time with Notts County. So did Vaughan, at Huddersfield, after quickly ending with Chesterfield an eleven-club career in which successive Cambridge United promotions were the highlights. Armstrong made only half-a-dozen first-team appearances for Chesterfield, his home club, and was loaned to Ilkeston Town and Bradford PA before assisting several other teams outside the League.

Chesterfield's interest in the other main domestic knock-out competition, for the League (Worthington) Cup, was also short-lived in the 1999-2000 season, but they reached a Northern semi-final of the Auto Windscreens Shield before losing to Stoke, who went on to beat Bristol City in the final at Wembley. In the League, Chesterfield were up against it right from the start, beaten in both their first two matches with only a Reeves penalty to show for their scoring efforts. Two more spot-kicks helped Reeves to net all four next time out, at home to Cambridge, but only one more win, though against Preston's coming champions, was gained in the next twenty matches.The sequence of eighteen without a victory, thirteen of them without scoring, was the longest in the club's history, not broken until early January – and then by just one goal (Reeves again) against Brentford.

There were then just two more wins in the next seventeen games. Back they sank to last place after a defeat at Oxford on 19 February, and there they stayed. Relegation was already inevitable when, on 11 April 2000, after four successive defeats near the end of that second depressing run, the curtain was brought down on the seven years of John Duncan's second coming. Nicky Law's return to the club as commercial officer, after increasing his number of League appearances to 530 with his free transfer to Hereford, made him immediately available, but he was not officially appointed the new manager until 16 May. That was ten days after the season had ended with a draw away to Blackpool, another of the clubs to go down. These were the final positions at the bottom of the Nationwide Division Two:

Season 1999-2000	P	W	D	L	F	A	Pts
20. Oxford	46	12	9	25	43	73	45
21. Cardiff	46	9	17	20	45	67	44
22. Blackpool	46	8	17	21	49	77	41
23. Scunthorpe	46	9	12	25	40	74	39
24. Chesterfield	46	7	15	24	34	63	36

A decline in form to such an extent after finishing in the top half of the table (just) in each of the four previous seasons since promotion was not entirely surprising, considering that such important players as Mercer, Dyche, Carr, Mark Williams, Jules, Lormor and Holland had moved on – soon to be followed by Curtis, who made the last few of his 250-plus appearances for the club during the slump to relegation. Curtis, who left with the distinction of having scored Chesterfield's 5,000th League goal, his second of the game, after a 40-yard run in a home win against Bournemouth in November 1998, went to Portsmouth for £50,000 in August 2000.

The most regular members of the side that plunged back to Division Three were Reeves, who was absent from only three matches, Hewitt, Breckin, Blatherwick, Beaumont and Ryan Williams, who were all into the 30s for games. Those with appearances in the twenties were Chris Perkins, who had rejoined from Hartlepool, Gayle, Tony Carss, a midfielder from Cardiff City, Steve Woods, a full-back from Stoke, and Willis.

Incredibly, Chesterfield bounced straight back up again in 2001. Why incredibly? Well, because they did so amid a traumatic upheaval behind the scenes which began one bleak morning in the late January of that year when a Mr Bean arrived unannounced at Saltergate. This Mr Bean was no comic character, nothing like the one depicted by Rowan Atkinson on television. Far from it. He was Graham Bean, the Football Association's compliance officer. He was accompanied by three investigators, and what a complex web of financial irregularities was revealed when Chesterfield officials were told to open their files and hand over all documentation for inspection by this joint FA-Football League inquiry. As Vivek Chaudhary remarked in his report in *The Guardian*, after seven days of exhaustive research Mr Bean concluded that it was not just the spire of Chesterfield's famous church that was crooked.

17

Former chairman Darren Brown sent to prison

Rumours of financial irregularities at Chesterfield FC had been circulating for several months before Graham Bean's surprise visit. Football League officials had received a number of anonymous telephone calls alleging that all was not as it should have been in the club's affairs, from the method of paying players to the manner in which gate receipts were declared.

Consequently, League officials had been monitoring the gate receipts and attendance figures registered at their Preston headquarters each week by Chesterfield, in accordance with the accepted procedure that applied to all member clubs, for at least two months. This revealed that at times Chesterfield would report receipts below what would have been appropriate for the submitted crowd figures. During that 2000-01 season, in which immediate promotion was so amazingly gained despite such distracting drama behind the scenes, the average attendance at Saltergate was 4,846, an increase of almost 2,000 on the previous one of relegation. Home gates ranged from a lowest of 3,796 at a draw with lowly Carlisle to a highest of just over 7,000 who saw victory over Brighton's coming champions.

It transpired that at least three of the turnstiles at Saltergate were not connected to a main computer that recorded attendance figures, and that cash was collected at these turnstiles. Sharon Wood, who was then manager of the Chesterfield lottery, Blue On The Move, confirmed: 'I was involved in the payment of cash bonuses to the team managers and certain players, and I knew that the cash used for those bonuses came out of the gate receipts from a home match against Exeter.' She claimed that 'Darren Brown's got me doing this.'

Brown was to be exposed as the central figure in this calamity. He was a 29-year-old would-be entrepreneur who had bought the club from the ageing Norton Lea in May 2000 and taken over from him as chairman. Some of those close to Brown regarded him as a charming family man. One of them described him as 'a guy that you want to work for', adding: 'I don't think there was anything deliberate. I think it just got too big for him.' To say that Brown over-reached himself was quite an under-statement. As for charm, well the nearest word to that for Chesterfield and their fans in relation to Brown was harm. And what an under-statement that was!

The findings the inquiry first announced were alarming in the extreme. No fewer than about 90 charges were brought against Darren Brown, manager Nicky Law, and eighteen players. Riding high as Chesterfield were in the Third Division, there were fears of the imposition of a points penalty so big that the club would be banished from the League. However, most of those initial findings, including the alleged illegal payments to players and an agent's receipt of £10,000, were not proven by an inquiry panel at Hillsborough. Even so, on 11 April 2001 a Football League disciplinary panel found the club guilty of irregularities over the £150,000 purchase during the 2000 close season of striker Luke Beckett from Chester City, who had just been relegated from the League, and of failing to divulge the correct gate receipts. Eight League regulations were found to have been broken. Chesterfield had nine points deducted and were fined £20,000.

The fee for Beckett, some £75,000 of which had still to be paid, was set by a tribunal. At that hearing Chesterfield presented a contract for the player that showed he was to earn £500 a week and receive a £21,000 signing-on fee. But those were not the real figures. The false ones had been put forward to reduce the size of the transfer fee. In fact, Beckett was paid £1,000 a week and a signing-on fee of £54,000. This was revealed by Dean Newman, one of the three directors (David Wood and Mike Warner were the others) who had resigned before all these shenanigans had begun to unravel.

In evidence, Newman stated that he had asked Ian Banks, manager Law's new assistant, why Beckett had two contracts. 'Ian said that when they were at the tribunal to set Beckett's transfer fee Luke's agent had said that one of the tribunal's determining factors when setting the fee was the player's contract terms. If it looked as though Beckett was earning less than he actually was, this would significantly reduce the transfer fee Chesterfield would have to pay.'

Beckett, who had been a free-transfer bargain from Barnsley for Chester, and won the Sealand Road club's Player of the Season award in 1999-2000, scored 22 goals in the 62 League games he played for Chesterfield before moving to Stockport in 2002. His 45 goals in 84 appearances for Stockport persuaded Sheffield United to pay £50,000 for him towards the end of 2004, but he spent much of the next two seasons on loan to Oldham and Huddersfield. He scored the winning goal against Bradford City that saved Oldham from relegation in 2005. Huddersfield became his last League club, for a transfer fee of £85,000. From there he went to Gainsborough Trinity, Worksop Town on loan, and Goole. His final tally of League goals was not far short of 150.

Darren Brown, who had stepped down as Chesterfield's chairman the month before the League announced the penalties they had imposed, expressed delight, along with the newly appointed chief executive, John Green, at what they believed to be the clearing of their names by the disciplinary panel's verdict, and at the acquittal of twenty of the club's other employees. But for both there was to be complete disillusionment. On 23 April, less than a fortnight after the outcome of the League's deliberations, Green had only just completed his monthly ritual of convincing the players that they would be paid when he was himself suspended for four days by the new owner, Andy Cooke, a businessman in the motor trade to whom Brown had transferred his Chesterfield shares. The reasons for the ban remained unclear. 'I'm devastated,' said Green. 'I've become the scapegoat for the political manoeuvring within the club.'

He added that the mood of the players had turned 'rebellious' when the wages had failed to appear. Only an assurance from Cooke to Law had placated them. Green revealed that the club had been compelled to take loans from the Professional Footballers' Association in order to cover wages. The first one had been repaid, but the second, of £36,000, was still outstanding.

For Darren Brown, the repercussions were far greater. Events eventually caught up with him in September 2005, when he was sentenced to four years in prison for his actions in driving the Chesterfield club to the brink of ruin in the few months during which he had been chairman. It transpired that Lea had agreed to sell out to him for £1.2 million, payable in instalments. Brown had made a £384,000 down payment, but £399,000 had gone out of the club to Brown's printing company.

Following investigations by Derbyshire Police after a complaint from the FA in March 2001, Brown had pleaded guilty to two charges of fraudulent trading, to having taken £800,000 of Chesterfield's money to repay those from whom he had borrowed to meet the first instalment, to clear the debts of the ice hockey team Sheffield Steelers he owned, and to live in style. This miner's son, who had left Old Hall Comprehensive School in Rotherham at sixteen for a job with British Gas, had also used the Chesterfield club's cash for a £55,000 deposit on a spanking new house, ordered Mercedes, Land Rover and BMW club company cars for his own use, and spent, among other excesses, £2,500 on a lawnmower.

The taking-over of the investigation by the Serious Fraud Office led to nineteen more charges, including false accounting, supplying false information, and theft. Brown pleaded not guilty to three charges and fourteen were left on file. Andy Marples, an accountant who worked for Brown and Chesterfield, was sentenced in 2003 to 240 hours' community service after FA investigators had found a dozen false invoices in his briefcase, for £470,000 purported management and consultancy services from Brown's other companies. Brown had been banned from British ice hockey for his 'total mismanagement' of Sheffield Steelers, who were facing financial ruin after being fined £50,000 by the Superleague, and he had stepped down as head of the UK Sports Group which owned the Steelers and another ice hockey team, Hull Thunder. The Sheffield Sharks basketball team, another of Brown's former concerns, also had financial problems.

It was, however, at Chesterfield FC that the main damage was done. And great credit for its exposure was due to Jim Brown, the commercial manager, and three women, bookkeeper Joan Muir, and her young assistants, Aimee Miles and Joanne Hadley, who worked with him in the office at Saltergate. They defied Darren Brown to record all the money that was going out of the club for no valid reason. 'We'd worked for the previous board,' Jim Brown told *The Guardian*'s David Conn, 'so we knew the proper way to run the club. In the very first week Darren Brown was paying money out with no invoices, so we began to keep a log.' This supported the charges later brought against Darren Brown after being handed to the police and Serious Fraud Office, and there can be little doubt that if Jim Brown and his colleagues had kept quiet Darren Brown would have driven the club out of business. There would have been nobody else to stop him. Former goalkeeper Jim Brown clearly made his greatest 'save' for the club on that occasion, but that was not properly acknowledged in the anxiety to put the whole appalling affair out of mind. The absence of a testimonial for him was presumably an oversight.

Jim Brown was left feeling hard done by for another reason. 'We had to stand up in front of Darren Brown and tell the truth, which we did to get him out and save the club,' he said. 'Afterwards, we were very disappointed that nothing was immediately being done to stop him, and then we had to go to work the following day for him. The girls showed great courage to do the right thing, but nobody from the League has said "Thank you" or shown appreciation for the risks the staff took.' Joan Muir later went to work for Norton Lea, and the two other women also left the club.

A League spokesman conceded that 'those who gave evidence clearly made a very important contribution, and perhaps it's fair to accuse the League of being too inward-looking in the immediate aftermath of the Chesterfield tribunal.'

How very different it had all appeared when Darren Brown had swept in promising to boost Chesterfield's fortunes as part of his much vaunted UK Sports Group. With the attack sharpened by Beckett's link-up with Reeves, the defence strengthened by the signing of goalkeeper Mike Pollitt from Rotherham, and the midfield spruced up with Sean Parrish from Northampton and Lee Richardson from Livingston, the Spireites soared straight to the top of the Third Division and were twelve points clear of second-placed Brighton, if with four games more played, when Graham Bean came calling. Other signings, made soon after the season had got under way, included defenders Rob Edwards, from Huddersfield, and Steve Payne, from Macclesfield.

Only one defeat was suffered in the first 21 League games – and that, by the odd goal of three, at home to Barnet, a club heading back to the Conference as wooden spoonists. That, though, was just a minor setback compared with the seven-goal thrashing Barnet handed out to Blackpool, who went up through the play-offs.

After their Barnet blip on 2 September, Chesterfield went sixteen matches unbeaten, beginning with six wins in a row, before a 2-3 slip-up at Southend on the third Saturday of December. They then played fourteen more without defeat until they conceded three goals without reply at Plymouth in early March. From that point, however, the growing awareness of the turmoil building up in the club's affairs had such a detrimental effect on the team's performances that only two more victories were gained, both at home, in the remaining nine matches. The first of those was by Beckett's lone goal against League newcomers Kidderminster, the other on the final day by 3-0 against Halifax Town, who would have dropped out of the League instead of Barnet if the Hertfordshire club had ended with a win at home to Torquay. Three down at half-time, Barnet made a great effort to avoid being the ones to be replaced by Rushden & Diamonds, that season's Conference champions, but they were left two points adrift of Halifax in failing to claw back more than two goals.

Chesterfield's lapses on the run-in enabled Brighton and Cardiff to push the Derbyshire club into the third automatic promotion place. Understandably, there was a widespread feeling of injustice that the Spireites' nine-point penalty was made meaningless. There was even a suggestion that it might be increased, but that came to nothing. Hartlepool United had reason to feel most aggrieved, finishing three points behind Chesterfield in fourth place after their club record sequence of 21 games undefeated, and then losing to Blackpool, the lowest of the four play-off qualifiers, in both legs of their semi-final.

Brighton were never out of the top three from mid-October, nor Cardiff from January. It was away to Brighton, in their penultimate match on May Day, that Chesterfield clinched promotion despite being beaten, Hull's challenge fading in a draw at Southend. Smart saves by Pollitt, and a fine chance missed by Brighton's top scorer, Bobby Zamora, delayed the deciding goal until twelve minutes from time, when Danny Cullip headed home from Paul Watson's corner-kick. These were the teams:

Brighton: Kuipers; Watson, Mayo, Cullip, Crosby, Carpenter, Zamora, Rogers, Hart (Steele), Oatway (Melton), Brooker (Thomas). Subs not used: Jones, Wicks.

Chesterfield: Pollitt; Pearce, Edwards, Payne, Beaumont) Breckin, Ebdon, Williams, R, Reeves, Howard, Ingledow.

Beckett substituted for Howard; Beaumont and Williams were replaced by two youth trainees – Danny Barrett, who had few other opportunities before joining Matlock Town, and Andy Rushbury, who moved to Telford United. Goalkeeper Armstrong and Mike Simpkins, a former Wednesday defender later with Cardiff, were the unused subs. Final positions at the top of the Third Division:

Season 2000-01	P	W	D	L	F	A	Pts
1. Brighton	46	28	8	10	73	35	92
2. Cardiff	46	23	13	10	95	58	82
3. Chesterfield*	46	25	14	7	79	42	80
4. Hartlepool	46	21	14	11	71	54	77
5. Leyton Orient	46	20	15	11	59	51	75
6. Hull	46	19	17	10	47	39	74
7. Blackpool	46	22	6	18	74	58	72
8. Rochdale	46	18	17	11	59	48	71

* Nine points deducted

For all the aggrieved feelings elsewhere, those figures emphasised Chesterfield's worthiness of promotion – not only in being able to absorb their penalty punishment but also in having the fewest defeats in the division, scoring more goals than the champions, gaining more victories than the runners-up, and having a healthy goal-difference. Beckett was their leading scorer with sixteen goals, plus two in the Worthington Cup. Reeves totalled fifteen, all but two of them in the League, followed by Párrish (ten and one Worthington goal), Ryan Williams (eight) and Howard and Willis (five apiece). Three of Reeves' goals were penalties. Parrish and Williams both converted one.

Pollitt alone played in all 46 League games, and in all but one of the club's nine ties in the knock-out competitions (the first leg in the opening round of the Worthington Cup, away to Port Vale, for which Armstrong deputised). But that was Pollitt's only season with Chesterfield. Back he went to Rotherham, where he was rated as arguably the best keeper in the club's history, with a record number of clean sheets. Later he was with Wigan in the Premiership, and helped them to the 2006 Carling Cup final in which they lost to Manchester United, the club with which he had begun his professional career – but without appearing in their first team.

Breckin also missed only one of Chesterfield's matches in the promotion season of 2000-01, but that was in the League, in the defeat at Southend shortly before Christmas. He was an ever-present in the knock-out ties: the 0-1 home defeat in the FA Cup by Bristol City (who were owed more than £16,000 of their share of the gate); the two-leg games of the first two rounds in the Worthington Cup, ending with a 0-4 beating at Fulham after a 1-0 win at home; and in an LDV Vans Trophy run that reached a fourth game, lost 1-4 at Lincoln in the Northern semifinal, after a 'sudden death' 104th-minute goal by Ryan Williams had retrieved the surrendering of a 3-0 half-time lead in the first round at Rotherham.

The next most regular member of Chesterfield's team that season was Marcus Ebdon, a Welsh Under-21 midfielder who had been signed from Peterborough in March 1977, during Duncan's time as manager, for a fee said to be £100,000. He made 41 Third Division appearances and was absent from only that Rotherham marathon in the knock-outs. His total of games for the club amounted to around 200 before his move to Leyton Orient in 2003. He retired from playing two years later while with Tamworth, but was persuaded back into action in being reunited at Alfreton Town with former Tamworth managers Gary Mills and Darren Gee. In January 2007, Ebdon was appointed Alfreton's manager for the rest of the season after Gee had joined Mills as assistant manager at Tamworth, and the trio came together again the following summer when Ebdon moved to that Staffordshire club as youth development officer.

After Ebdon in the Spireites' list of 2000-01 League appearances came the former Tranmere forward Ryan Williams (39, plus six as sub), Beckett (38, plus three), Blatherwick (38), Reeves (34 plus three), Edwards (34), Parrish and Payne (both 33 plus two) and Richardson (30).

The promotion that those players, and sixteen others who were called upon, helped to achieve in such traumatic circumstances gave supporters an unexpected silver lining to the black cloud cast by the transformation of the club's finances from solvency to huge debts. But it was not until after the formation of a supporters' trust, the Chesterfield Football Supporters Society, at an emotional meeting attended by more than 1,000 fans at the town's Winding Wheel theatre in March 2001, that the true scale of the liabilities became widely known.

Within five days of that meeting, which turned into something of a revivalist rally with the singing of 'We Can Build Our Dreams', a song from the FA Cup semi-final year, Andrew Cooke, Darren Brown's business associate who had become the new owner, recognised the fans' solidarity and offered the football club to the trust. To save it, the trust bought it, but then discovered that the Saltergate ground had been hocked to guarantee a loan, and that the debts were as high as £2 million, including a £439,000 loan from the UK Sports Group. Fears that the ground would be repossessed by the moneylenders spurred several wealthy supporters, including Barrie Hubbard, Mike Warner, Phil Taylor and Alan Walters, to pay them off.

The only thing the Supporters Society could do in view of the desperate situation caused by Darren Brown's catastrophic chairmanship was to put the club into administration. After the payment of the debts and overdue tax, it was agreed to give the remaining creditors the three £183,000 instalments due from the Football League's lucrative television deal with ITV Digital, but when that collapsed in April 2002 it was immediately obvious that the debts could not be met. Phil Tooley, a founder member of the CFSS board, commented: 'A fan-owned club can achieve a great deal when starting from scratch, as the relative successes of AFC Wimbledon, AFC Telford and FC United have shown, but the experience at York, Stockport, Chesterfield and elsewhere shows that if you start with massive debt it's very difficult. We believe CFSS kept the club in existence, restored its good name, and then we were pragmatic about what was needed.'

The Supporters Society remained the club's owners, having bought it for £6,240, but handed management control to Hubbard, Warner, Walters and Jason Elliott, a fan who had won the club's lottery. Those four loaned enough to pay creditors and service the ongoing struggle to keep operating. In 2005, at about the time Darren Brown was starting his prison sentence, CFSS agreed to dilute their ownership, distributing shares equally to the 2,000 members. Four years later, a controlling 80 per cent stake was bought by Dave Allen, a friend of Hubbard's who owned a 99.9 per cent share of the A&S Leisure Group that ran casinos across England and the greyhound racing track at Sheffield's Owlerton Stadium. According to the *Sunday Times*, Allen was the 944th richest person in

Britain in 2006, said to be worth £60 million, but by the following year he had dropped out of the country's top 1,000 richest.

Allen was a substantial holder of Sheffield Wednesday shares, but he had resigned from that club's board in November 2007 because, as chairman, he had no longer been prepared to put up with the abuse he had been getting from supporters of the Owls who had criticised him and his colleagues on websites. He had taken legal action, but most of the charges had been dismissed by Richard Parkes QC, a High Court judge, as 'trivial' and the outcome of no more than 'saloon bar moanings', and all had eventually been dropped.

This animosity between Wednesday's chairman and supporters had stemmed from the fans' opinion that Allen had put less money into the club than they had expected. Against that, the aggrieved Allen resented the unpopularity he had incurred at Hillsborough because of the formidable task the board had faced when he had joined it during 2000 following the departure of Sir David Richards to become the Premier League's chairman. Wednesday had then been £20 million in debt and on the brink of inescapable relegation. The debt was reduced while Allen was chairman, and Wednesday rose first to Division One, then to the Championship.

After all the ill-will he encountered over in Yorkshire, Allen was attracted to Chesterfield by the feeling of being associated with a happier legacy. 'I came to a couple of games,' he said, 'and found there are a lot of nice people at the club. I agreed to put some money in, take Chesterfield to the Championship in five years, then sell and make a profit.' That fitted in perfectly with his description of himself as 'a businessman through and through', but he did add that he might stay involved – as he did to the extent of eventually becoming chairman. As the Spireites' supporters readily recognised, in sharp contrast to how those at Hillsborough had felt, Allen was actually more generous than he had originally indicated. He paid £4 million to the club for the new shares, and afterwards loaned £3.5 million at five per cent interest.

Yet, as he admitted in an interview with the *Chesterfield Post*, 'football was the last thing on my mind after Sheffield Wednesday when Barrie Hubbard approached me to see if it was interested in going to Chesterfield. He originally asked me to look after the catering side of the business, as that's our speciality, but he eventually offered me the chance to get involved with the whole lot. I wasn't bothered at first, but he brought me some plans and it was after seeing them that I decided to get involved.'

Allen continued to own ten per cent of Sheffield Wednesday until

December 2010, when he sold his shares to the club's new owner, Milan Mandaric. The initial price was £750,000, but to be doubled with a return to the Premiership.

Alan Walters took over from John Green as Chesterfield's chief executive under the new Saltergate set-up. He also succeeded Stephanie Otter as secretary, and continued in that role when further administrative changes were made in 2003. Mike Warner then became chief executive. Barrie Hubbard was reinstated as chairman, with Jason Elliott vice-chairman, before Hubbard handed over to Allen on being made the club's life president in 2012. By that time David Jones had become vice-chairman, Warner managing director, and Walters financial director.

In 2004 the Creditors' Voluntary Agreement that had been hanging over the club for the past three years was paid off, thanks to financial input from the Chesterfield Council.

Meanwhile, as we shall be coming to in the next chapter, there were further changes of manager, a lot of belt-tightening as great reliance had to be put on loans or free transfers, and hair-raising escapes from the relegation they could not elude in 2007, before Chesterfield FC became a force to be reckoned with again. And, as if all that were not enough, there was the exciting brand new beginning in the offing with the move to the B2net stadium at 1866 Sheffield Road, Whittington Moor.

18

An influx of players from abroad

Chesterfield went increasingly close to relegation through the first three seasons after winning promotion under the handicap of their nine-point penalty, and also had two more changes of manager.

In January 2002, Dave Rushbury, the club's physiotherapist, who also held a UEFA 'A' licence, filled the vacancy left by Nicky Law's departure to manage Bradford City, taking his assistant Ian Banks with him. Rushbury's appointment was originally as caretaker, with Lee Richardson as his assistant and Jamie Hewitt, who was awarded a thoroughly deserved testimonial in 1999, moving up from youth team physio to fill the same role with the senior players. Rushbury was confirmed as manager after seeing Chesterfield to Division Two safety, three points clear of the relegation zone in eighteenth place, but the team became involved in an even more fraught struggle against the drop the following season, and he departed in April 2003, complaining of abuse from supporters.

There were then only two games to go, and from them Chesterfield preserved their status, though with only two points to spare immediately above the trapdoor, by winning 2-0 at home to third-placed Bristol City (who missed promotion from the play-offs) and drawing 1-1 at mid-table Blackpool. Nine days after that final match the new manager was named: Roy McFarland, the former Derby and England centre-half. He had just resigned at Torquay after the Devon club's chairman, Mike Bateson, had decreed that McFarland's assistant must also be a player – and that had meant the undesired departure of David Preece, who had only recently given up playing. McFarland was also a very convenient choice for Chesterfield because, although he was a Liverpudlian, he considered himself 'a Derbyshire person'. He had lived in the county since joining the Rams from Tranmere Rovers in 1967, and had made his home at Quarndon, a village a few miles north of Derby, since his marriage in 1973.

As a player, McFarland had been right at the forefront. He feared he had made the biggest mistake of his life by signing for Derby, then Second Division strugglers, instead of waiting for the call he hoped for from high-flying Liverpool, after the Rams' manager, the volatile Brian Clough, had got him out of bed and refused to leave without having his name on the transfer form. But it turned out anything but a mistake. Fresh from helping Tranmere out of the Fourth Division, McFarland went on to play more than 500 times for Derby, a dominant figure when they were League champions for the first time, and 28 for England. And there would have been more games for both club and country but for injuries – the worst of which, an Achilles tendon severely damaged against Northern Ireland at Wembley, caused McFarland to miss all but the last four matches of the 1974-75 season in which the Rams won the First Division title for the second time in four years.

As a manager, McFarland had mixed fortunes. He took Bradford City to promotion as Fourth Division runners-up in 1981-82, but rejoined Derby as assistant manager in controversial circumstances. They were fined £10,000 by the League and had to pay the Bradford club £55,000 in compensation for alleged poaching. McFarland subsequently became the County's manager – first temporarily when Peter Taylor left, then when Arthur Cox, to whom he had also been assistant, resigned because of back trouble – but he was dismissed on missing the play-offs the year after defeat by Leicester in the Division One final at Wembley. Next, he lasted only six months at Bolton as they headed for relegation from the Premier League to which they had just risen under the management of his former Derby team-mate Bruce Rioch. After that, McFarland preceded his time at Torquay with another promotion, for Cambridge United as Third Division runners-up in 1998-99, but he was sacked early in 2001 amid a struggle, ultimately successful, for survival.

Later that year, life for Chesterfield back in the Nationwide Division Two ran into trouble right from the start of six matches without a win as they also strove to protect their newly won status. Colchester's visit on the opening day came as a particular shock for the new goalkeeper, Nathan Abbey, who had to pick the ball out of his net six times. Abbey, a Londoner, had been a first-team regular in only one of his six seasons with Luton Town, who had released him after descending into the League's basement, but despite that discouraging debut for Chesterfield and the team's inability to escape from the bottom half of the table, he won the club's Player of the Year award and did what his predecessor, Mike Pollitt, had done – played in all 46 League games. Like Pollitt, too, he stayed for only the one season. He failed to agree a new contract and set off doing the rounds with a dozen other clubs, ranging from Northampton to Kettering.

Other Chesterfield newcomers in the 2001-02 season included Glynn Hurst, a striker from Stockport County, Mark Innes, a defender from Oldham Athletic, and Stuart Howson, a midfielder from Blackburn, each on a free transfer. With the purse strings as tight as ever, great dependency was again placed on loans, the most notable of which brought the return from Oldham of Mark Allott as a prelude to his free re-signing in February. On the day of Allott's comeback, 19 December, Dave Reeves ended his first spell with Chesterfield by going in the opposite direction, also originally on loan before being signed. Among the last of some 50 goals Reeves had by then scored in more than 170 games for Chesterfield was a 93rd minute 'sudden death' decider against Kidderminster Harriers that earned an LDV Vans Trophy quarter-final at home to Blackpool, but it was the Seasiders who went on to success in the final at Cardiff's Millennium Stadium.

With Chesterfield's source of goals also depleted by the transfer of the adaptable Ryan Williams to Hull City for a reported £150,000 (almost double the price said to have been paid for him), Glynn Hurst headed the scorers with just nine goals in his first Chesterfield season. Hurst was born at Barnsley but spent some time in South Africa, representing that country at Under-23 level, before returning to England and joining Tottenham Hotspur as an apprentice. He was back at Barnsley for his entry into League football, though only briefly, and his 84 appearances at that level for Chesterfield (29 goals) before leaving for Notts County were the most he made for one club before getting within four of a century for Bury.

The most regular members of the Spireites side after Abbey in 2001-02 were Steve Payne, Ian Breckin, Martyn Booty and Rob Edwards. Booty, a defender, gained experience with Crewe and Reading before arriving from Southend, and he had more than 300 League games behind him by the time, in 2003, he moved on to Huddersfield. Peter Jackson, newly reappointed as the Yorkshire club's manager, saw him as a key player in the rebuilding necessary after two relegations in three seasons, but Booty was appointed to the coaching staff instead after soon dropping out of the team through injury. Buxton were among the non-League clubs with which he was subsequently associated.

The 'new' goalkeeper who replaced Nathan Abbey made his 23rd League appearance for Chesterfield in their opening match of the 2002-03 season. After his stints on loan, from first Leicester, then Stoke, Carl Muggleton came back as a signed player, hailed by manager Dave Rushbury as 'a mature goalkeeper who will provide the voice of experience behind our younger defenders'. That maturity came from over 200 games spread among more than a dozen clubs, most of which Muggleton had played for on loan, and one England Under-21 match, won 7-3 against France at Toulon in 1990.

After being confined to a half-century of first-team appearances in seven years with Leicester, his home club (including the 1992 Second

Division play-off final against Blackburn in which he saved a penalty but ended on the losing side), Muggleton made over 170 in seven more years with Stoke, who paid £150,000 for him during the 1994 close season. On being released by Stoke in 2001 he joined Cheltenham, but was unable to dislodge Steve Book as first choice and went on loan to Bradford City before again becoming available. That was when Chesterfield stepped in, and he exceeded 120 games for them before leaving 'by mutual consent' in 2006. He then guarded Mansfield's goal in just over 50 games, taking his career total beyond 550, but was not retained after the Stags' relegation to the Conference National at the end of the 2007-08 season.

Muggleton would almost certainly have been an ever-present in his first season as a Chesterfield player, as well as his second, but for being out of action for about six weeks with a double stress fracture of the fibula suffered during a narrow defeat at Brentford in mid-December. The local-born Andy Richmond, who had been taken on as a youth trainee, made his League debut as substitute and he stood in for the next three matches before Ben Williams was obtained on loan from Manchester United. 'We must be doing something right,' said Rushbury, 'because United don't let players out on loan unless they are confident they will be properly looked after.'

Williams was allowed to stay at Saltergate until Muggleton was fit to return for Chesterfield's last five matches of that 2002-03 season. There was never room for Williams in the first team at Old Trafford, but he got into a third century of appearances in a career that took him to Crewe, Carlisle and Colchester before he went into the Scottish League with Hibernian. While at Crewe he made a full recovery after being taken ill with meningitis; at both Carlisle and Colchester he was voted Player of the Year.

With Chesterfield, however, Williams had the misfortune to be pitched into a team heading for decline after making a promising start to the season. In late September the Spireites were as high as fifth after beating Blackpool at the end of a run of eight games in which the only goals they conceded were the three to which they could muster no reply at Luton. They were still in the top half of the table, ninth, after Williams' first game for the club, won at home to Luton on New Year's Day, but ten more matches then went by before another victory was gained. Hence the desperate struggle to stay up that led to Rushbury's exit shortly before safety was so slenderly snatched. The win against Bristol City in the penultimate match, avenging one of the club's biggest defeats of the season, by 4-0 at Ashton Gate, was the only one Chesterfield gained in their last seven games.

In four of those seven, in succession, Chesterfield failed to score, a symptom of the big weakness that resulted in nineteen blanks in all and a minus goal-difference of 30. Again the club's top scorer in the League fell short of double figures, in a team total of 43 – ten fewer than the previous season. This time the way was led by Dave Reeves, welcomed back from Oldham for another couple of seasons before going into Northern Ireland football with Ards. Reeves managed eight, one of them a penalty. Next, both with seven, came Hurst and Chris Brandon, a newcomer on a free transfer from Torquay who was voted Chesterfield's top player of that 2002-03 season. The Bradford-born Brandon was a late starter in League football. After being released from Bradford City's youth academy he was with Bradford PA, Farsley Celtic and Stafford Rangers before joining Torquay in 1999 at the age of 23.

Brandon, though specialising in 'wonder' goals, was never a prolific scorer (fewer than 50 in his career of more than 350 games), but he did get into double figures in that first of his two Chesterfield seasons with the addition of the Worthington Cup equaliser that earned a replay lost at West Ham by 4-5 on penalties, and his two goals of an LDV Vans Trophy tie in which Port Vale also had the better of a spot-kick shoot-out, by 4-3. Brandon might also have headed the League list but for a damaged hamstring. Chesterfield finished with only nine men when Brandon and Caleb Folan, a free signing from Leeds, were both injured during a home defeat by Brentford at a crucial late stage of the battle for survival. All three substitutes, of whom Folan was one, had already been used.

Brandon attracted interest from Nottingham Forest before leaving in 2004 for Huddersfield Town, who had been promoted straight back to the Second Division (on penalties in the play-off final) after being one of the clubs relegated below Chesterfield in 2003. That quickly pitted him against the Derbyshire club, coincidentally on his home debut for the Terriers, and Muggleton had to make a couple of smart saves to deny him a goal in a scoreless draw. Brandon was later with Blackpool, on loan, and Bradford City before going into the Thailand Premier League. Folan also went abroad, to the United States with Colorado Rapids, after following just over 100 games for Chesterfield with service at Wigan (who paid £500,000 for him in January 2007), Hull and on loan to Middlesbrough. He was born at Leeds, but after leaving Chesterfield he played for the Republic of Ireland, eligible through the Irish nationality of his grandparents.

The other players Roy McFarland inherited when he took over as manager on 12 May 2003 included two products of the North-East,

Kevin Dawson, a free-transfer defender from Nottingham Forest, and Mark Hudson, a midfielder signed only that March from Middlesbrough after a spell on loan. Alan O'Hare, who hailed from Drogheda in the Irish Republic, had also joined after being on loan, opting for regular first-team football with Chesterfield, again with no transfer fee, instead of being confined to Bolton's reserve side. Naturally left-footed, O'Hare fitted in at left-back, but also played at centre-back with some success. All three were in the team McFarland fielded on the first day of the 2003-04 season, drawn goalless at Wrexham: Muggleton; Uhlenbeek, O'Hare, Dawson, Blatherwick, Payne, Brandon, Hudson, Allott (Reeves), Hurst, Evatt.

Ian Evatt was McFarland's first target on being appointed. He made the short journey from Derby that July, having started out with the Rams at the age of eleven and been a professional since his seventeenth birthday in November 1998. He came with Premiership experience – albeit only in two appearances as a sub, and one full one in relegated Derby's final match of the 2001-02 season. He would win Chesterfield's top-player award of 2003-04, rise to the captaincy, and come back after a second hernia operation, before moving to QPR for £150,000 in June 2005 only because there was a clause in his contract that allowed him to move if a six-figure bid were received.

Evatt was later with Blackpool, originally on loan, and twice helped them to promotion via the play-offs – to the Coca-Cola Championship in 2007, and to the Barclays Premier League in 2010. This time he had a fuller taste of life among the elite, to the extent of being the Seasiders' only player to take part in all their 38 matches of 2010-11, two of them as substitute. That, though, was as far as it went. Immediate relegation was a cruel outcome of the club's first rise to the top flight for more than 40 years.

The fact that O'Hare now had a Dutchman as his full-back partner was, of course, a sign of the times, with an ever-increasing number of players from abroad entering the British game. Gus Uhlenbeek was born at Paramaribo in the former Dutch colony of Suriname, but he grew up in Amsterdam. He first played in England for Ipswich Town, who had most successfully looked to Holland for Arnold Muhren and Frans Thijssen when, during the late 1970s, soccer talent in the Football League from outside the UK had been a contrasting novelty. Uhlenbeek was also with Fulham, Sheffield United, Walsall (on loan) and Bradford City before having just the one season with Chesterfield, and he completed his dozen years in England with Wycombe, Mansfield and Halifax. His League appearances totalled just under 380.

Chesterfield's other foreign imports during the early years of the 21st century included two Germans, Thomas Hitzlsperger and Felix Bastians, Hungarian Janos Kovacs, Frenchman Sebastien Grimaldi, Australians Aaron Downes and Nicky Rizzo, Val Teixeira, who was born in Lisbon, Davide Somma from South Africa, and Tcham N'Toya, who came from Kinshasa in the Democratic Republic of Congo (formerly Zaire). There was also Ishmel Demontagnac. With a name like that – so lengthy that there was room for only Ishmel on the back of his shirt – he appeared to be an obvious addition to this list, but he was born in the Newham borough of London and played in England's Under-18 and 19 teams. The same deceptive first impression was given by the names of three other Londoners who played for Chesterfield: Mark DeBolla, of Italian and French ancestry, Jamal Campbell-Ryce who played for Jamaica by parentage, and Kieran Djilali, whose father was a Jamaican and his mother of Moroccan/Welsh parents.

Of those players, the one who made most appearances for Chesterfield, by a considerable margin, was Aaron Downes, a defender who was given trials by Bolton Wanderers and had a short spell with Frickley Athletic before McFarland signed him on the first day of August in 2004. By the time he was released at the end of the 2011-12 season, soon after being loaned to Bristol Rovers, he had played for the Spireites in some 200 games, 174 of them in the League, and succeeded to the captaincy in 2007 when Mark Allott moved to Oldham. Downes had also played almost a dozen times for the Australian Under-23 team and featured in the 2005 FIFA world youth championship in the Netherlands. His compatriot Rizzo, a midfielder, was capped by Australia and played in the Nationwide First Division for Crystal Palace, but turned out only four times for Chesterfield while on loan from Milton Keynes Dons.

Next behind Downes for League games with Chesterfield among that overseas talent came Janos Kovacs, a 6ft 4in defender. He was also signed by McFarland, in 2005, from the Budapest club MTK, but had his only season as a regular member of the side, with 41 of his 57 games, in 2007-08, by which time McFarland had left. Although offered a new contract, Kovacs decided against it when prospects of keeping his place faded with the signing of Kevin Austin from Swansea, and he was transferred to Lincoln for a fee of £17,500 decreed by tribunal. He subsequently had two spells with Luton divided by a season with Hereford.

N'Toya, a striker, was another who had his first experience of English football under McFarland's management, moving from the French club Troyes in 2004. He also completed a half-century of appearances, then was given a free transfer to Notts County after loans to York and Oxford.

Steve Thompson, then the Notts manager, welcomed him as 'an untapped talent with outstanding pace and strength', but he added only one League goal to the eight he had scored for Chesterfield before having an unsuccessful trial with St Mirren and then going into the Israeli Premier League.

DeBolla, who was born at Camberwell, began as a 16-year-old trainee striker with Aston Villa. He was then snapped up by Charlton Athletic, but failed to break into their first team despite impressing in the Under-19 side. Having first joined Chesterfield on loan in September 2003, he was signed on a free transfer the following March and had one season as a regular choice before also leaving for Notts County. From there he drifted out of the Football League, but had a match to remember in scoring a dramatic late winner for AFC Wimbledon against Staines Town in the 2008 Isthmian League play-off final.

Of those others from abroad who played for Chesterfield, on short-term loans, the one with the most impressive background was Hitzlsperger, a midfielder from Munich who graduated through Germany's Youth and Under-21 teams to play in 52 full internationals. He made only five League appearances for Chesterfield during the 2001-02 season while on loan from Aston Villa, with whom he was just one short of 100 more before returning to his home country with Stuttgart. After that he was briefly in Italy with Lazio before moving back into England at West Ham.

For home-grown talent, Roy McFarland followed up his signing of Ian Evatt by going back to Derby for Marvin Robinson, a Crewe-born striker who played for England Under-18 Boys while at Wolverhampton Grammar School. Robinson, a strapping six-footer, turned professional with Derby in June 1998, but he had the misfortune to break a leg while on loan to Stoke and was out of action for eighteen months before making a scoring comeback at Sunderland in the Rams' last match of the 2001-02 season. His second-half goal as a substitute, his only one for the club in just a dozen games, earned a point, but Derby were already doomed to relegation from the Premiership. In his one season with Chesterfield Robinson made fifteen of his 32 League appearances as a sub, and was their second-highest scorer with just six goals to Hurst's thirteen. He netted another in an LDV Vans victory over Macclesfield that led to a frustratingly late defeat at Lincoln City. The Imps equalised at 3-3 with an 85th-minute penalty, then won 'on slow death' in the fifth minute of extra-time.

After being with half-a-dozen other clubs, Robinson rejoined his former Derby manager Jim Smith at Oxford, but while out on loan to

Cambridge he again broke a leg, and also bruised his lungs, in a car crash. On recovering he played for several non-League teams – most effectively with four goals in Hednesford Town's record 9-0 win against Weymouth.

Another McFarland recruit in his first season as Chesterfield's manager also had to overcome adversity – to a greater degree heathwise. This was Derek Niven, a Scottish midfielder who played only once in the first team for Raith Rovers, and not at all for Bolton, but did so more than 300 times for Chesterfield before being released at the end of the 2011-12 season. He had made 199 of his 297 League appearances for the Spireites when, in November 2008, the club confirmed that he was undergoing treatment for testicular cancer. His return to the team the following March was marked by a 'wonder' winner fifteen minutes from the end of a home match with Grimsby Town. Just over a year later, as we shall be coming to in its proper turn, he scored another memorable goal, one that gave him a unique place in the history of Chesterfield football.

Before that special occasion for club and Niven, however, McFarland was unable to inspire a Saltergate revival. Indeed, the first season under his management ended with an even closer brush with relegation than the previous one. Again Chesterfield finished twentieth, this time with only one point to spare. And their fate was in the balance right to the 88th minute of their very last match, in which Glynn Hurst at last broke the deadlock against visitors from Luton. But for his lone goal Grimsby would have stayed up instead of Chesterfield, despite ending with defeat away to ten-man Tranmere Rovers after leading at half-time. Only a few weeks earlier the Mariners had been held 4-4 at Saltergate by the 90th-minute second penalty in a Dave Reeves hat-trick. These were the final figures on the relegation fringe:

Season 2003-2004	P	W	D	L	F	A	Pts
20. Chesterfield	46	12	15	19	49	71	51
21. Grimsby	46	13	11	22	55	81	50

The others to go down were Rushden & Diamonds (48 points), Notts County (42) and Wycombe Wanderers (37).

After starting with four drawn games, Chesterfield lost six in a row, and went through thirteen altogether before gaining their first League win – by 3-0 at home to Swindon in mid-October, four days after the ice had been broken with the Vans victory against Macclesfield. Eight more matches then passed before the next success, by the odd goal of three at home to Peterborough on Boxing Day. The old year ended with another win, by a Hurst goal ten minutes from time at Barnsley, only for the new one to begin with a 7-0 trouncing by the leaders and coming champions at Plymouth. It was Argyle's record winning margin, equalling their 8-1 defeats of Millwall in 1932 and Hartlepool United in 1994. Six of the goals came in the first half.

Not until the beginning of February did Chesterfield escape from the drop zone, during their only run of three consecutive victories, but they plunged back into it from the first Saturday of April until that dramatic last-day snatching of three vital points.

Ironically, the avoidance of a descent into the Nationwide Division Three was followed by 'promotion' to the Coca-Cola Division One before another ball had been kicked. This was due to the new set-up whereby the change of Football League sponsorship turned the Nationwide Division One into the Coca-Cola Championship, the two other League divisions being numbered one and two instead of two and three. In each of the first two seasons under this arrangement Chesterfield steered six points clear of relegation, but third time was not lucky for either them or their manager. Down they went in 2007, and on 12 March that year Roy McFarland was sacked – exactly a month after his former Derby defensive partner Colin Todd was dismissed by Bradford City, relegation companions who finished on the same number of points as Chesterfield but with an inferior goal difference.

19

Premiership scalps in Cup,
but another demotion

Having so precariously weathered his first season as Chesterfield's manager under the almost constant threat of relegation, Roy McFarland appeared to be getting things right during the first few months of the next one, 2004-05. Right up to the middle of January the Spireites were in the top half of the new Coca-Cola First Division – as high as second after a home draw with Milton Keynes Dons early in September, third after a home victory against Walsall later that month, and sixth after winning at Peterborough during December.

But how wrong it all went after that. Of their last twenty League games Chesterfield won only five. Nine were lost, six drawn. Down they slipped to a final seventeenth place, but six points clear of relegation. Nor was there any comfort to be gained from the knock-out competitions. They went out of all three in the first round.

Scoring was again the big problem. In fourteen matches Chesterfield failed to find the net, and Stockport, who finished a poor last in the table, were the only club against which they managed as many as four goals. In a season's total of 55 N'Toya was top scorer with just eight. Next, with seven and six respectively, came two of the newcomers, Shane Nicholson and Wayne Allison. Caleb Folan also netted six. All but one of Nicholson's goals came from the penalty spot.

This, in fact, was the second time Nicholson had joined Chesterfield. He was first signed by them in August 1998 on the lifting of a ban imposed on him while with West Bromwich Albion for failing a drugs test that revealed traces of amphetamines. He had got to know his new colleagues at Saltergate in training with Chesterfield after being sacked by Albion, but on that occasion he stayed for only one season before being given a free transfer to Stockport County. His previous moves had cost £100,000 from Lincoln City to Derby County, and £150,000 from the Rams to WBA.

Nicholson became Lincoln's youngest League player at the age of sixteen years and 172 days before being substituted in a defeat at Burnley on 22 November 1986, but that was the season in which the club dropped out of the League for the fourth time in their then 95-year history – the first to be banished to the GM Vauxhall Conference under the new arrangement whereby the champions of the Conference, in this case Scarborough (managed by former Chesterfield player Neil Warnock), were automatically promoted to the League's lowest division in place of its bottom club. Torquay forced Lincoln into that predicament only on goal-difference, and only because Paul Dobson snatched an equaliser against Crewe in the injury-time of their final match. And that extra-time would not have been added if Jim McNichol, a Torquay defender, had not needed attention to a bite from a dog that had strayed onto the pitch.

Lincoln, however, produced what in those circumstances might be termed a dogged response. They returned to the League in 1988 as Conference champions, and Nicholson made more than 130 appearances for them at that level before his move to Derby. He was unable to hold a regular place with either the County or Albion, but totalled another century of League games between them before adding a dozen in his first stay with Chesterfield. He was brought back to Saltergate from Tranmere Rovers after also being with Sheffield United besides Stockport, each of those moves being made on a free transfer. His impressive form on his return to Chesterfield elevated him to the captaincy, but in the 2005-06 season he had to have emergency treatment for a leg infection following keyhole surgery. No sooner had he recovered and accepted a year's extension of his contract than he injured a knee in a friendly match with Sheffield Wednesday.

After that, Nicholson played in only three more first-team games for Chesterfield, each as a substitute. On 23 November 2006 he rejoined Lincoln on loan, twenty years and a day since his debut for them, and he was also with Boston United on a short loan before announcing his retirement as a player, after more than 500 League appearances, in the 2007 close season. Whereupon Chesterfield, for whom he had played in almost 100 of those games, kept him in their ranks as rehabilitation and fitness coach.

Wayne Allison, nicknamed 'The Chief', had some 700 games and more than 200 goals behind him in League and Cup when he was signed by Chesterfield, on a free transfer from Sheffield United, just a few days before Nicholson's return to Saltergate in June 2004. The Spireites were the eighth and last League club for which Allison played. The Blades had also obtained him on a free transfer, but his moves between the first six of those clubs, from Halifax to Tranmere via Watford, Bristol City, Swindon and Huddersfield, had totalled £1.975 million in transfer fees according to figures given at the time of those deals. The costliest of the lot took him to Huddersfield, his home club, for £800,000, but Bristol City benefited most from the five years he spent with them. He repaid the

Ashton Gate club's investment of £150,000 (Mark Gavin, valued at £250,000, went to Watford in exchange) with nearly 60 goals in more than 200 games, and they raked in a fee of £475,000, set by tribunal, when he moved to Swindon.

With Chesterfield, Allison completed another century of appearances, and scored more than two dozen goals, before leaving at the end of February in 2008. His first-team opportunities had dwindled, and he had applied unsuccessfully to become assistant manager. That summer he obtained a Certificate of Applied Management after completing UEFA 'A' and 'B' licenses, and early the ensuing season he was appointed manager Simon Davies' assistant at Chester City. He was also taken on as a player, but unused in the only three games for which he was among the substitutes. In November 2008, with Chester tumbling towards the loss of League status for the second time since the turn into the 21st century, Allison became caretaker manager when Davies was sacked, but he made it clear he did not want the job on a regular basis. Neither did he take up the offer for him to remain when Mark Wright, a former England central defender, was reappointed to the post. Instead, he switched to coaching with, in turn, Bury, Tranmere Rovers and Bradford City.

The team with which Chesterfield embarked upon the 2004-05 season with a 3-1 home win against Brentford in which Allison made a scoring debut included another newcomer in full-back Alex Bailey. Only Mark Allott played in as many League matches as this young Londoner for the club that season, both missing just one of the 46, yet Bailey had not previously appeared at that level during his three years with Arsenal despite having been a prominent member of the Gunners' FA Youth Cup-winning side in 2001. Bailey, who had attended the same school as Jermain Defoe, the Tottenham and England forward, also stayed for three years with Chesterfield. He then left for Halifax Town, and was later with St Albans City.

Other additions to Chesterfield's playing staff during McFarland's second season as manager were made on loan apart from the signing near the March transfer deadline of Jamie McMaster, who had himself been on loan. McMaster, an attacking type of midfielder, cost an undisclosed fee from Leeds United. Sydney-born, he was part of the Australian 'invasion' that also brought Harry Kewell and Mark Viduka into English football, but he was unable to establish himself with any of the five clubs for which he played (Coventry, Swindon and Peterborough were the others, also on loan) after committing his international prospects to England and winning Under-18 and Under-20 caps. He also stayed with AGF Aarhus in Denmark for only a short time before returning to Australia.

Sammy Clingan, a midfielder of the more defensive kind, became a particular favourite of Chesterfield fans during the two periods for which he was loaned out by Wolverhampton Wanderers to gain experience. Twice an unused sub was the closest he came to Wolves' first team, but the encouraging form he showed for the struggling Spireites led him to a regular place with Nottingham Forest, who signed him in January 2006 – and later that year to the first of the senior Northern Ireland caps he has added to those gained in the Under-21 side, which he captained.

Clingan's progress was checked when he broke an ankle in March 2007, during Forest's 5-1 defeat of Huddersfield, but he was back as a key member of the team that won promotion to the Championship the following season. Against Forest's wishes, he moved to Norwich that summer, but asked for another transfer when the Canaries were relegated to Division One at the end of his first season with them. His choice of Coventry, thinking they would give him his best chance of playing in the Premiership, backfired when, in 2011, Norwich got there instead. Coincidentally, Coventry were Norwich's visitors on the last day of the East Anglian club's promotion season, and Clingan had to endure taunts that he could have been going up with them if he had stayed. Even so, he was by then into his third century of League appearances in addition to being an established international, and although Chesterfield regretted their inability to hold on to him, they had the satisfaction of knowing that they had enabled him to kick-start his career.

Among the other players taken on loan by Chesterfield during the 2004-05 season was Mark Stallard, a Derby-born striker who had entered League football as a substitute with the Rams back in 1991. Since then, Stallard had been with half-a-dozen other clubs, twice commanding a six-figure transfer fee, playing in some 350 more games, and scoring just over 100 goals. He was nearing his 30th birthday when he reached Chesterfield from Barnsley, however, and after scoring two goals in only ten matches, in three of which he was substituted, he spent the rest of the season back on loan with Notts County, the club with which he had enjoyed most success in a stay of almost five years. His return to Meadow Lane took him past 200 games and 70 goals for the Magpies. After that he was released by Barnsley, and completed his League career with Shrewsbury and Lincoln before winding down in the Conference National and North with Mansfield Town and Corby. He then became a consultant for Paul Kerr Associates, a company that offers financial advice to professional footballers.

In his preparations for the 2005-06 season Roy McFarland pulled off a smart deal in his attempt to pep up his attack by bringing in Paul Hall, a Manchester-born Jamaican international, on a free transfer from Tranmere Rovers. Hall had been around quite a bit, having played for seven other clubs since making his debut for Torquay in 1990, and he turned 33 in the summer Chesterfield signed him. Neither was his scoring rate all that impressive up to that time – 88 goals in 524 League games – but he was a striker who played on the right wing, and he ended his first season with the Spireites as their leading marksman with fifteen goals. Allison chipped in with eleven in a team total increased to 63 as a final sixteenth place was secured, again six points from relegation.

As before, however, Chesterfield promised more than they achieved. This time they were at their best in the middle of the season, though their unbeaten run of fifteen games from November to February included eleven draws, eight of them in succession. They were next to the foot of the table during a depressing start of five defeats in seven matches, and won only one of their last eleven – and that, with two Hall goals, away to Huddersfield, who qualified for the play-offs. In between they were eighth in September, sixth in October, and fourth in November. They won more times on their travels than at Saltergate, eight to six, and their number of home defeats, ten, was the highest in the division. Victory by an only goal against Bradford City on 7 January was the last fans saw at home that season. Of the remaining ten League matches there, seven were lost and three drawn.

The heaviest defeats for McFarland's men were both inflicted by Swansea, who, like Huddersfield, reached the play-offs but missed promotion (Barnsley accounted for both, beating Huddersfield in their semi-final after losing the first leg at home, then squeezing through against the Swans on penalties in Cardiff). Against Chesterfield, Swansea won 5-1 at their new Liberty Stadium, incongruously immediately before the Derbyshire club began that undefeated fifteen-game sequence, then scored four times without reply in the return match on the season's final day.

There were two other new faces besides Hall's in the side that opened Chesterfield's season with a 3-1 win at Blackpool. Muggleton gave way in goal to Barry Roche, a Dubliner who had been in Leeds United's youth team before following Paul Hart to Nottingham Forest in 2001, and Reuben Hazell, a defender from Torquay United, went on as substitute for Adam Smith, a Huddersfield-born winger who had come through Saltergate's youth ranks.

Roche's League opportunities with Forest had been limited to an unlucky thirteen, but with Chesterfield he was an automatic choice, apart from a brief loss of form during the 2006-07 season, and he still had a year left on his contract when he moved to Morecambe in the summer of 2008. With Morecambe he surpassed the 126 League appearances he had made for Chesterfield, became club captain, and won their Player of the Season award.

Hazell, a nephew of a former Wolves and QPR defender, had been with Tranmere before Torquay after starting out as an Aston Villa trainee in his native Birmingham, and he had played at Wembley for the Birkenhead club in the 2000 Worthington Cup final won by Leicester City. He captained Oldham after leaving Chesterfield in September 2007, and was later with Shrewsbury Town. Smith, spotted playing for Kirkheaton after having trials with Huddersfield and Oldham in his mid-teens, scored in the penalty shoot-out that Chesterfield lost to Port Vale when he made his first-team debut as a substitute in the LDV Vans Trophy competition in November 2002. He then looked set for a promising career with the Spireites, but was beset by injuries. In that first match of 2005-06 he was making a comeback after having a cartilage operation, but his opportunities were restricted by further knee trouble, confirmed as severe patella tendonitis, and he was loaned to Lincoln at the beginning of 2008 following more surgery. On being released by Chesterfield that summer, he embarked upon a course in sports massage therapy and went on to continue his career with several clubs outside the Football League.

Hall, Allott, Niven and Roche were joined in making more than 40 League appearances for Chesterfield in the 2005-06 season by Colin Larkin, whose 41 included ten as a substitute. Larkin, a cousin of Keith Gorham, a caddy for golfer Tiger Woods in the late 1990s, hailed from Dundalk in the League of Ireland. A central striker or winger, he scored within eight minutes of coming off the bench for his Wolves debut in a Worthington Cup-tie lost to Wycombe Wanderers in 1999, but he failed to maintain that bright start and, after being loaned to Kidderminster Harriers, he moved to Mansfield Town for a six-figure fee during the 2002 close season. In three seasons at Field Mill he scored 25 goals in almost 100 League matches, then fell out with the club and joined Chesterfield on a two-year contract. After 90 matches, but only thirteen goals, for the Spireites he was with Northampton Town, then Hartlepool United.

Phil Picken, a full-back, was another player frequently used by Chesterfield in 2005-06. He came for the full season on loan fresh from being one of Manchester United's champions in the North Section of the FA Premier Reserve League, then was promptly signed when the Old Trafford club released him. He completed a century of appearances in remaining a regular choice for the next two seasons, but fell out of favour in 2008-08 and went on loan to Notts County. Another change of Chesterfield manager brought him back to Saltergate for a final spell at right-back before his free transfer to Bury in August 2010.

It was in the May of that year that the Portsmouth team beaten by Chelsea in the FA Cup final included a player on loan who had been loaned to Chesterfield for three months during the 2005-06 season. Jamie O'Hara, a Dartford-born England Under-21 midfielder who was also eligible for the Republic of Ireland in having Irish grandparents, made both those temporary moves (and also those to Millwall and Wolves) while with Tottenham, whom he had joined after coming through the Arsenal academy. He was unable to make much impact with Chesterfield, who won only three of their last nineteen League games in which he played from mid-January in 2006, but he was voted Portsmouth's top player of 2009-10, and, after recovering from back surgery, he was valued at £3.5 million in his move from Spurs to Wolves in 2011.

That dismal end to what would be Roy McFarland's last full season as Chesterfield's manager was an all-too-accurate portent of what was to come. The start to 2006-07 was tormentingly deceptive. A 3-0 win at Bournemouth and a goalless home draw with Carlisle were followed by a 5-1 defeat of Millwall that hoisted the club to the dizzying height of third place. But only one victory in the next six games plunged them to seventeenth, and after that it remained downhill all the way to a final 21st place, four points from safety. They failed to score in 21 of their 46 League matches; only two wins were gained in their last fourteen. These were the final positions at the foot of the table:

Season 2006-2007	P	W	D	L	F	A	Pts
20. Leyton Orient	46	12	15	19	61	77	51
21. Chesterfield	46	12	11	23	45	53	47
22. Bradford C	46	11	14	21	47	65	47
23. Rotherham*	46	13	9	24	58	75	38
24. Brentford	46	8	13	25	40	79	37

* ten points deducted

Caleb Folan played in only half Chesterfield's League games, four of them as a sub, yet his eight goals were enough to make him their leading scorer He netted three more in the Carling Cup, and another in the Johnstone's Paint Trophy – competitions in which the woeful League form was so surprisingly but gratefully contradicted. In the FA Cup, in which Chesterfield also failed to score, there was the embarrassment of a first-round defeat at home to Basingstoke Town, such humble members of the Nationwide South Conference that only goal-difference saved them from relegation.

But in the Carling Cup Chesterfield's victory by 6-5 in a penalty shoot-out with Wolves, one of the Coca-Cola Championship's play-off semi-finalists, was followed by defeats of two Premiership clubs, Manchester City and West Ham, before going out 3-4 on penalties to another, Charlton Athletic. And in the JPT they reached a North semi-final in which Hall made the score 2-2 after 84 minutes, only for Crewe's Luke Varney to complete a winning hat-trick with a goal in each of the last two minutes.

Of the three Premiership clubs Chesterfield met in the Carling Cup, Charlton, ironically, were the ones heading for relegation. And all three were soon to have a change of manager, the Spireites' shock successes having some influence on the dismissal of Stuart Pearce at City and Alan Pardew at West Ham. It was said at the time that Pearce 'appeared to have jumped to the front of the queue' as the favourite for Premiership dismissal after City's lead had been wiped out by Folan, and Derek Niven had smashed a spectacular 25-yard decider, but he survived until just after the end of the season.

Pardew was sacked by the Hammers less than two months after Chesterfield had again come from behind in also beating his team 2-1, Folan poking home the winner in the 87th minute, but he promptly bounced back by replacing Iain Dowie as Charlton's manager shortly after the shoot-out that Wayne Allison so sensationally made necessary against the Addicks with an equaliser, at 3-3, in the last minute of extra-time. Dowie had been in the Charlton job only fifteen games; his predecessor, Alan Curbishley, who followed Pardew at West Ham, had held it for fifteen years (in partnership with Steve Gritt for the first four).

The home games with the three Premiership clubs each attracted a crowd of at least 7,000 (almost 8,000 for Manchester City's visit), whereas the average for the League season at Saltergate was not much more than 4,000 – a slight decrease on the 2005-06 figures.

Coupled with the marked lack of success on the field, that declining support spelled the end for Roy McFarland in March 2007. The bitter pill of dismissal was sweetened, however, by what chairman Barrie Hubbard had to say: 'Roy has helped return respect from the football world, and we thank him for that. During my long involvement with the club I have made a number of mistakes, but appointing Roy McFarland as manager was not one of them. He helped a club recovering from the shenanigans of a previous regime.'

Lee Richardson, described by Hubbard as 'a loyal assistant who deserves his chance after working hard to achieve the relevant qualifications', was moved up to take over as caretaker manager for the remaining nine games of the season. Of these, the club won two, drew three, and lost four. Richardson was confirmed in the appointment on 26 April, two days before relegation became inescapable despite a 3-0 beating of Bradford City in the club's penultimate match of the season, the final one at home. Cheltenham's recovery from two down to win 4-2 at Rotherham made survival impossible for both the Spireites and their victims.

The first two of the goals against the visitors from Valley Parade were scored by Jamie Ward, McFarland's last important signing for Chesterfield, for an undisclosed fee from Torquay United, on the last day of January 2007. Here was another English-born player (Solihull) with Irish ancestry, qualified for Northern Ireland. Ward, a 5ft 5in bundle of energy and craft, began as a trainee with Aston Villa and was in their team beaten by Middlesbrough in the FA Youth Cup final of 2004. He turned professional the next year after recovering from injuries suffered in a car crash, but, although he captained the Reserves, he did not get into Villa's first team before his move to Torquay in 2006 following a few games on loan to Stockport.

Ward's impressive form in his two years with Chesterfield resulted in his transfer to Sheffield United for a fee about £70,000 below the £400,000 that would have taken him to Barnsley if he could have agreed personal terms with the Oakwell club. His stay with the Blades was blighted by his sending-off for twice handling the ball during their defeat by Burnley in the 2009 Championship play-off final, but two years later, while on loan to Derby County before costing them another big fee, he helped to save the Rams from the relegation Sheffield United at the same time were unable to avoid.

For Lee Richardson's successor to himself as assistant manager, with the then 38-year-old Wayne Allison giving support, Chesterfield appointed Alan Knill, who only a fortnight earlier had been sacked as manager of a Rotherham United team at the bottom of the Coca-Cola First Division without a win in fourteen games. Rotherham had been the last of the six League clubs for which Knill had played in central defence, the others including three, Halifax, Bury and Scunthorpe, for each of which he had made more than 100 appearances. While with another, Swansea City, he had played his one game for Wales, in a World Cup qualifier against the Netherlands at Amsterdam in September 1988.

From Chesterfield, Knill went back into management in his own right with two of his old clubs. In his first full season of 2008-09 in charge at

Bury the Shakers missed automatic promotion from Division Two by only one goal on goal-difference, and were then beaten 3-4 on penalties by Shrewsbury in a play-off semi-final. At the end of March in 2011, Bury were just one point from the play-offs, with eight games remaining, when Knill left to manage Scunthorpe. Bury went on to win promotion to a League One then sponsored by Npower, as runners-up to Chesterfield. Scunthorpe, beaten 0-6 at Norwich in Knill's first match at the helm, went down with Sheffield United from the Championship, finishing last.

That 2010-11 promotion of Chesterfield's League Two champions was achieved under yet another manager, the club's sixth of the decade, and at their long-overdue new home. But first there was the not inconsiderable matter of a month-long twice-abandoned FA Cup-tie of controversial goals, a mass brawl, and an ending from which the losers emerged as winners.

20

The strangest cup-tie of the season

So abysmal had Chesterfield's FA Cup record been since reaching the last four in the 1996-97 season that it came as an almost overwhelming relief when they appeared to have an excellent chance of at last again getting among the big boys of the third round in 2008-09. Only twice in the intervening period had they avoided falling at the first fence, and on both those occasions they had done so against the non-League opposition of Northwich Victoria and Stalybridge Celtic. What was more, three of their immediate exits had been enforced by other clubs from that lower sphere, Enfield, Morecambe (four years before their promotion from the Conference) and Basingstoke – all at Saltergate.

Now, after six successive seasons of first-round defeats, here they were through that barrier with a 3-1 home win against Mansfield Town, a club newly relegated to the Blue Square Premier, and again favoured with a home draw against Droylsden, humbler members still of the Blue Square North. What could possibly go wrong? Especially as Chesterfield were fresh from an unbeaten run of six League games that had included victories by 5-1 at home to Aldershot and 6-1 at Exeter.

But how horribly wrong it did go, even though the Spireites wriggled into the third round despite once more being beaten. Yes, that is what actually happened, in what was inadequately described as 'the strangest cup-tie of the season'. It all began on the last Saturday of November 2008, when play had to be abandoned at half-time because of fog that reduced visibility to less than 50 yards. Droylsden, first-round replay winners against Darlington, who could have reached the Division Two play-offs but for being docked ten points for going into administration the following February, were then one goal ahead, and their chairman-manager, Dave Pace, was not slow to vent his anger at the decision. 'If it had been the other way round,' he said, 'with Chesterfield winning, I don't think it would have been called off.'

Even greater controversy was stirred up in the rearranged game on Tuesday, 9 December. Jamie Ward gave Chesterfield a first-half lead, but Brown levelled five minutes after half-time. Then, in the 79th minute, came a goal that sparked a mass protest. Droylsden sportingly put the ball out of play when a Chesterfield player was injured, but from the resulting throw-in Jack Lester, a free scorer from Forest, accidentally lobbed the ball over goalkeeper Mawson into the net in attempting to pass it back to him. Order having been restored out of the chaos that reigned for several minutes, Chesterfield also showed the sporting sprit in allowing Halford to walk the ball into their net to make the score 2-2. And that was how it stayed, taking the teams to a replay at Droylsden's ground in Greater Manchester on the next Tuesday, 16 December.

It sounded ominous enough that this ground was named after the Butcher's Arms public house behind which it was situated (the club had been originally formed with an the invitation to play there from Joseph Cropper, then the licensee). There was also Droylsden's daunting nickname of The Bloods, derived from their colours of red and white. But this time Chesterfield were in no mood to let slip what had seemed such a good opportunity to progress against a club from the sixth tier of English football. Piling into the attack from the kick-off, they again took the lead in the first half and increased it in the second.

But all to no avail. After 72 minutes play again had to be abandoned. The floodlights failed. Now it was Chesterfield's turn to complain bitterly. Theories about a conspiracy were freely bandied about, the timing of the black-out regarded as very convenient, but Pace was quick to point out that the power had been steadily lost in other areas of the ground during the evening.

So they had to try yet again a week later, on 23 December, and this drawn-out saga at last appeared to have been brought to a conclusion when Droylsden held on to the 2-1 lead that left-back Sean Newton gave them with a 55th-minute penalty after his first goal in the 31st minute had been equalised by Lester in the 35th. But no! Chesterfield wasted no time at the final whistle in complaining to the FA about Newton, who had been booked for the fifth time that season during the 2-2 draw between the clubs. That meant, according to the FA, that he was suspended for one game from – yes, 23 December. The investigation carried out by an FA Cup committee six days later, in response to the Derbyshire club's appeal, could therefore come to only one conclusion. Droylsden were expelled from the competition for fielding an ineligible player, and Chesterfield were reinstated.

This situation would never have arisen if the lights had not gone out. The aborted replay had yet to be needed when Droylsden faxed confirmation of Newton's suspension to the FA and stated that he would serve it against Vauxhall Motors on Boxing Day. They had thought (or, rather, hoped) that this arrangement still applied, though it clearly could not do so once the intervening replay was arranged, coincidentally and naively, for that very day, two before Christmas, from which the FA had deemed the ban should start.

Dave Pace, predictably, was furious about it. He had ploughed a lot of his money into the club, and was looking forward to a prolonged Cup run with at least one good gate (only just under 5,700 saw the 2-2 draw at Saltergate, and fewer than 3,000 attended each of the ties at Droylsden). But the appeal he lodged was bound to fail, and, although some sympathy may have been felt for the non-Leaguers, it has to be said that they should have been well aware of the changed circumstances once 23 December was decided upon for the replay caused by the second abandonment.

Chesterfield, too, were not free from criticism. Quite apart from the fact that they should not have found it so difficult to account for supposedly inferior opposition, they knew about Newton's ban and the date it was due to begin, but made no fuss about it until after they had been beaten. Neither did the reprieve work in their favour. Out of the third round they went to three second-half goals at Ipswich, where at the same stage of the competition two seasons earlier the Championship club had also defeated (in a replay), a team, Chester City, that had benefited from the expulsion of one to which they had lost, Bury, for including an ineligible player. A coincidence fit to round off a tale to stretch the imagination of the most inventive writer of schoolboy fiction.

With their defeat in Suffolk, Chesterfield were in their all-too-familiar position of quickly having no interest in the season's three knock-out competitions. They had gone straight out of the Carling Cup, 0-2 at Preston, and lost 1-4 on penalties after a 2-2 home draw with Grimsby Town in the first round of the Johnstone's Paint Trophy. At least there was some slight improvement in that respect compared with the previous 2007-08 season, the first full one of Lee Richardson's management, when they had also made an immediate exit from the FA Cup, at home to Tranmere.

During that campaign Chesterfield had a new assistant manager, Scott Sellars, a son of Sheffield, succeeding Alan Knill. Sellars had been a talented midfielder in almost 550 League games, mainly shared between Blackburn and Bolton after coming through Leeds United's youth ranks. While with Blackburn from 1986 to 1992 he played for England Under-21s and was in Rovers teams that won the finals of the Full Members Cup and a Second Division play-off. He then helped both Newcastle, in 1993, and Bolton, in 1997, to the First Division title. After that he played for Huddersfield and the Danish club AGF Aarhus, then appeared in the last half-dozen games of Mansfield's push to the third promotion place from Division Two in 2002. Injuries restricted his subsequent appearances for the Stags, so he turned to coaching the club's youngsters, and after leaving Chesterfield in 2009 he continued in that role with Manchester City's Under-18 team.

New additions to Chesterfield's playing staff for that first 2007-08 season of the Richardson-Sellars partnership most influentially included Peter Leven, Jack Lester and Steve Fletcher. Leven had struggled to hold a place in Kilmarnock's midfield after failing to advance beyond Glasgow Rangers' youth team, but his free transfer to the Spireites brought him the regular first-team football he had sought in rejecting Killie's renewed offer to stay with them. He was second only to Barry Roche for Chesterfield appearances that season, missing just five of the club's 49 games to the goalkeeper's one. He was also given the captaincy when Aaron Downes, although not often absent, was a little below his best during the opening weeks.

That, however, was the only season Leven spent at Saltergate. He turned down a contract extension when Chesterfield missed promotion and moved to Milton Keynes Dons, also on a free transfer. He was voted by sports writers as the Npower League One Player of the Year for the 2010-11 season in which the Dons were losing play-off semi-finalists, but that summer he again declined the renewal of his contract and joined Oxford United. It also did not take him long to become a firm favourite there. The winning goal he scored from the halfway line against Port Vale was one of the best seen in the first ten years at the Kassam Stadium.

Chesterfield's bid for promotion in 2007-08 looked well on track until as late as their last match of March in which a 3-0 away win against Dagenham & Redbridge kept them in the seventh and last of the play-off places. Before that they had occupied all the leading positions except the top one, and been as high as fourth in early January. But they won only one of their last five games, drawing three and losing the other. That left them on 69 points, a disquieting nine immediately outside the play-offs. Deep as the disappointment was in north Derbyshire, it could hardly compare with that in the south of the county. For that was the season in which Derby County won only one of their 38 matches in crashing out of the Premiership with a mere eleven points and twenty goals.

Peter Leven was not alone in staying with Chesterfield for only the 2007-08 season. Steve Fletcher also refused a new contract at the end of it, 'for family commitments.' This 6ft 2in Hartlepool-born forward, a grandson of Jack Howe, the former Derby and England full-back, then spent eight months with Crawley Town in the Blue Square Premier before rejoining Bournemouth, the club to which he had first moved from Hartlepool United in 1992, and for which he holds the record for League appearances. He exceeded Sean O'Driscoll's 423 in 2004, reached

500 on 24 February 2009, and topped 600 in his third game of the 2011-12 season, on 16 August. Twice he played a key role in the Cherries' promotion. No wonder they renamed the North Stand at their Dean Court ground after him.

With the addition of his 32 games and four goals for Hartlepool, and 38 and five for Chesterfield, Fletcher had respective overall League totals of 686 and 112 before playing in another six matches, but scoring no goals, while on loan to Plymouth in 2012. That temporary move, after resigning as assistant to Bournemouth manager Lee Bradbury in November 2011 to concentrate on playing, reunited him with his former Cherries clubmate Carl Fletcher, who was then Argyle's manager. Having helped the Devon club to stay in League Two, avoiding a second successive relegation, he was recalled to Bournemouth by the club's new manager, Paul Groves, and played in their last League match of the 2011-12 season, as a substitute. That game, won 1-0 at home to Preston with a Charlie Daniels penalty, was Steve Fletcher's 617th for the club, in which he had scored 103 goals.

Throughout his long career, Fletcher was employed predominately as a target man, using his height and strength to unsettle defences and create openings for his team-mates. He was therefore a fine foil for Jack Lester, whose 23 goals in 2007-08, plus two in the Cups, made him the consistent sharpshooter for whom Chesterfield had for so long been searching. Mind you, Lester was by then a thoroughly seasoned professional, having formed other effective strike partnerships for Grimsby Town, Nottingham Forest and, to a lesser extent, Sheffield United in a career dating back to 1994, and in 2008-09, without Fletcher, he maintained his form with 23 more goals, three of them in the knock-out competitions. He thus became the first Chesterfield player to score as many as twenty goals in two successive seasons since Jimmy Cookson 82 years before.

Two of Lester's League goals came in the second half of the 6-1 win at Exeter on the last Saturday of October in 2008 that was the biggest Chesterfield had ever gained in an away match. This was the team that achieved it: Carson; Gray, Austin, Kerry, Page, Downes, Lowry, Winter (Harsley), Lester (Currie), Ward (Niven), Goodall. The other scorers were Winter, Goodall, Ward and Currie.

Quite a few names there not previously mentioned. Trevor Carson, a Northern Ireland Under-21 and 'B' international goalkeeper, was on loan from Sunderland – originally for the season, but recalled in the January because of the Black Cats' sudden shortage of keepers due to injuries. His return to the North-East opened up the way again for Tommy Lee, who had started the season as Barry Roche's successor after being released by Macclesfield Town, but soon afterwards had needed surgery on having his jaw broken when attacked during a night out in Sheffield. Carson was later loaned to four other clubs before being signed by one of them, Bury; Lee, a former member of Manchester United's trophy-winning junior side, had also gained experience on loan. Just over two months before joining Chesterfield (on a one-year contract, but booked for a longer stay as he quickly became popular with the fans), he had been at Wembley in the Rochdale team narrowly beaten by Stockport in the League Two play-off final.

Dan Gray, the right-back, began as a central midfielder. This Mansfield-born six-footer had limited opportunities in his six seasons with Chesterfield after a short spell at Alfreton, and he spent part of them on loan to Macclesfield. Chesterfield were the tenth club for his partner, Londoner Kevin Austin, an imposing figure, also just over six feet tall, who was dubbed The Doorman. Austin, primarily a central defender, had twice had to overcome an Achilles tendon injury – first suffered shortly after moving to Barnsley (in a game against Lincoln, the club he had just left), and then while on international duty for Trinidad & Tobago in the Cayman Islands. That recurrence caused a proposed transfer from Barnsley to Oxford to fall through, and Austin was also dogged by injury with Cambridge United before regaining fitness and form for Bristol Rovers and Swansea. After two seasons with Chesterfield he went into the Conference Premier with Darlington, then the Conference North with Boston United.

Midfielder Lloyd Kerry also signed for Chesterfield, his home club, on a two-year deal (after first being on loan from Sheffield United), and he was also later in the Conference North, with Hinckley United. Considerable experience was introduced to Chesterfield's defence with the arrival from Huddersfield of Robert Page, 41 times a Welsh international, but he was then nearing his 34th birthday, and the Spireites would be the last of the six clubs with which he totalled more than 500 appearances in an eighteen-year career that began at Watford in 1993. Page captained the Hornets to two promotions, marshalling their defence when they won the Second Division title in 1997-98 and reached the FA Carling Premiership a year later by beating Bolton in the play-off final. Immediate though relegation was, he still topped the poll as Watford's Player of the Season.

A £350,000 fee took Page to Sheffield United in 2001, and he followed his 200-plus games for Watford with more than 100 for the Blades before also playing for Cardiff and Coventry before going to

Huddersfield. He captained Sheffield United (managed by former Spireite Neil Warnock) to third place in the Nationwide First Division of 2002-03, but they were beaten by Wolves in the play-off final in Cardiff. That was the season in which the Bramall Lane club also reached the semi-finals of the Worthington Cup and FA Cup, losing respectively to Liverpool, after winning the first leg, and to Arsenal by an only goal at Old Trafford.

With Coventry, Page's progress was checked by a knee injury and major hip surgery. He also missed matches through suspension for fighting with Southampton's Darren Powell, displaying a fiery temperament that got him into further trouble when, as captain, he fought with his vice-captain, Michael Doyle, at the Sky Blues' training ground. He also captained Huddersfield, elevated to that position by caretaker manager Gerry Murphy following Andy Richie's departure, but left for Chesterfield after failing to agree contract terms with the new manager, Stan Ternent. He was also given the Spireites' captaincy by Lee Richardson, but lost it, and temporarily his place in the team, after giving several disappointing displays and being sent off in a defeat at Dagenham. In July 2009 Port Vale's manager Micky Adams, his former manager at Coventry, offered him the job of player-coach, and, although he decided to stay with Chesterfield at that time, it was with Vale that he became youth-team coach after retiring from playing in 2011.

Jamie Lowry was born in Cornwall, at Newquay, so he would have been an unlikely recruit for Chesterfield but for the fact that he was recommended to the club by his grandfather, who came from the Derbyshire town. After two weeks' work experience, Lowry accepted the offer of a place in the Youth Academy, and he was given a two-year contract following the completion of his youth scholarship in 2006. Originally a full-back or right-sided midfielder, he was used in central midfield towards the end of Richardson's time as manager, but during an unlucky thirteenth match of the 2009-10 season, lost at Hereford in October, he suffered a cruciate knee ligament injury that put him out of action until he was sent on as a substitute in the added time of a 2-0 win at Lincoln in February 2011.

Neither Jamie Winter nor Paul Harsley, his replacement in that record victory at Exeter, made much of a mark with Chesterfield. Winter, a Dundee-born midfielder, also failed to impress at Leeds, Aberdeen, and on loan to St Johnstone, before his move to Saltergate in July 2007. With the Spireites he was best remembered for the piledriver with which he scored at Exeter and two strikes from long range in an FA Cup defeat of non-League Mansfield. On not having his contract renewed in 2009

Winter returned to Scotland with Fortmarine United in the Highland League and Broughty Athletic, a Dundee junior club. Harsley was a Third Division play-off winner with Scunthorpe, and Player of the Year with Northampton, Macclesfield and Port Vale, but only twenty of his 400-plus career appearances were made for Chesterfield before he went on loan to Darlington with Danny Hall. After also being loaned to York, he bowed out with North Ferriby United in the Northern Premier League.

Darren Currie, another of the subs used at Exeter, made Chesterfield his twelfth League club when he moved from Luton after the Hatters' relegation to the Blue Square Premier in 2008 under the handicap of a ten-point penalty for going into administration. This nephew of Tony Currie, the former Sheffield United, Leeds and England player, had cost Shrewsbury £70,000, Wycombe Wanderers £200,000, and Ipswich £250,000, but joined both Luton and Chesterfield on a free transfer. He turned down Brighton & Hove Albion in his preference for the Spireites, but was soon on his way again, to Dagenham & Redbridge in November 2009. He did not get into the Daggers' team that defeated Rotherham in the 2010 League Two play-off final at Wembley, and was released when they were promptly relegated. After an unsuccessful trial with Southend he went into the Conference South with Boreham Wood, as both player and assistant manager, then into the Isthmian League with Hendon.

Alan Goodall was also signed by Chesterfield from Luton Town. A Merseysider, he had gained most of his previous League experience with Rochdale after being in Bangor City teams that lost to Barry Town in the Welsh Cup final, to FK Sartid in the UEFA Cup, and to Gloria Bistrita in the UEFA Intertoto Cup. Although chiefly a defender, he scored on his debut for Luton, and in his third home game for Chesterfield netted the winner against Rotherham in the fourth minute of the time added for stoppages. He rejoined Rochdale during the 2010 close season, but was loaned to Newport and had a short spell with Stockport before being in the first Fleetwood Town team to reach the Football League as the Blue Square Premier champions of 2011-12.

The record win at Exeter came during Chesterfield's best spell in the first half of the 2008-09 season, a run of six matches unbeaten, and just one defeat in fifteen from February lifted them into the last of the play-off places with only three games to go. But they lost all three, failing to score in each of them (and also the previous two). So the final position was tenth, six points from the play-offs, and it was not good enough to keep Lee Richardson in his job. The loyalty he had shown the year before in declaring himself 'focused on Chesterfield' and refuting rumours linking him with the managerial vacancy at Huddersfield, one of the clubs for which he had played, counted for nothing when directors thirsting for the promotion he had twice failed to deliver decided not to renew his contract. Chairman Hubbard was even quoted as saying: 'I'm very sorry that he's gone because I think he's done well at Chesterfield. He's had some bad luck, and he's had some good luck, but I don't think some of the players he's signed have come up to the expectations he had for them.'

Richardson, though naturally expressing disappointment, said it had not come as a complete surprise to him. 'We've had tough times over the two years I've been manager in terms of pressure on the chairman and board to make a change in the midst of what I think have been two decent seasons. But it's not the end of the world. I've got three wonderful kids and a lovely wife, and life goes on. I've gained from the experience.' He might have added that he had been Manager of the Month for March, just two months before his dismissal, and had only narrowly been beaten to the award the previous October by Lincoln's Peter Jackson.

The path out of Saltergate led Richardson away from football into cricket by way of Rugby League after he had shown unrewarded interest in the vacancies at Burton and Port Vale. He had been with eight other clubs before Chesterfield after starting in 1987 as an energetic midfielder with his local team, Halifax Town, for which his younger brother Nick had also played (briefly in the same side). Of those eight, the elder Richardson had enjoyed most success with Aberdeen, when they finished second to Rangers in all three Scottish competitions in 1992-93, and Oldham. As a psychologist, he turned to working with Warrington Wolves in Rugby League, and with Lancashire CCC, but also found another niche in soccer. Sam Allardyce, who had been his manager at Blackburn, took him south after being put in charge at West Ham.

Peter Moores, Lancashire's cricket coach, considered that Richardson made a significant contribution behind the scenes to the club's winning of the County Championship in the 2011 season. 'He impressed both me and skipper Glen Chapple when we met him during the winter, and the same goes for the rest of the lads,' said Moores. 'The fact that he's been there and done it in professional sport is a big help when it comes to relating to players and what they are going through. He's our sort of bloke, and he's fitted in with what we're trying to do really well.'

Meanwhile, Chesterfield FC were going through another most eventful era under new management, bringing the promotion that so fittingly coincided with the move to their new home, and a trophy triumph at Wembley that relieved some of the depression of immediate relegation.

21

Goodbye Saltergate! Move to new stadium

John Sheridan, Chesterfield's choice to follow Lee Richardson as manager, took only two seasons, 2009-11, to achieve the promotion that carried the club halfway towards the declared aim of Dave Allen, the major shareholder and coming chairman: 'A place in the Championship within a few years.' On 25 March 2012, Sheridan also steered the Spireites to a shock win at Wembley in the final of the Football League Trophy competition sponsored by Johnstone's Paint.

But, in the aftermath of speedy relegation at the end of his third season in charge, 2011-12, and only three games, all lost, into his fourth, Sheridan was out of a job. His dismissal on 28 August 2012 served up yet another classic case of a footballing vote of confidence transformed into a 'kiss of death'. In his interview with the *Chesterfield Post*, at a time around Christmas in 2011 when Chesterfield were firmly entrenched at the foot of League One, Allen had been quoted as saying: 'I had insisted that the chairman [then Barrie Hubbard] give the management team an extended contract because I didn't want to lose them. I had no intention of sacking John [Sheridan], and never will do. You will get one or two calling for his head. People are entitled to their opinion, and they pay their money, but you don't become a bad manager overnight. John's a good manager, and was a good footballer. You don't get 30-odd caps for Ireland without being a good footballer.'

With Sheridan put on 'gardening leave' while the financial terms of his contract, which still had three years to run, were sorted out, Chris Turner, who had been the club's chief executive since December 2011, announced that Tommy Wright, Sheridan's assistant, would stay on to manage the first team as caretaker and have the help of goalkeeper Mark Crossley with the coaching. Wright, a former Scotland Under-21 winger, and Crossley, an Englishman (born Barnsley) who played for Wales, had both followed Sheridan from Oldham, where Wright had also been assistant manager and Crossley a coach as well as goalkeeper. Crossley would not have still been with Chesterfield to go into his behind-the-scenes partnership with Wright but for the Derbyshire club's failure to agree a compensation fee when Birmingham City sought to make him their new goalkeeping coach in July 2012.

Wright, a native of Dunfermline, began his senior career of more than 400 League games with Leeds United in 1982. He fell just short of

100 appearances for the Elland Road club, but got into three figures with both Oldham and Leicester before also giving Middlesbrough and Bradford City the benefit of his expert crossing of a ball. Twice he rejoined Oldham. He first went back there briefly as a player before returning to Scotland with St Johnstone and Livingston, then was with Doncaster for their first season of 1998-99 in the Conference after relegation from the League. Wright's next recall to Boundary Park was to coach the under-16s, so, in June 2006, at the age of 40, he was on the spot when John Sheridan appointed him as his assistant in taking over as manager following a couple of spells as caretaker. They had played together at Leeds and shared a house there.

'I always said that if I went into management I would take him with me,' said Sheridan. 'Tommy has a terrific record of bringing young players through the Leeds club, and, like myself, is very excited about the future.'

Mark Crossley's playing career lasted from 1988 to 2011, during which time he played in 451 League games, the last four of them for Chesterfield, and went beyond 500 with the inclusion of FA Cup, League Cup, and the four European ties in which he took part while with Nottingham Forest. It was for Forest that he made most of his appearances, approaching 400 in all in a dozen years, and he earned some notoriety on 24 March 1993 by becoming the only goalkeeper to save a penalty taken by Matthew Le Tissier, the Southampton spot specialist who made no mistake with the 47 other kicks of his career. Crossley had quite a reputation for saving penalties. The save he made against Gary Lineker, of Tottenham, at Wembley in 1991 made him one of only three goalkeepers – the others Dave Beasant (Wimbledon) and Peter Cech (Chelsea) – to have kept out a penalty-kick in an FA Cup final. That is apart from the shoot-outs that decided the finals of 2005 and 2006 in favour of Arsenal and Liverpool.

Crossley also had that rare achievement among goalkeepers (though, as already noted, shared by Jim Brown) of straying from his job of preventing goals by scoring one. His was a dramatic late equaliser for Sheffield Wednesday at Hillsborough on 23 December 2006, when he charged upfield for a corner and snatched a 3-3 draw with Southampton. Against that, he had the dubious distinction of scoring the FA Premier League's first own-goal, in Nottingham Forest's 1-4 defeat at Blackburn on 5 September 1992.

Crossley, or 'Norm,' as he was known to Forest fans because of his supposed resemblance to Manchester United's Norman Whiteside, started out with the Old Trafford club as a trainee in 1987. He was loaned back to United, but without breaking into their first team, before becoming a Forest regular. Although he played in the 1991 FA Cup final defeat by Tottenham, he missed the following season's finals of the Rumbelows Cup and Zenith Data Systems Trophy because they coincided with a period when he was out of favour for a breach of club rules. It was with great reluctance that he left Forest in 2000, a victim of financial troubles that enforced a reduction of the wage bill. After that he was with Middlesbrough, Fulham and, on loan, Stoke and Wednesday, before he first combined coaching with playing at Oldham.

As an international, Crossley's dual qualification enabled him to guard the England Under-21 goal in a tournament at Toulon in 1990, and start eight games for Wales while chiefly an understudy for Neville Southall and then Paul Jones. His most memorable match at that level was against Scotland in 2004 at Cardiff, where he played in the first half of Wales' 4-0 win.

John Sheridan and his younger brother Darren, who helped Barnsley to what turned out to be their only season, so far, in the Premier League (1997-98), were both born in the Stretford district of Manchester. Their nephew Sam joined Stockport. John signed for Leeds United on leaving school in July 1981 and was rarely out of their team after making his League debut in November the following year. In the 1986-87 season he was an outstanding and hugely popular member of the side that reached the last four of the FA Cup, losing to winning finalists Coventry by the odd goal of five after extra-time, and failed by the odd goal of three (Sheridan scored) in the replay of their play-off final against Charlton after finishing fourth in Division Two.

After 272 games and just over 50 goals, Sheridan ended his eight-year stay at Leeds on 3 August 1989, when he fell out with manager Howard Wilkinson and was transferred to Nottingham Forest for £650,000. That took him to a First Division club for the first time, but, as Pete Attaway put it in his *Forest Complete Record* (1865-1991), published by Breedon Books, 'for some reason known only to [manager] Brian Clough,' he was never given a League game before being moved on to Sheffield Wednesday three months later. The Owls indicated that they paid around £500,000 for him, though the actual sum was probably nearer £400,000. There obviously was some friction between Clough and Sheridan, but my old friend and former colleague Keith Farnsworth, who was in close touch with Wednesday in those days, has told me that Sheridan refused to talk about it when he arrived at Hillsborough.

Sheridan's only first-team appearance for Forest was made in the first leg of a Littlewoods Cup-tie at home to Huddersfield Town. Both that match and the second leg were drawn, but Forest won on the away-goals rule at the start of their path to victory in the final against Oldham.

Ironically, that was the season in which Leeds returned to the top flight, but Sheridan finally reached that level when Wednesday took the third promotion place behind Oldham and West Ham in 1991 – and also won the Rumbelows Cup with a spectacular goal, a Sheridan special, against Manchester United. Sheridan played some of his best football in turning out almost 250 times for Wednesday, but he was in the team less often when David Pleat took over as manager, and he was loaned to Birmingham City (then managed by Pleat's predecessor, Trevor Francis) before costing Bolton £180,000 in November 1996.

With the Wanderers, Sheridan immediately shared in another promotion, as First Division champions, only for them to go straight down again, and he briefly teamed up once more with Tommy Wright by moving to another club, Doncaster, that had just been relegated – out of the League into the Conference. It was from there that he joined Oldham, and over the next six seasons he made the last 163 of his career total of 733 League and Cup appearances (103 goals) before retiring from playing at the conclusion of the 2003-04 campaign, a few months short of his 40th birthday. He had represented the Republic of Ireland 34 times, and two of his five international goals had been of extra significance. The one against Bolivia at Lansdowne Road in 1994 was the Republic's 100th. And they would not have qualified for that year's World Cup if he had not scored in a 1-3 defeat by Spain. That goal tipped the balance in the Republic's favour on goal-difference, whereas a 0-3 result would have meant expulsion.

Towards the end of 2003 Sheridan took over the coaching of Oldham's first team, along with fellow veteran David Eyres, when manager Iain Dowie left for Crystal Palace. They were both replaced after only a few months following the appointment as Dowie's successor of Brian Talbot, a former England midfielder who had uniquely been an FA Cup winner with two clubs, Ipswich and Arsenal, in consecutive seasons, but Sheridan became manager in the summer of 2006 after Talbot had resigned and his successor, Ronnie Moore, had left because of poor season-ticket sales in the wake of a narrow escape from relegation. Moore most made his mark with Rotherham, as both player and manager.

Sheridan twice had Oldham in line for promotion. They lost to Blackpool, winners against Yeovil at Wembley, in a Coca-Cola Division One play-off semi-final in 2007, and they were again going well, in fifth place, in March 2009 when there were reports of a fight involving players and Sheridan at a racetrack. Sheridan described them as 'overblown', but after only one more game, lost 2-6 at Milton Keynes, he was called to talks with Simon Corney, the club's managing director, and agreed to step down.

He was widely tipped to fill the coinciding Chesterfield vacancy, and the door duly opened for him there on 9 June 2009, with a three-year contract. Although he brought Wright and Crossley with him, he retained Jamie Hewitt as physiotherapist and Dave Thompson as scout. One of the first things Sheridan did on the Spireites' behalf was to form a strong defensive partnership by bringing back Ian Breckin from Nottingham Forest and reinstating Robert Page, who had been made open to offers after being dropped and relieved of the captaincy by Lee Richardson. Sheridan also recalled another old favourite, Mark Allott rejoining Chesterfield for the second time on being released by Tranmere Rovers only eight weeks after becoming their first signing of the 2009 summer transfer window.

The first League side Sheridan fielded as Chesterfield manager was: Crossley; Picken, Austin; Niven (Gritton), Page, Breckin, Lowry, Allott, Talbot, McDermott, Currie (Bowery). Only three remained from the team that started the last match of the previous season, Austin, Lowry and Talbot, with Bowery again a substitute, though Tommy Lee was immediately available to resume in goal and missed just three more games that season.

That opening match, lost to two Torquay goals at Plainmoor on 8 August 2009, was Drew Talbot's eighteenth in the League for Chesterfield, but his first as one of the club's own players. He had been taken on loan from Luton, for the rest of the previous season, on 27 January 2009, the day before he had been due for a pay rise under the terms of his contract. Sheridan moved in to sign him when he failed to agree a new deal with the Hatters. Until then Talbot had been mainly used as a striker, but Sheridan preferred him as a right-back or right-winger, roles in which he went into a second century of appearances before the manager's departure.

Chesterfield bounced back from their opening-day defeat with a home win against Northampton gained with a goal from Donal McDermott, an Eire Youth forward on loan from Manchester City, and they were encouragingly entrenched among the play-off places by the time the setback at Torquay was avenged in the return game in January 2010 with a goal scored on his debut by Barry Conlon, another Irishman. Conlon was then into his 32nd year, and Chesterfield were his thirteenth club of a career in which he had made the most of his League appearances, just over 400, for Darlington, 134 in two spells.

Conlon originally joined Chesterfield on loan from Grimsby after the Mariners had offered him to Accrington Stanley in the hope of obtaining striker Michael Symes in exchange as part of a six-figure deal that the Lancashire club rejected. Conlon became a Spireite a few weeks later when his contract with Grimsby was cancelled by mutual consent, but he was among the dozen players Sheridan released after the failure to qualify for the Coca-Cola League Two play-offs in 2010. He might have expected better after finishing second top scorer behind Jack Lester's twelve, in only nineteen games (four as sub), though all but two of his seven goals came from penalties.

Two of those spot-kicks brought victory against Rochdale, who were automatically promoted with Notts County and Bournemouth, but Chesterfield won only one of their remaining seven matches – at home to Bournemouth on the final day – in tailing away to eighth, two points outside the play-offs but with a goal-difference inferior to that of Dagenham & Redbridge, who won the Wembley final as the seventh and last of the qualifiers. Chesterfield were as high as third after another Conlon penalty had earned victory at Cheltenham in early March, only for their costly slump to set in immediately afterwards. The wins against Rochdale and Bournemouth were the only ones they gained in their last dozen matches, the six defeats of that lean spell including a five-goal pounding by Port Vale. It was their heaviest home setback since Wrexham's 6-0 victory at Saltergate in 1976.

Conlon left Chesterfield with 432 League games and 121 goals to his name. Stockport became his final League club during the 2010 close season, but he was released only five months later, shortly after being fined £1,175 and banned from driving for 3½ years, for speeding in his Mercedes while above the drink limit. A venture into Belgium with a Third Division 'B' side was also soon over, and a trial back in the Republic of Ireland with Monaghan United failed to secure a contract.

Wade Small was another Sheridan signing of the 2009-10 season who did not stay to share in the runway promotion success that promptly followed. Sheridan hailed him as 'an exciting player, versatile and pacey, who is capable of causing problems for opponents', but he spent 2010-11 with Aldershot Town before going out of the League with Lewes, then Tooting and Mitcham. A product of the Wimbledon academy, he enjoyed his most profitable stints with Milton Keynes Dons (as Wimbledon were renamed) and, despite injuries, Sheffield Wednesday. Two of his six goals for Chesterfield came in a 5-1 win at Burton at the start of a run in the Johnstone's Paint Trophy competition that brought some compensation for first-round knock-outs in the FA Cup and Carling Cup. It ended in the Northern quarter-finals at home to Carlisle, runners-up to Southampton in the Wembley final.

The win against Bournemouth at the end of the 2009-10 season, 8 May, holds a special place in Chesterfield's soccer annals because it was the last one the club played at the dear old, but run-down, Recreation Ground at Saltergate. Goals from Jack Lester and Derek Niven secured a fitting farewell, but they did not come until ten minutes from time and tbe sixth minute of injury-time after Bournemouth had led from the 42nd minute with an own-goal conceded by Drew Talbot. Niven's winner was greeted by a pitch invasion, and there was another one as emotions spilled over at the final whistle in celebration and to say goodbye. The crowd numbered 4,998, and these were the teams:

Chesterfield: Lee; Whing, Austin, Niven, Page, Breckin, Demontagnac, Allott, Lester, Conlon (Bowery, 66), Talbot (Rundle, 78). Unused substitutes: Crossley, Picken, Gray, Boden (S), Small. Full-back Andy Whing was on loan from Brighton.

AFC Bournemouth: Jalal; Bradbury, Cummings (Garry, 84), Hollands, Pearce, Cooper, Bartley, Robinson, Pitman, Fletcher, Feeney (McQuoid, 70).

The record attendance for a match at Saltergate had been set on 12 February 1938, when 30,561 were packed in for a fifth-round FA Cup-tie in which Chesterfield drew 2-2 with Tottenham, then fellow members of Division Two, but lost the replay by the odd goal of three. Four goals were also equally shared when Spurs visited in the League that season. The record was at first said to have been broken for the League game with Newcastle United on 7 April 1939, but that gate was subsequently reduced from 30,968 to 'only' 28,636.

Plans had been drawn up in 1996 for a 12,000-seat stadium, leisure and retail complex, at Wheeldon Mill, the town's former greyhound stadium, on the outskirts of Chesterfield, but the Borough Council had refused planning permission. All was not lost, however. The Council pledged £1 million towards the club's stadium development plans, and in July 2008 they did grant permission for the new home to be built on Whittington Moor, on the site of the former Dema Glassworks. This had emerged as a possible location four years earlier, and the Council viewed it as part of a master plan to regenerate the A61 corridor, an area to the north of the town centre that included the Chesterfield canal.

The land having been decontaminated after being handed over in the following February, construction began, overseen by GB Development Solutions, on Thursday, 23 July 2009 to the designs of Sheffield-based architects, Ward McHugh Associates, who had previously undertaken commissions on the redevelopment of the South Stand at Twickenham and Everton's Goodison Park stadium. The work was completed in time for the 2010-11 season, with an all-seat capacity of about 10,600, at a cost of £13 million. The naming ceremony took place on 14 August 2009. It became known as the B2net Stadium under the initial sponsorship, but after the acqusition of B2net by the Swedish company Proact the renaming as the Proact Stadium was officially announced on 13 August 2012. Hailed as north Derbyshire's premier venue, it hosted the biggest concert ever staged in the town when, in June 2012, more than 15,000 attended the Elton John performance.

Buildings erected at the same time as the stadium included a Tesco Extra superstore, Tesco petrol station, a KFC Enterprise car rental, and other office facilities. The stadium consists of four stands, each equipped with multiple television screens. The West Stand incorporates conference and banqueting rooms, one of which has been named the Leengate Legends Lounge. Leengate Valves have agreed a six-figure sum and five-year deal. Up to 400 guests can be catered for. A cafeteria, soft-play area for youngsters, and a classroom resource centre for local education, are among the features of the East (Community) Stand extension that was built at a cost of £750,000. This stand was opened for use by several community organisations, Chesterfield being part of a national pilot scheme working with underprivileged young people through football.

John Croot, the club's community director, who had been a CFSS founder board member, recalled that his first involvement with the Spireites had been as an eleven-year-old programme seller at the foot of Saltergate's centre stand steps. 'I always felt the club should be united with its supporters, and a central part of the community,' he said. 'It's been a long journey over ten years.'

It was announced in October 2010 that the new stadium would have been used for the 2013 European Championship finals at Under-21 level, but England failed with their bid to host the event. On 10 September 2012, however, it was the venue when England restarted their qualifying campaign for this championship with a 1-0 win against Norway. An international match was first staged at the ground on 8 February 2011, when England lost 0-1 to Germany in an Under-19 friendly.

The leaving of Saltergate was also marked with a celebration of the club's history at the Pomegranate theatre.

22

Down again, but Trophy triumph at Wembley

To Craig Davies, newly signed after having his Brighton contract cancelled by mutual consent, fell the distinction of scoring the first goal at the B2net Stadium, in a friendly match with Derby County on Saturday, 24 July 2010. He also had a first of a very different kind, however, in being ordered off on his competitive debut for Chesterfield against Barnet in the first League game to be played at the ground on 7 August 2010.

The Rams' visit was well worthy of such an historic occasion, a highly eventful encounter of nine goals. Davies' opener was quickly equalised by Kris Commons, but Simon Ford, a Jamaican international brought back into English football after six years with Kilmarnock as replacement for Kevin Austin, who had departed to Darlington, regained the lead, and Mark Allott increased it in the 34th minute. The balance then tipped decisively in Derby's favour. From 1-3 down they went 5-3 ahead with goals from trialist Connor Doyle, Chris Porter, John Brayford and a Commons penalty. Derek Niven had the last word for Chesterfield with their fourth goal near the end, but County held out for a thrilling win. These were the teams, with subs in brackets:

Chesterfield: Lee (Redmond 58); Hunt (Niven 54), Breckin (Page 54), Ford, Morris (Timmins 78); Talbot (Darikwa 78), Allott (Gray 62), Mattis (Clay 62), Whitaker, Lester (Boden S 62), Davies (Bowery 78).

Derby County: Bywater; Brayford, Hulse (Moxey 63), Anderson (O'Brien 71), Roberts, Doyle (Cywka 57), Green (Deeney 88), Savage, Bailey, Commons (Martin 71), Porter (Varney 71).

Davies was quite a catch. His goals were the springboard from which Chesterfield launched their successful bid for promotion in 2010-11. There were 23 of them, seven in the first dozen League 2 games of the season that boosted the club to the top of the table. They took over there with a 2-1 win at Wycombe, Davies scoring both their goals, on 16 October – and there they stayed. After unbeaten runs of seven and ten matches, the climb was clinched with four games to spare, and without playing, when Wycombe, who went up in third place, were held to a draw at Torquay on 22 April. Chesterfield cemented their position by drawing with Oxford the next day, and although they lost at home to runners-up

Bury next time out, a point at Torquay and three at home to Gillingham, carried them five clear as champions in the final reckoning.

The 3-1 defeat of Gillingham completed the double over the Kent club – and thereby hung the harrowing tale of that season's visit to the ground where they had suffered their record defeat nearly a quarter of a century before. They were originally scheduled to play there on 18 December, but a heavy snowfall made a postponement inevitable, and conditions were so treacherous on the roads that the Chesterfield players and officials had a journey home that revived memories of the depressing retreat from that ten-goal hammering of September 1987. It began at 11.45am on the Saturday and lasted until almost 2.30 on the Sunday morning – after which several of the players still had some distance to travel to get home. For seven hours there was no chance of a break for a meal until a service area was reached near Luton. Full credit to Arthur the driver for getting them all back to Derbyshire safely.

The match was rearranged for 25 January, when Chesterfield won 2-0 with goals from Deane Smalley, a 6ft striker from the Chadderton district of Manchester. He had been on loan from Oldham Athletic since the beginning of November, but would leave after contributing ten other goals to the winning of promotion. The new contract Oldham offered him at the end of the season was rejected in favour of signing on for two years with Oxford United, who paid the compensation to which Oldham were entitled because he was under the age of 24.

Another Chesterfield newcomer, Dwayne Mattis, not only scored the opening goal in the first League appearance at the new stadium but was also on the mark the club's next two games – against Middlesbrough in the Carling Cup and Port Vale back in the League. Mattis, who had represented the Republic of Ireland at Under-21 level, gained the lead halfway through the first half against Barnet, at close range from a Talbot pass. Jack Lester made it 2-0 on the hour, beating two men before coolly firing home, but the issue was put back in doubt when Glenn Poole halved the deficit in the 70th minute – especially after Davies' dismissal for a late tackle on Steve Kabba. Barnet piled on the pressure against the ten men for the remaining fourteen minutes, the last seven of them the time added on for stoppages through injury, but the fresh legs Sheridan brought on by substituting Jordan Bowery for Lester helped Chesterfield to ensure a winning League start at their new home.

The Nottingham-born Bowery, whose father Bert had been a Forest striker under Brian Clough's management before moving into the North American League in 1976, was an exciting prospect who had made his Chesterfield debut at the age of seventeen in 2008. In September 2011 he signed a contract extension up to June 2014, but, shortly after completing a century of appearances for the Spireites, he was transferred to Aston Villa in August 2012 for a fee of about £500,000. This was how they lined up on that first day of League football at the B2net Stadium:

Chesterfield: Lee; Ford, Breckin, Hunt, Allott, Whitaker, Mattis, Morris (Griffiths, 67), Davies, Lester (Bowery, 86), Talbot. Subs not used: Redmond, Page, Niven, Gray, Boden S.

Barnet: Cole; Devera, Parkes (Dennehy, 63), Uddin, Leach, Jarvis (Holmes, 54), Southam, Poole, Byrne, Marshall, Kabba (Kelly, 85). Subs not used: Carpenter, Clovis Kamdjo, Hughes, Cox.

The crowd numbered 6,431, and the average attendance over the season almost doubled from the previous season's 3,800 to 6,900. The gate for Gillingham's visit on the final day soared to 10,023, but the record for the ground was raised to 10,089 for Rotherham's visit on 18 March 2011.

Defensive strength has been a feature of Chesterfield's most successful teams, but, significantly, their promotion seasons, and near-misses, have been built on increased scoring power. The club record of 102 was set up by the Third North championship side of 1930-31, and the century was again reached when they finished third in 1925-26. Three totals in the 90s included 92 by the title winners of 1935-36. In 2010-11, 85 goals were scored in the 46 games, an increase of 24 on the previous season and the club's highest number since the 86 of 1933-34, when they finished second to Barnsley in the 42 matches of the Third North.

Prominent amid this goal rush was a 5-5 home draw with Crewe Alexandra on 2 October 2010. Not the least surprising aspect of this remarkable game was that it was not the most high-scoring of the day. Accrington Stanley won 7-4 at home to Gillingham. Crewe were 3-0 up in thirteen minutes. Behind for the first time in the League at the B2net Stadium, Chesterfield conceded more goals in that spell than in their four previous home games that season. Jack Lester reduced the deficit after 23 minutes from a cross by Dean Morgan, who was on loan from Milton Keynes, but Shaun Miller rounded Tommy Lee to make it 4-1 three minutes later and that was the score at half-time. Another Lester header after 74 minutes and a 79th minute penalty by Whitaker after Morgan had been fouled gave the Spireites renewed hope, but Clayton Donaldson tapped in at close range to make it 5-3 to Crewe five minutes after going on as a substitute after 75 minutes.

Chesterfield dominated the second half. The draw was snatched with a goal in the 89th minute and another in the third of four minutes of stoppage time. After Morgan had hit the bar, Whitaker converted another penalty and a 25-yarder from Craig Clay, a sub for skipper Breckin on the half-hour, produced the dramatic equaliser. This was the first League goal for Clay, a product of the club's youth policy. He rejected a move to Mansfield to sign a new contract in May 2012 after being on loan to Barrow (with Tendayi Darikwa) and Alfreton Town.

'You can look at it both ways,' said John Sheridan. 'After being 1-4 down in the first half we should have gone on to win. The goals we conceded today were very poor. I'll look at the goals and I'll show the players, but to come back from 1-4 does them credit.'

That total of 85 goals by Sheridan's promoted team brought Chesterfield the luxury of having four players into double figures. After Davies, who took his aggregate to 25 by netting twice in the knock-out competitions, came Lester, with seventeen in only 29 starts (plus eleven as a sub), Danny Whitaker, whose fifteen included eight penalties and a hat-trick against Hereford in his second home game, and Deane Smalley (twelve). Whitaker, a former Academy midfielder with Manchester United, had made around 400 appearances in service with Macclesfield, Port Vale and Oldham Athletic. Smalley was also obtained from Oldham, but only on loan.

Whitaker scored on his debut for Macclesfield, with whom he turned professional in 2001, and in five years he topped 200 appearances for them before making another 100 for Port Vale. His three goals for Macclesfield in a 4-1 League Cup defeat of Barnsley in 2002 were special because they all came in the second period of extra-time.

Goalkeeper Lee was an ever-present in Chesterfield's promotion season of 2010-11. Talbot missed two games, Whitaker three. Davies made 41 appearances, and Mattis, Allott and Ford each got into the 30s.

Other important roles were played by Derek Niven, Scott Griffiths, a defender on loan from Peterborough, and Gregor Robertson, a former Forest, Rotherham and Scotland Under-21 defender who had been signed while Lee Richardson was manager.

These were the final positions at the top of the table:

Season 2010-11	P	W	D	L	F	A	Pts
1. Chesterfield	46	24	14	8	85	51	86
2. Bury	46	23	12	11	82	50	81
3. Wycombe	46	22	14	10	69	50	80
4. Shrewbury	46	22	13	11	72	49	79
5. Accrington	46	18	19	9	73	55	73
6. Stevenage	46	18	15	13	62	45	69
7. Torquay	46	17	18	11	74	53	68
8. Gillingham	46	17	17	12	67	57	68

As the players went off for their well-deserved summer break, prospects for the club's future could scarcely have seemed brighter, so emphatically had promotion been gained: only eight defeats (just one short of the record set up in 2000-01), the best goal-difference in the division, and a lead of five points over the runners-up. It therefore came as a shock of catastrophic proportions when the conquerors of 2010-11 were transformed into the no-hopers of 2011-12, with victories culled from 24 to ten (three of them in succession in the closing weeks when the outcome was as good as decided), and defeats increased from eight to 24 in the plunge straight back to the League's lowest tier. This was how the bottom of the table looked after the matches on the season's last day of 5 May:

Season 2011-2012	P	W	D	L	F	A	Pts
19. Walsall	46	10	20	16	51	57	50
20. Leyton Orient	46	13	11	22	48	75	50
21. Wycombe	46	11	10	25	65	88	43
22. Chesterfield	46	10	12	24	56	81	42
23. Exeter	46	10	12	24	46	75	42
24. Rochdale	46	8	14	24	47	81	38

Allott, Lee, Talbot and Whitaker, and to a lesser extent, Ford, Lester and Robertson, remained from the nucleus of the promoted team, but the decrease of 29 goals in the 'for' column was largely explained by the loss of Craig Davies to Barnsley and the drop in Jack Lester's output to just three goals in the League (if from only sixteen starts). This from a combination that had produced 42 goals in their only season together. Reading were prominent among the Championship clubs to show an interest in Davies after his success with Chesterfield, but it was Barnsley's Keith Hill who tempted the young striker to put pen to transfer form in July 2011. He soon showed what the Spireites were missing with eight goals in as many games for the Colliers.

At international level, Davies, who was born in England, at Burton-upon-Trent, but was eligible for Wales, joined John Hartson, Lee Jones and Ched Evans as the only players to do the hat-trick for the Under-21s. That earned him his call-up into the senior squad, after having incurred a five-game international ban on being sent off in an Under-21 defeat by Israel in 2008.

In defence, where goals conceded rose by 30, Ian Breckin was sadly missed. The departure of this faithful long-server, released at the end of the 2010-11 season after some 300 appearances in two spells, was inevitable with his 37th birthday looming. His League Two championship medal with Chesterfield came after an Autoglass Shield triumph with his home club Rotherham and a Division Two title with Forest (with whom he was also twice a runner-up in the League).

To fill the gap left by Davies, John Sheridan looked no further than Nottingham, birthplace of Craig Naptali Westcarr, who had played for Forest as a youth and helped Notts County to the League Two title in 2009-10. He became Forest's youngest first-teamer when he turned out against Burnley on 13 October 2001 at the age of sixteen years and 257 days. From Forest he moved to Cambridge United in 2005, but after only one season he rejected the offer of a contract extension and went into the Conference North with Kettering Town. In his first season with the Poppies they finished second but lost in the promotion play-offs; in his second he was their top scorer, having been switched from the wing to central striker, as they rose to the Conference National.

That attracted the attention of Stevenage Borough, whom he joined in the Blue Square Premiership. He did well in pre-season games, only to find himself unsure of a first-team place when striker Steve Morison changed his mind about leaving. Unsettled, he jumped at the chance to rejoin Kettering, and they headed the table during the season he spent back there before returning to the Football League with Notts County.

In September 2011, the month after snapping up Westcarr from the Meadow Lane club for an undisclosed fee, Sheridan also acquired another striker, the much-travelled Leon Clarke, on a three-month loan from Swindon Town, taking advantage of trouble behind the scenes at the Wiltshire club. After a defeat at Southampton, Clarke was involved in an altercation with Claudio Donatelli, Swindon's fitness coach. Manager Paolo Di Canio, the Italian who had played in Britain for Celtic, Sheffield Wednesday, West Ham and Charlton, intervened, and was seen on television arguing with Clarke before being separated by members of the coaching staff. Swindon's chairman, Jeremy Wray, later confirmed that the club would be looking to offload Clarke, who was also told he would never play again for the Town while Di Canio was manager.

So it was that this Wolverhampton-born six-footer, a product of Wolves' youth academy, made Chesterfield his eleventh club, including loans. Those to which he was transferred had included Sheffield Wednesday, with whom he had most made his mark despite their being relegated. The drop from the Championship was confirmed on 2 May 2010, when he dislocated a toe, and had to be substituted, in kicking an advertising board as he celebrated his goal in a 2-2 draw with fellow strugglers Crystal Palace.

Clarke scored on his Chesterfield debut in a 3-0 win at Bournemouth, netted again with a winner against Bury in his midweek home debut, and on the following Saturday did the hat-trick in a 4-1 defeat of visitors from Carlisle. Quite a start, but, alas, a deceptive one. In fourteen games before he left to sign for Charlton Athletic in part-exchange for Paul Benson, Clarke totalled nine goals – and that made him Chesterfield's leading scorer of the season. Even so, they were at the foot of the table when he departed, and never escaped from the relegation positions into which they had first descended after just four matches. The next highest scorers, with eight apiece in the League, were Jordan Bowery, who added one in the FA Cup and three in the Johnstone's Paint Trophy, and Westcarr, who also scored three times in the Trophy triumph. Whitaker also reached eight goals with the inclusion of three in knock-out competition and four penalties.

Drew Talbot made most League appearances, absent only three times. Next came Allott (36), Lee (35), Westcarr (32, plus six as sub) and a French winger, Alex Mendy. It was for trials with Leeds United that Mendy originally came to England after helping Mlada Boleslav to win the Czech Republic Cup for the first time, on penalties. He impressed in all four friendlies in which he played, demonstrating the skill and pace for which he was noted, but manager Simon Grayson eventually decided that he had to prioritise his transfer budget to sign players for other positions. That let in Chesterfield, who took him on a one-year deal up to the end of June in 2012.

Mendy and Westcarr were involved in the goals that gave Chesterfield their shock 2-0 victory over Swindon Town in the League Trophy final, sponsored by Johnstone's Paint, in front of a Wembley crowd of 49,602 on Sunday, 25 March 2012. Two minutes into the second half, Mendy collected the ball after it had run loose following goalkeeper Foderingham's save from Bowery, turned his marker, and delivered a powerful low centre that was prodded into his own net by midfielder Oliver Risser. Then, in injury-time Westcarr, on as sub for Lester after half-an-hour, raced clear to put the issue beyond doubt.

There were many anxious moments for the Spireites, however. Lee did well to palm a deflected shot by Lee Holmes to safety as the League Two leaders began to settle, and Swindon had a bright spell of twenty minutes in the first half without finding a way through. Tommy Lee again excelled with a superb finger-tip save from Alessandro Cibocchi's header, but Holmes wasted a particularly good opportunity by tamely shooting straight at the goalkeeper. Alan Connell also erred in volleying wide when well placed. For Chesterfield, Westcarr had two of the best chances before converting Randall's long forward pass. Jack Lester and Simon Ford were the unluckiest. Lester had the ball in the net after eight minutes in following up a Ford effort that rebounded off the crossbar, but was narrowly ruled offside.

With Swindon trailing on the hour, their manager, Di Canio, crouched on the Wembley turf and clasped his hands in prayer. 'I was praying I could change eight of the players,' he admitted later, 'but I would also change the manager.' He took off Risser and played three at the back, with substitute Ronan Murray operating just behind the front two. All to no avail. Swindon, the firmest of favourites, were undone by a club with whom they were to exchange places in the League, and who on the day played well above the wretched form that brought immediate relegation. Di Canio labelled it all 'long ball', to which Sheridan responded: 'It doesn't matter what competition you're playing in. To come here and win a trophy can only do you good. The League position's always in the back of my mind, but I'll enjoy today.' These were the teams:

Chesterfield: Lee; Hurst (on loan from Walsall), Smith N (a newcomer from Yeovil), Moussa (Randall), Thompson, Ford, Talbot, Allott, Lester (Westcarr), Bowery (Boden S), Mendy.

Swindon Town: Foderingham; Devera, McEveley (Cibocchi), Smith J (Bostock), Risser (Murray), McCormack, Ritchie, Ferry, Benson, Connell, Holmes.

To reach the final, offsetting immediate exits from the FA and Carling Cups, Chesterfield won 3-1 at Notts County, then beat Tranmere 4-1 in the Northern quarter-final, drew 1-1 at Preston in the Northern semi-final, but won 4-2 on penalties, and accounted for Oldham 3-1 over the two legs of the Northern final. Jamie Lowry moved to Crewe on loan in November 2011, but was recalled on 30 January and the same evening played in the 1-0 win in the second leg against Oldham at Boundary Park. On being released at the end of the season he joined Plymouth Argyle.

It was within three months of that Big Day Out (though not big enough to safeguard Sheridan in his job), that Dave Allen became chairman, the appointment confirmed at a board meeting early in June 2012. 'Barrie Hubbard asked if I would be willing to take over the chair,' he said, 'and as I have heavily invested in the club it seemed the sensible thing to do. Over the years Barrie has worked very hard for the club, and he can feel proud of his achievements, but he has indicated he is now ready for a rest. We all wish him a long and happy retirement. It's fair to say I didn't expect to be taking over as chairman of a football club again, but I am comfortable with it as we have a good bunch of supporters at Chesterfield. I intend to give 100 per cent in my efforts to achieve what the fans want, which is Championship football as soon as possible. This will require careful planning and hard work by everyone at the club to ensure we bring the success we all want.'

There was, however, to be no retirement yet for the 73-year-old Hubbard, who had spent most of the past 29 years on the board – a period during which there had been three promotions, four relegations, two Wembley play-off finals, an historic FA Cup semi-final, and the winning of the Johnstone's Paint Trophy. Only a week after he had stepped down came the news of his appointment as the new life president of Chesterfield FC in recognition of his achievements as a director and chairman over three decades. His lasting legacy was to have masterminded the move to the B2net (now Proact) stadium after 139 years at Saltergate. At the same time, His Grace the Duke of Devonshire became the club's first patron, thus maintaining the 'proud association' with Chatsworth.

So the club look forward with increasing confidence despite the swift setback after promotion. They have bounced back before, and will surely do so again.

Appendix 1
CHESTERFIELD HONOURS

Midland League champions 1909-10 and 1919-20
Third Division North champions 1930-31 and 1935-36
Third Division play-off winners 1994-95
Fourth Division champions 1969-70 and 1984-85
Division Two champions 2010-11
Anglo-Scottish Cup winners 1980-81
Derbyshire FA Centenary Cup winners 1994-95, 2000-01, 2001-02, 2009-10
Bass Charity Vase winners 1900-01
Derbyshire Senior Cup winners 1898-99, 1920-21, 1921-22, 1924-25, 1932-33,
    1936-37
Banner Jones Middleton Cup winners 2003-04, 2004-05, 2005-06, 2006-07, 2007-08,
    2008-09, 2009-10, 2010-11
North & Midlands East Conference Youth winners 2005-06, 2008-09, 2010-11
FA Youth Cup runners-up 1955-56
FA Cup Giantkillers Trophy 1996-97

Appendix 2
CHESTERFIELD IN THE FA CUP

1894-95 Lost to Middlesbrough (a) 4-0, 1st rd
1895-96 Lost to Newcastle United (h) 4-0, 1st rd
1900-01 Drew 1-1 at Kettering; lost replay 2-1, 1st rd
1905-06 Drew 0-0 at Clapton Orient; won replay 3-0, 1st rd
    Lost 3-0 at home to Everton 2nd rd (Everton beat Newcastle 1-0 in final)
1906-07 Drew 1-1 at Derby; lost replay 4-0, 1st rd
1907-08 Won 4-0 at home to Stockton, 1st rd
    Lost 2-0 at Bristol Rovers, 2nd rd
1908-09 Lost 2-0 at home to Glossop, 1st rd
1909-10 Drew 0-0 at home to Fulham; lost replay 2-1, 1st rd
1910-11 Won 2-0 at Bolton, 1st rd
    Lost 4-1 at home to Chelsea, 2nd rd
1912-13 Lost 4-1 at home to Nottingham Forest, 1st rd
1913-14 Lost 8-1 at West Ham, 1st rd
1925-26 Lost 1-0 at home to Clapton Orient, 3rd rd
1926-27 Lost 4-3 at Fulham, 3rd rd
1928-29 Lost 7-1 at home to Huddersfield Town, 3rd rd
1929-30 Drew 1-1 at home to Middlesbrough; lost replay 4-3, 3rd rd
1930-31 Lost 2-1 at home to Notts County, 1st rd.
1931-32 Won 5-2 at home to Nottingham Forest, 3rd rd
    Lost 4-2 at home to Liverpool, 4th rd
1932-33 Drew 2-2 at Sheffield Wednesday; won replay 4-2, 3rd rd
    Won 2-0 at Darlington, 4th rd
    Lost 1-0 at Burnley, 5th rd
1933-34 Drew 2-2 at home to Aston Villa; lost replay 2-0, 3rd rd

1934-35 Lost 2-1 at Swindon, 3rd rd

1936-37 Lost 5-1 at home to Arsenal (holders), 3rd rd

1937-38 Drew 1-1 at Bradford City; drew replay 1-1 aet; won 2-0 at Bramall Lane

    Won 3-2 at home to Burnley, 4th rd

    Drew 2-2 at home to Tottenham Hotspur; lost replay 2-1, 5th rd

    Record Saltergate attendance v Spurs; 30,123, 12 February 1938

1938-39 Drew 1-1 at home to Southend (aban 73 min); drew replay 1-1, lost 4-3

1945-46 Drew 1-1 at home to York 1st leg; lost 3-2 aet 2nd leg, 3rd rd

1946-47 Won 2-1 at home to Sunderland, 3rd rd

    Lost 2-1 at Middlesbrough, 4th rd

1947-48 Lost 2-0 at Derby, 3rd rd

1948-49 Lost 6-0 at Wolverhampton (winning finalists), 3rd rd

1949-50 Won 3-1 at home to Yeovil Town, 3rd rd

    Won 3-2 at home to Middlesbrough, 4th rd

    Drew 1-1 at home to Chelsea; lost replay 3-0, 5th rd

1950-51 Lost 2-1 at Brighton, 3rd rd

1951-52 Won 2-0 at Barrow, 1st rd

    Lost 3-1 at Norwich, 2nd rd

1952-53 Won 1-0 at home to Workington, 1st rd

    Drew 1-1 with Shrewsbury; lost replay 4-2, 2nd rd

1953-54 Won 4-1 at Gainsborough Trinity, 1st rd

    Won 2-1 at Southend, 2nd rd

    Won 2-0 at home to Bury, 3rd rd

    Drew 0-0 at Sheffield Wednesday; lost replay 4-2, 4th rd

1954-55 Lost 1-0 at Hartlepools United, 1st rd

1955-56 Won 1-0 at home to Chester, 1st rd

    Lost 2-1 at home to Hartlepools United, 2nd rd

1956-57 Lost 7-0 at Burnley, 3rd rd

1957-58 Lost 1-0 at York, 1st rd

1958-59 Lost 2-0 at Colchester, 3rd rd

1959-60 Lost 2-1 at South Shields, 1st rd

1960-61 Drew 0-0 with Blackburn Rovers; lost replay 3-0, 3rd rd

1961-62 Won 4-0 at Doncaster, 1st rd

    Drew 2-2 at home to Oldham Athletic; lost replay 4-2, 2nd rd

1962-63 Won 4-1 at home to Stockport County, 1st rd

    Lost 2-1 at Barnsley, 2nd rd

1963-64 Won 2-1 at Crook Town, 1st rd

    Drew 1-1 at Netherfield; won replay 4-1, 2nd rd

    Lost 1-0 at Oxford United, 3rd rd

1964-65 Won 2-0 at home to South Shields, 1st rd

    Won 2-1 at home to York City, 2nd rd

    Lost 3-0 at home to Peterborough United, 3rd rd

1965-66 Lost 2-0 at home to Chester, 1st rd

1966-67 Lost 3-2 at Wrexham, 1st rd

1967-68 Won 2-0 at home to Barnsley, 1st rd

    Won 1-0 at Chester, 2nd rd

    Lost 2-1 at Blackpool, 3rd rd

1968-69 Won 2-0 at home to Skelmersdale, 1st rd
    Won 2-1 at home to Wrexham, 2nd rd
    Lost 3-0 at Portsmouth, 3rd rd
1969-70 Lost 3-0 at Tranmere Rovers, 1st rd
1970-71 Won 2-0 at home to Halifax Town, 1st rd
    Drew 0-0 at home to Workington; lost replay 3-2, 2nd rd
1971-72 Won 1-0 at home to Oldham Athletic, 1st rd
    Drew 0-0 at Barnsley; won replay 1-0, 2nd rd
    Lost 2-1 at Stoke, 3rd rd
1972-73 Won 4-2 at home to Rhyl, 1st rd
    Drew 2-2 away to Grimsby; lost replay 1-0, 2nd rd
1973-74 Drew 0-0 at home to Barnsley; lost replsy 2-1, 1st rd
1974-75 Won 3-1 at home to Boston United, 1st rd
    Won 1-0 at home to Doncaster Rovers, 2nd rd
    Lost 2-0 at Sunderland, 3rd rd
1975-76 Lost 1-0 at Bradford City, 1st rd
1976-77 Won 2-1 at Scunthorpe United, 1st rd
    Drew 1-1 at home to Walsall; drew replay 0-0 aet; lost 1-0 at Derby, 2nd rd
1977-78 Won 1-0 at home to Halifax Town, 1st rd
    Lost 1-0 at Blyth Spartans, 2nd rd
1978-79 Drew 1-1 at Darlington; lost replay 1-0, 1st rd
1979-80 Drew 1-1 away to Grimsby; lost replay 3-2, 1st rd
1980-81 Drew 2-2 with Wigan; won replay 2-0, 1st rd
    Drew 1-1 at Sheffield United; won replay 1-0, 2nd rd
    Drew 1-1 at Peterborough; lost replay 2-1, 3rd rd
1981-82 Won 4-1 at home to Preston NE, 1st rd
    Lost 1-0 at home to Huddersfield Town, 2nd rd
1982-83 Drew 2-2 at home to Peterborough; lost replay 2-1, 1st rd
1983-84 Won 2-1 at Chester City, 1st rd
    Drew 2-2 at home to Burnley; lost replay 3-2, 2nd rd
1984-85 Won 3-1 at Whitby, 1st rd
    Lost 1-0 at Walsall, 2nd rd
1985-86 Drew 2-2 at Tranmere Rovers; lost replay 1-0, 1st rd
1986-87 Lost 2-0 at Walsall, 1st rd
1987-88 Drew 3-3 at Notts County; lost replay 1-0, 1st rd
1988-89 Drew 0-0 at Bolton; lost replay 3-2, 1st rd
1989-90 Won 3-2 at Shrewsbury Town, 1st rd
    Lost 2-0 at home to Huddersfield Town, 2nd rd
1990-91 Won 3-2 at home to Spennymoor United, 1st rd
    Lost 4-3 at home to Bolton Wanderers, 2nd rd
1991-92 Lost 2-1 at Darlington, 1st rd
1992-93 Drew 0-0 at Macclesfield; 2-2 in replay; lost 3-2 on penalties, 1st rd
1993-94 Lost 1-0 at home to Rochdale, 1st rd
1994-95 Drew 0-0 at home to Scarborough; lost replay 2-0, 1st rd
1995-96 Won 2-0 at Scarborough, 1st rd
    Lost 3-2 at Wrexham, 2nd rd
1996-97 Won 1-0 at home to Bury, 1st rd

Won 2-0 at home to Scarborough, 2nd rd

Won 2-0 at home to Bristol City, 3rd rd

Won 3-2 at Bolton, 4th rd

Won 1-0 at home to Nottingham Forest, 5th rd

Won 1-0 at home to Wrexham, 6th rd

Drew 3-3 with Middlesbrough at Old Trafford, semi-final; lost replay 3-0 at Hillsborough

1997-98 Won 1-0 at home to Northwich Victoria, 1st rd

Drew 2-2 away to Grimsby; lost replay 2-0, 2nd rd

1998-99 Lost 1-0 at Wycombe Wanderers, 1st rd

1999-2000 Lost 2-1 at home to Enfield, 1st rd

2000-01 Lost 1-0 at home to Bristol City, 1st rd

2001-02 Won 3-0 at Stalybridge Celtic, 1st rd

Drew 1-1 at home to Southend United; lost replay 2-0, 2nd rd

2002-03 Lost 2-1 at home to Morecambe, 1st rd

2003-04 Lost 3-2 at home to Tranmere Rovers, 1st rd

2004-05 Lost 2-0 at Scunthorpe, 1st rd

2005-06 Drew 0-0 at Leyton Orient; lost replay 2-1, 1st rd

2006-07 Lost 1-0 at home to Basingstoke, 1st rd

2007-08 Lost 2-1 at home to Tranmere Rovers, 1st rd

2008-09 Won 3-1 at home to Mansfield Town, 1st rd

Losing 1-0 at home to Droylsden when abandoned ht (fog), 2nd rd

Drew 2-2 at home to Droylesden, 2nd rd

Led 2-0 in replay when lights failed after 72 minutes, 2nd rd

Lost 2-1 at Droylesden, 2nd rd

Droylesden banned from Cup for fielding a suspended player

Lost 3-0 at Ipswich Town, 3rd rd

2009-10 Lost 3-1 at home to Bournemouth, 1st rd

2010-11 Won 2-0 at Harrow Borough, 1st rd

Lost 3-1 at Burton Albion, 2nd rd

2011-12 Lost 3-1 at home to Torquay United, 1st rd

Appendix 3

CHESTERFIELD'S RECORD IN THE FOOTBALL LEAGUE

P W D L F A Pts Pos

Season Division Two

1899-1900 34 16 6 12 65 60 38 7th

1900-01 34 9 10 15 46 58 28 14th

1901-02 34 11 6 17 47 68 28 16th (out of 18)

1902-03 34 14 9 11 67 40 37 6th

Record victory: 10-0 v Glossop North End, 17 Jan 1903

1903-04 34 11 8 15 37 45 30 11th

1904-05 34 14 11 9 44 35 39 5th

1905-06 38 10 8 20 40 72 28 18th (out of 20)

1906-07 38 11 7 20 50 66 29 18th

1907-08 38 6 11 21 46 92 23 19th

1908-09 38 11 8 19 37 67 30 19th
Lincoln City elected in place of Chesterfield
Division Three North
1921-22 38 16 7 19 48 67 35 13th
1922-23 38 19 7 12 68 52 45 4th
G Beel top scorer in division with 23 goals
1923-24 42 22 10 10 70 39 54 3rd
1924-25 42 17 11 14 60 44 45 7th
1925-26 42 25 5 12 100 54 55 4th
J Cookson League top scorer with 44 goals
1926-27 42 21 5 16 92 68 47 7th
1927-28 42 13 10 19 71 78 36 16th
1928-29 42 18 5 19 71 77 41 11th
1929-30 42 22 6 14 76 56 50 4th
1930-31 42 26 6 10 102 57 58 1st
Division Two
1931-32 42 13 11 18 64 86 37 17th
1932-33 42 12 10 20 61 84 34 21st (out of 22)
Record defeat: 1-9 v Port Vale, 24 September 1932
Division Three North
1933-34 42 27 7 8 86 43 61 2nd
Barnsley promoted with 62 points
1934-35 42 17 10 15 71 52 44 10th
1935-36 42 24 12 6 92 39 60 1st
Division Two
1936-37 42 16 8 18 84 89 40 15th
1937-38 42 16 9 17 63 63 41 11th
1938-39 42 20 9 13 69 52 49 6th
Second World War, 1939-45
1946-47 42 18 14 10 58 44 50 4th
1947-48 42 16 7 19 54 55 39 16th
1948-49 42 15 17 10 51 45 47 6th
1949-50 42 15 9 18 43 47 39 14th
1950-51 42 9 12 21 44 69 30 21st
Division Three North
1951-52 46 17 11 18 65 66 45 13th
1952-53 46 18 11 17 65 63 47 12th
1953-54 46 19 14 13 76 64 52 6th
1954-55 46 24 6 16 81 70 54 6th
1955-56 46 25 4 17 94 66 54 6th
1956-57 46 22 9 15 96 79 53 6th
1957-58 46 18 15 13 71 69 51 8th
Division Three
1958-59 46 17 10 19 67 64 44 16th
1959-60 46 18 7 21 71 84 43 18th
1960-61 46 10 12 24 67 87 32 24th
Division Four

1961-62 44 14 9 21 70 87 37 19th
1962-63 46 13 16 17 70 64 42 15th
1963-64 46 15 12 19 57 71 42 16th
1964-65 46 20 8 18 58 70 48 12th
1965-66 46 13 13 20 62 78 39 20th
1966-67 46 17 8 21 60 63 42 15th
1967-68 46 21 11 14 71 50 53 7th
1968-69 46 13 15 18 43 50 41 20th
1969-70 46 27 10 9 77 32 64 1st
Division Three
1970-71 46 17 17 12 66 38 51 5th
1971-72 46 18 8 20 57 57 44 13th
1972-73 46 17 9 20 57 61 43 16th
1973-74 46 21 14 11 55 42 56 5th
1974-75 46 16 12 18 62 66 44 15th
1975-76 46 17 9 20 69 69 43 15th
1976-77 46 14 10 22 56 64 38 18th
1977-78 46 17 14 15 58 49 48 9th
1978-79 46 13 14 19 51 65 40 20th
1979-80 46 23 11 12 71 46 57 4th
1980-81 46 23 10 13 72 48 56 5th
1981-82 46 18 10 18 57 58 64 11th
1982-83 46 8 13 25 43 68 37 24th
Division Four
1983-84 46 15 15 16 59 61 60 13th
1984-85 46 26 13 7 64 35 91 1st
Division Three
1985-86 46 13 14 19 61 64 53 17th
1986-87 46 13 15 18 56 69 54 17th
1987-88 46 15 10 21 41 70 55 18th
Record League defeat: 10-0 at Gillingham, 5 Sept 1987
1988-89 46 14 7 25 51 86 40 22nd
Division Four
1989-90 46 19 14 13 63 50 71 7th
1990-91 46 13 14 19 47 62 53 18th
1991-92 46 14 11 17 49 61 53 13th
1992-93 46 15 11 16 59 63 56 12th
Division Three
1993-94 46 16 14 12 55 48 62 8th
Divisions rejigged under change of sponsorship
1994-95 46 23 12 7 62 37 81 3rd
Promoted from play-offs
1995-96 46 20 12 14 56 51 72 7th
1996-97 46 18 14 14 42 39 68 10th
1997-98 46 16 17 13 46 44 65 10th
1998-99 46 17 13 16 46 44 64 9th
1999-2000 46 7 15 24 34 63 36 24th

Division Three
2000-01 46 25 14 7 79 42 80 3rd
Nine points deducted for financial irregularities. Fined
£20,000.
Division Two
2001-02 46 13 13 20 53 65 52 18th
2002-03 46 14 8 24 43 73 50 20th
2003-04 46 12 15 19 49 71 51 20th
Division One
2004-05 46 14 15 7 55 62 57 17th
Change of sponsor, from Nationwide to Coca-Cola.
2005-06 46 14 14 18 63 73 56 16th
2006-07 46 12 11 23 45 53 47 21st
Division Two
2007-08 46 19 12 15 76 56 69 8th
2008-09 46 16 15 15 62 57 63 10th
2009-10 46 21 7 18 61 62 70 8th
2010-11 46 24 14 8 85 51 86 1st
Division One
2011-12 46 10 12 24 56 81 42 22nd

Appendix 4
CHESTERFIELD MANAGERS

1891-95 E Russell Timmens (secretary-manager)
1895-1901 Gilbert Gillies
1901-02 E F Hind
1902-06 Jack Hoskin
1906-07 W Furness
1907-10 George Swift
1911-13 G H Jones
1913-17 R L Weston
1919 T Callaghan
1920-22 J J Caffrey
1922-27 Harary Parkes
1927 Alec Campbell
1927-32 Teddy Davison
1932-38 Bill Harvey
1938-45 Norman Bullock
1945-48 Bob Brocklebank
1948-52 Bobby Marshall
1952-58 Teddy Davison
1958-62 Duggie Livingstone
1962-67 Tony McShane
1967-73 Jimmy McGuigan
1973-76 Joe Shaw
1976-80 Arthur Cox

1980-83 Frank Barlow
1983-87 John Duncan
1987-88 Kevin Randall
1988-91 Paul Hart
1991-93 Chris McMenemy
1993-2000 John Duncan
2000-01 Nicky Law
2002-03 Dave Rushbury
2003-07 Roy McFarland
2007-09 Lee Richardson
2009-12 John Sheridan

Appendix 5
TRANSFER RECORDS

Record fee received: £
100 Ellis Gee to Everton, March 1898
400 Joe Ball to Bury, December 1903
500 William Egerton to Lincoln City, January 1914
1,000 Jacky Fisher to Burnley, March 1922
1,000 Joe Cooper to Notts County, March 1923
1,000 Billy Marshall to Grimsby Town, May 1923
1,500 Willis Edwards to Leeds United, March 1925
2,000 Cyril Oxley to Liverpool, October 1925
2,500 Jimmy Coookson to WBA, June 1927
3,000 Albert Malam to Huddersfield Town, September 1934
8,500 Harry Clifton to Newcastle United, June 1938
10,000 Billy Whitaker to Middlesbrough, June 1947
10,600 Harold Roberts to Birmingham City, December 1947
20,000 Gordon Dale to Portsmouth, July 1951
50,000 Alan Stevenson to Burnley, January 1972
90,000 Jim Brown to Sheffield United, March 1974
177,500 Alan Birch to Wolverhampton W, August 1981
750,000 Kevin Davies to Southampton, May 1997

Record fees paid: £
400 Joe Ball from Bury, August 1905
1,500 Alan Sliman from Bristol City, March 1932
2,000 Walter McMillen from Manchester United, December 1930
4,500 Norman Kirkman from Rochdale, November 1947
8,500 Walter Harrison from Leicester City, December 1950
10,000 Arthur Bellamy from Burnley, July 1972
15,000 Frank Barlow from Sheffield United, August 1972
20,000 Ricky Green from Scunthorpe United, February 1977
35,000 Geoff Salmons from Leicester City, August 1978
150,000 Phil Bonnyman from Carlisle United, March 1980
250,000 Jason Lee, from Watford, August 1998